Einstein

FOR

DUMMIES®

Einstein
FOR
DUMMIES®

by Carlos I. Calle, PhD

WILEY

Wiley Publishing, Inc.

Einstein For Dummies®

Published by
Wiley Publishing, Inc.
111 River St.
Hoboken, NJ 07030-5774
www.wiley.com

For general information on our other products and services, please contact our Customer Care Department within the U.S. at 877-762-2974, outside the U.S. at 317-572-3993, or fax 317-572-4002.

For technical support, please visit www.wiley.com/techsupport.

Wiley also publishes its books in a variety of electronic formats. Some content that appears in print may not be available in electronic books.

Library of Congress Control Number: 2005923739

ISBN: 978-0-7645-8348-3

10 9 8 7 6 5

1O/QT/RQ/QV/IN

WILEY

About the Author

Carlos I. Calle, PhD, is a senior research scientist at NASA Kennedy Space Center and the founder and director of NASA's Electrostatics and Surface Physics Laboratory. He holds a doctorate in theoretical nuclear physics from Ohio University. He is the recipient of numerous NASA awards, including the Spaceflight Awareness Award in 2003 for exceptional contributions to the space program. With his laboratory staff, he has developed new testing techniques for the Space Shuttle Thermal Control System and for the thermal shrouds on the International Space Station modules.

Calle has been working on the physical properties of the lunar and Martian soil and is currently designing and building instrumentation for future planetary exploration missions. As one of the world experts on the electrostatic properties of the lunar and Martian dust, he has been working on methods to keep dust from the space suits and equipment being planned for the lunar exploration missions.

Calle is the author of *Superstrings and Other Things: A Guide to Physics,* a book on physics for the general reader. He has authored over 100 scientific papers in nuclear physics, relativity, particle electrostatics, the properties of the Martian soil, and the lunar surface dust.

He has lectured on physics and relativity at several colleges and universities and is a regular speaker at the physics department at Florida Institute of Technology.

When he is away from his lab at NASA, Calle likes to spend his time drawing, painting, and sculpting, usually from life. He is married to Luz Marina Calle, also a NASA scientist. Their son and daughter-in-law, Daniel and Emily, are software engineers.

Dedication

To my wife and fellow NASA scientist, Dr. Luz Marina Calle. Your constant support and encouragement truly made this book possible.

Author's Acknowledgments

My warm thanks go first to my editor, Joan Friedman, for her invaluable and efficient editing of this book. Her intelligence, her insightful remarks, and her attention to detail enhance the clarity of the book.

I also wish to thank Joyce Pepple at Wiley and the outstanding team that she put together for this book. Kathy Cox, acquisitions editor at Wiley, believed in the project and provided support and editorial assistance; Lisa Reed created the beautiful and accurate illustrations; and Heather Dismore provided helpful editorial support. Finally, Dr. Brian Murphy of Butler University reviewed the entire manuscript and provided helpful insights, suggestions, and corrections.

I wish to acknowledge also the professional reviews of Dr. Scott Hyman at Sweet Briar College and Dr. Jim Mantovani at Florida Institute of Technology. Their important and helpful suggestions improved the book.

Many other people, directly or indirectly, made possible the completion of this book. I am grateful to my agent, Susan Protter, for her support throughout the project. Special thanks to my son, Daniel, and to his wife, Emily, for their enthusiasm and support. Thanks also to Dr. Dominique Leveau and to Tanya Leveau for their warm understanding.

Publisher's Acknowledgments

We're proud of this book; please send us your comments through our Dummies online registration form located at www.dummies.com/register/.

Some of the people who helped bring this book to market include the following:

Acquisitions, Editorial, and Media Development

Project Editor: Joan Friedman

Acquisitions Editor: Kathy Cox

Technical Editor: Brian Murphy, PhD

Editorial Supervisor: Carmen Krikorian

Editorial Manager: Michelle Hacker

Editorial Assistants: Hanna Scott, Melissa S. Bennett

Cover Photos: © Abbie Enneking/2005

Cartoons: Rich Tennant (www.the5thwave.com)

Composition Services

Project Coordinator: Adrienne Martinez

Layout and Graphics: Carl Byers, Andrea Dahl, Kelly Emkow, Joyce Haughey, Stephanie D. Jumper, Heather Ryan, Mary Gillot Virgin

Special Art: Lisa Reed

Proofreaders: Leeann Harney, Jessica Kramer, Dwight Ramsey, Aptara

Indexer: Aptara

Special Help
Heather Dismore

Publishing and Editorial for Consumer Dummies

> **Diane Graves Steele,** Vice President and Publisher, Consumer Dummies
>
> **Joyce Pepple,** Acquisitions Director, Consumer Dummies
>
> **Kristin A. Cocks,** Product Development Director, Consumer Dummies
>
> **Michael Spring,** Vice President and Publisher, Travel
>
> **Kelly Regan,** Editorial Director, Travel

Publishing for Technology Dummies

> **Andy Cummings,** Vice President and Publisher, Dummies Technology/General User

Composition Services

> **Gerry Fahey,** Vice President of Production Services
>
> **Debbie Stailey,** Director of Composition Services

Contents at a Glance

Table of Contents

Part VI: The Part of Tens 319

Chapter 20: Ten Insights into Einstein's Beliefs on Religion and Philosophy 321

Chapter 21: Ten Women Who Influenced Einstein 329

Introduction

● ❖ ● ❖ ● ❖ ● ❖ ● ❖ ● ❖ ● ❖ ● ❖ ● ❖ ● ❖ ● ❖ ● ❖ ● ❖ ● ❖ ● ❖ ● ❖ ● ❖ ● ❖ ● ❖ ●

*I*n this book, I aim to give you a clear understanding of Einstein's beautiful work. Everyone knows that Einstein invented the theory of relativity and that he came up with that famous $E = mc^2$ equation. And everyone thinks that you need to be almost an Einstein to understand either one.

I am here to tell you that the theory of relativity isn't really that difficult to understand. (Actually, there are two theories of relativity, the special and the general, and neither one is beyond your grasp.) And as for the famous equation, it too can be understood without using math.

In this book, I use Einstein's own simple examples to explain his discovery that time slows down and distances shorten when you move fast. (I mean *really* fast — not just a steady jog.) I also tell you why, even if no one can ever reach the speed of light, a future astronaut may be able to circumnavigate the entire galaxy in a human lifetime. (*Her* lifetime, that is; hundreds of millions of years will pass for the Earthlings who stay behind.) That's a form of time travel to the future, without the possibility of returning to the present. I also discuss whether it's possible to really travel to the past or future and get back to the present.

About This Book

This book is intended as a guide to all of Einstein's work, not just relativity and $E = mc^2$. Einstein did much more than invent his theory of relativity and discover his famous equation. He started quantum physics, invented the principle of the laser, came up with the first model of the universe, and showed us that space is curved. And these are just the big-ticket items. There's hardly any field in physics that's untouched by his discoveries.

My aim with this book is to present and explain all the scientific contributions that Einstein made in his life in plain and simple English. My aim is also to tell you why Einstein's discoveries are so important and why he deserves to be as famous as he is.

Einstein's life was fascinating, so as I discuss his work I also give you an overview of the main events during different periods of his life. I tell you about Einstein's views on religion and philosophy, as well as his interactions with the women in his life.

What You're Not to Read

You don't need to read this book from cover to cover. I've tried to make the chapters self-contained, so you can read about a specific topic in Einstein's work and be able to follow the discussion.

Don't read anything you don't want to read. If you're reading the book because you're curious about what Einstein did, read about what you'd like to know. If you're reading it because you're taking a physics class and need to complement your textbook, read the parts that match your text.

You may just want to know about special relativity or what the $E = mc^2$ equation means. Or you may be interested in what Einstein did during his miracle year. By all means, read what piques your interest. I promise I won't test you on what you are learning. And I hope you'll enjoy reading whatever you decide to read.

Of course, if you do decide to read this book from cover to cover, nobody will stop you. And no one will complain about how much you know about Einstein's work.

Foolish Assumptions

I'm assuming that you bought the book (or borrowed it or maybe got it as a gift) because you always wanted to know about Einstein's theories but you don't necessarily want to read about them in a more standard science book. I'm also assuming that, right now, you don't care to read a physics-type book with math or complicated diagrams in it. I'm also assuming that you are someone who enjoys learning new things. If this is the case, I hope you enjoy this voyage through Einstein's universe.

How This Book Is Organized

The book follows Einstein's life, to a certain extent. It starts with his miracle year and his unbelievable outburst into the world of physics, almost out of nowhere. During that year, Einstein started two revolutions in physics, the theory of relativity and quantum physics. The book follows the development of these two theories in a chronological order, and it ends with the impact of these two theories on the world of science.

Part 1: A Genius Awakens

This first part tells you who Einstein was and introduces Einstein's genius by following his life from birth to the search for a job after college graduation. This period in Einstein's life ends with his miracle year, which I present in Chapter 3.

Part II: On the Shoulders of Giants: What Einstein Learned in School

This part is an overview of physics from its early development, back when it wasn't called physics. I introduce the ancient Greeks' very modern ideas about the world, and I present the important developments through Einstein's time. I make stops to visit Galileo Galilei and Johannes Kepler, as well as a longer stay to see what the great Isaac Newton did. I follow the development of ideas on heat and energy, which Einstein changed. After that, I pay a visit to James Clerk Maxwell, the other great influence on Einstein. (Einstein skipped classes to read Maxwell's papers in the library, and he developed relativity from his studies of Maxwell's theories.) The part ends with what was known about the behavior of light before Einstein entered the picture.

Part III: The Special Theory of Relativity

You get to the real thing in this part: Einstein's special theory of relativity. First, I introduce you to the original idea of relativity, the relativity of Galileo. I then explain what Einstein's relativity is all about and how Einstein, at 26, went about developing it in a few weeks. In this part, you also see what $E = mc^2$ really means. (It's more than saying "energy equals mass times the square of the speed of light.")

Part IV: The General Theory of Relativity

The general theory of relativity is Einstein's masterpiece. Its math is complicated (even Einstein needed help with it), but the idea behind it is simple. I don't touch the math here. No need to. The ideas are beautiful, and you'll be able to see how it all works.

I show you how Einstein's ideas on time and space actually work and why Stephen Hawking says that black holes aren't really completely black. You can also read Einstein's theories about time travel. Finally, this part presents the major tests that NASA and other labs around the world have performed to check Einstein's theories.

Part V: The Quantum and the Universe

Quantum physics started with one revolutionary paper that Einstein wrote during his miracle year. You'll see why it was revolutionary and what it did to our understanding of reality. In this part, I also discuss Einstein's famous letter to President Franklin Delano Roosevelt about the possibility of an atomic bomb and Einstein's limited involvement with the bomb's development. Finally, I explain the relevance of Einstein's work and the important role it's still playing today in the current theories of the universe and in the unification of all of physics, Einstein's lifelong dream.

Part VI: The Part of Tens

This part is a staple in the *For Dummies* series. In this part, I explain ten views that Einstein held on religion and philosophy, and I give you short biographies of ten women who had an important influence on his life.

Icons Used in This Book

Throughout the book, you'll notice icons in the margins that are designed to help you navigate the text. Here's what they mean:

Our understanding of the physical world would be stagnant if scientists didn't occasionally think about things in a new way. This icon alerts you that a stroke of genius is nearby.

I think all the information in this book is important, but some nuggets are worth putting into your mental filing cabinet for future reference. This icon points them out.

Einstein had a knack for explaining his theories using simple pictures and examples. I aspire to do the same in this book, and when you see this icon, you know a helpful hint is close at hand.

This icon points out information that goes beyond the basics — information that may be tough to digest or go into more detail than you need. If your gray matter isn't up for the challenge, just skip past these paragraphs.

Chapter 1

Who Was Einstein?

In This Chapter

▶ Introducing Einstein

▶ Describing his work and why it was important

About a hundred years ago, an unknown civil servant in Switzerland decided that existing theories in the field of physics were not quite right, and he decided to fix them. What he did was so important that *Time* magazine selected him as the person of the 20th century, ahead of kings, queens, presidents, artists, movie stars, and religious leaders.

Who was Einstein, and what did he do? In this chapter, I introduce you to Einstein's genius, what he discovered, and the importance of his work — topics that get much more detailed attention in subsequent chapters.

Dissecting That Famous Brain

After giving birth to her only son in 1879, Albert Einstein's young mother thought for a moment that he was "a monster." The baby had a strangely shaped and large head. The doctor calmed her down, explaining that it's not uncommon for a baby to have a misshapen head right after birth, and assuring her that the size of his head was going to be just fine. The doctor was right about the size — in just a few weeks, the proportions evened out. But the angular shape of Einstein's head would remain for the rest of his life.

The unusual shape of Einstein's head didn't make him different than other boys. But his brain did. The way his brain worked was anything but ordinary.

When Einstein was alive, many people wondered if his brain was different than other people's. Einstein actually left instructions to make his brain available for research after his death. When Einstein died in 1955, pathologist Thomas Harvey preserved the brain and later performed studies of several tissue samples. Harvey didn't see anything out of the ordinary. However, in 1999, Sandra Witelson of McMaster University in Canada discovered that

Einstein's brain lacked a specific wrinkle that is found on most people's brains. The wrinkle is located in the region of the brain that's related to mathematical thinking and visual imagery.

Touring Einstein's Life

Einstein was apparently better equipped for mathematical and abstract thinking than most people, but it's likely that some other people have had similar native abilities. The shape of his brain alone doesn't explain Einstein's genius. The environment in which he grew up most certainly played a role.

Recognizing his own gifts

As I explain in Chapter 2, Einstein grew up as a fairly normal boy. He was not a child prodigy. He was, instead, a gifted and very independent student. He disliked the strict teaching methods used in the German schools he attended, which caused some friction with his teachers. His independence became teenage rebellion during his high school and college years. Several teachers and professors told him that he wasn't going to amount to anything.

Einstein knew that he was smarter than most people and, while in college, became arrogant and cocky. A couple of his high school teachers and at least one college professor recognized his brilliance. But as has been the case with all great men and women in history, no one ever predicted what he was going to become.

In college, Einstein lived the life of a normal European college student of the late 1800s, hanging out with friends at the local bars. (Some things don't change!) He was popular with women, who found him handsome and charming. He enjoyed being in their company, which caused trouble later in life, when he was married.

Surviving professional disappointment

"A happy man is too comfortable with the present to think much about the future," wrote Einstein in a high school paper for a French class. "If I were lucky enough to pass my college admission tests," he continued in very poor French, "I would attend the Polytechnic Institute to study mathematics and physics. I imagine myself becoming a teacher in those branches."

As I discuss in Chapter 2, when Einstein graduated as a physics major from the Polytechnic in Zurich, he had changed his mind somewhat. He wanted to be a university professor. However, one of the professors he clashed with at the Polytechnic was able to close all the academic doors for Einstein. So instead of becoming a professor, he became a clerk in a Swiss patent office.

From this position, alone and isolated from the academic world, Einstein burst into the world of physics and changed it forever. And he did so mostly in one year. That year, 1905, became known as his *year of miracles* (see Chapter 3).

Becoming famous

The publication of the special theory of relativity, of the famous formula $E = mc^2$, and especially of the general theory of relativity made Einstein famous. (I discuss these revolutionary ideas in detail in Parts III and IV of this book.)

Einstein became an icon. When people imagine a scientist, most think of him. Even the Hollywood portrayals of a scientist often show a middle-aged man, usually in a lab coat, who has disheveled hair, is unconcerned with his clothes, and is engrossed in the task at hand.

Does the stereotype reflect its model? Almost. But Einstein never wore a lab coat. He was a *theoretical* physicist, which means that he needed only a pen and paper — and his mind — to do his job.

Fame made Einstein mellow. He was very aware of his status as the greatest scientist in the world. But he never pulled rank. Most people who knew him found him to be kind and caring. As a physicist, I would've loved to have met him, but my life didn't overlap with his. However, I know a few scientists who were fortunate enough to meet him. The arrogance of his youth was long gone, and the Einstein they met was a gentle man who made them feel at ease.

Even people who were his professional equals, like Niels Bohr and Wolfgang Pauli, were in awe of him. In the late 1940s, Abraham Pais, then a young physicist at the Institute for Advanced Studies in Princeton, New Jersey (where Einstein worked after he immigrated to the United States), noticed a different attitude in both Bohr and Pauli whenever Einstein was around.

Lacking fortune

Einstein's fame didn't translate into wealth. He was never much interested in material things, but he did have a love for both music and sailing.

Even as late as 1922, Einstein couldn't put together the money to buy a weekend cottage on the water near Berlin and a sailboat. His salary as a professor at the University of Berlin wouldn't stretch enough to pay for these luxuries. He settled for renting a small house in the country.

For his 50th birthday, a group of friends bought Einstein a 21-foot mahogany-fitted boat. But Einstein would enjoy sailing it for only a few years. The threat of Nazi Germany forced him to leave Europe for the United States in 1933. His beloved boat was confiscated and sold by the Nazi regime as the property of an enemy of the state.

Einstein won the Nobel Prize in physics in 1922. The prize brought with it a considerable amount of money, which he gave to his former wife for the care of their children.

After Einstein came to the United States, his fortunes improved. His initial salary at the Institute for Advanced Studies was $16,000 a year, about twice that of a full professor at the time. (Because other recognized scientists also made high salaries, a few people commented that the institute was not just for "advanced study" but for "advanced salaries.") But Einstein's lifestyle continued to be modest. His house at 112 Mercer Street in Princeton was an average house in a middle class neighborhood.

Playing peaceful politics

Einstein used his fame to speak out on political causes that he felt strongly about. "My political ideal is democracy. Let every man be respected as an individual and no man idolized," he wrote in 1931. "It is an irony of fate that I myself have been the recipient of excessive admiration . . . through no fault, and no merit, of my own."

His two main political concerns were pacifism and the creation of a world government that would enforce disarmament. He long swore that he would never support wartime activities. But the rise of Nazi Germany changed his perspective somewhat, and he became what he called a "militant activist."

Although Einstein played no direct role in developing the atomic bomb, his $E = mc^2$ equation opened the door to its creation (but didn't lead directly to it). And Einstein did encourage the United States government to pursue an atomic weapon, out of fear that the Nazis might be doing the same. As I explain in Chapter 17, Einstein sent a letter to President Franklin Delano Roosevelt in 1939, bringing the threat of a Nazi atomic bomb to his attention. The letter didn't lead to the bomb's development, but nonetheless Einstein later called it "the greatest mistake" of his life.

Working and playing

Einstein had an uncommon ability to work even in the midst of personal tragedy. Even as a child, he was somewhat detached from external events. But he wasn't aloof or incapable of personal relationships. It's just that his work and his thinking came first. "Nothing tragic really gets to him," wrote his second wife, Elsa, after the death of her daughter (Einstein's stepdaughter). "He is in the happy position of being able to shuffle it off. That is also why he can work so well."

When Einstein was growing up, his mother made sure that he and his sister, Maja, were exposed to music. Einstein took violin lessons and later learned to play the piano on his own. Music became his lifelong love. He liked Mozart, Schubert, Bach, Beethoven, Vivaldi, Corelli, and Scarlatti.

Einstein also appreciated art, preferring the old masters. He thought that they were more "convincing." Of the modern masters, he was interested in the pre-cubist period of Picasso (the period around 1905, when Picasso's palette started to lighten, with paintings of clowns and harlequins).

In spite of two failed marriages and the rise of Nazism in his homeland, Einstein lived a generally happy life. For the most part, his life was his work, and his work was as meaningful as that of Isaac Newton's. (I discuss Newton's contributions in Part II of this book.) The two men have no equals in the history of science.

Appreciating His Contributions

The 18th-century mathematician Joseph-Louis Lagrange once complained that there was only one universe and Newton had already discovered how it worked. Einstein proved Lagrange (and other scientists, who thought that the field of physics was essentially complete) wrong. Einstein showed that Newton's laws didn't tell the whole story, and he proceeded to tell us how the universe really works.

The special theory of relativity

Newton's universe works like clockwork, obediently following the laws that Newton discovered. In this universe, clocks run at the same rate for everyone, and space is the stage where things happen.

With his special theory of relativity (which is called *special* to distinguish it from the extended *general* theory of relativity, which came later), Einstein showed us that time and space aren't fixed. Instead, each one of us measures time differently depending on how we move, and space contracts or expands as we speed up or slow down.

Einstein's strange conclusions came out of a single important insight: The speed of light is always the same, regardless of how fast you move toward or away from a light source. This assumption goes against common sense.

Consider these examples: Say you're in a car traveling 50 mph, and the car next to you is going at the same speed. If you look into the car next to you (without catching a glimpse of the horizon speeding by), it appears to be standing still. While both speedometers read 50, from your perspective, the other car isn't moving.

Now, say you're traveling on a spaceship at half the speed of light (which Einstein represents with the letter *c*). You see a beam of light traveling through space at 300,000 kilometers (186,000 miles) per second. What if you speed up? The speed of light remains the same. What if you slow down? No difference. No matter how fast you go, you still measure light traveling at *c*.

If you and I are moving relative to each other and we both measure the same speed of light, what does that mean? It means that your space and your time are different from my space and my time. In Einstein's universe, space and time are linked to each other, and when you change one, the other changes. But the combination of the two, the four-dimensional entity called *spacetime,* stays unchanged. Your spacetime is my spacetime, and your speed of light is my speed of light. In this way, not everything is relative, as many people think. Spacetime and the speed of light are not relative. They are absolute, as physicists say. And that's what makes everything in the universe work.

Einstein's conclusions about the nature of space and time have not only been seen and measured many times over the last half century; they are actually used in the design of delicate laboratory equipment. His special theory clarified our understanding of the world and corrected previous inconsistencies. I discuss the special theory in detail in Part III.

$E = mc^2$

This is the most famous equation of all. It's the one equation that most people on the planet can recognize. And it came out of Einstein's theory of relativity. You'd think that given its importance, it would take pages and pages of complicated mathematical derivations and a very long paper to present it. Einstein's paper on his equation was all of three pages long. And the math was simple (if you're good at math).

$E = mc^2$ says that mass and energy are the same thing and that objects usually have both. Mass can be converted into energy and energy into mass. The equation explains how the sun works, a mystery that had puzzled scientists until Einstein came along.

Einstein's mass-energy equation is used today by medical physicists to calculate the energies generated in particle accelerators used in cancer treatment. It's used in the design of machines like the positron emission tomography (PET) scanner. It's used in the design of smoke detectors.

And, as I note earlier in the chapter, the equation (but not Einstein) played a role in the calculations for the atomic bomb invented at Los Alamos National Laboratory and later dropped over Japan, ending War World II.

Quantum theory

In Newton's universe, if you had enough computing power at your disposal, you could input all the information that you know about the universe now, run a program based on Newton's laws, and be able to call up any event in the universe's past or predict any event in its future. You could input a time and place into your computer and get a complete description of that place at that time, even if the time were in the future.

Yes, that's right, you could predict the future! At first, that ability sounds wonderful. You could know what the first human colonies on Mars will look like or what civilization on Earth will be like in 500 or 1 million years. Or — even more importantly — you could find out who will win the Super Bowl next year. But would you like to know the exact details of the painful events that lie ahead? Wouldn't it be horrible to know exactly when and how they will happen?

Not to worry. Einstein took care of that dilemma for us. You can't predict the future. And nobody will ever be able to, regardless of how powerful their computers are. At least not if quantum physics is right. And all evidence tells us that, in its basic premise, it is.

Quantum physics began with Einstein's 1905 paper explaining the *photoelectric effect,* the principle behind photocells that convert sunlight into electricity. Einstein didn't just explain the effect. Characteristically, he went to the heart of physics and showed us how the world is made. In this paper, Einstein said that light is made up of indivisible bundles of energy that we now call *quanta*. What's more important, he said that when light interacts with matter, light is absorbed or emitted in the same indivisible energy bundles. This last assumption became the basis for the physics of the atom.

But Einstein's idea of the quantum of energy, which later on became known as the *photon,* encountered a great deal of resistance. Only when experiments 15 years later proved that Einstein was right, physicists finally came around and embraced the idea. Within a few months, quantum physics, the physics of the atom, was born.

Quantum physics says that you can't know at once everything you'd want to know about a subatomic particle. Matter is made up of things we call electrons and quarks and other equally exotic particles. And you are limited by nature in what you can know about them. The world has a built-in uncertainty that prevents you from knowing *exactly* how things are going to turn out. You can calculate only the probabilities of outcomes of events. If you measure an electron at one location, there's a certain probability that when you look for it at another location, you'll find it.

Subatomic particles and dust particles

A subatomic particle shares only its name with what we call *particles* in our regular daily experience. A dust particle, for example, has mass, size, shape, and even some color. A subatomic particle is called a particle only because that's what scientists thought they were looking at when they first began to learn about these entities during the late 19th and early 20th centuries. But the things that make up atoms turned out to be nothing like dust particles. Scientists figured this out only in the 1920s, after the term *particle* was widely used to refer to parts of the atom, so they didn't bother to invent a new name. They know what they mean when they use the word, even though nonscientists find it confusing.

Scientists have learned to work with these slippery particles and are able to manipulate them with great precision. A television set, for example, uses jets of electrons that are directed at different points on the screen to form the images that you see. (Of course, sometimes the images they form aren't worth seeing, but that's another discussion completely!)

If the only thing you know about these electrons is probabilities, you may be able to predict with good accuracy where the relatively few electrons in your TV set will hit the screen, but you won't be able to predict what the tremendous collection of electrons and other particles that make up your brain will do next. The future is as uncertain as you always thought it was, and no technological advances are going to change that. That's the way the world is.

Einstein, who started quantum physics, never really believed that this view of the world was the final word. He thought that quantum physics was temporary and that one day we would discover the hidden world underneath — a world that isn't probabilistic.

Sophisticated experiments done during the last 20 years have convinced physicists that, in this case, Einstein was wrong. The world that quantum physics shows us is the real world. And I give you a detailed introduction to that world in Part V.

The general theory of relativity

The special theory of relativity applies only when you're moving at a steady speed and along a straight line. If you turn or accelerate, special relativity ceases to apply. Einstein wanted to extend his theory to all motion, accelerated or not.

That proved difficult to do.

Whereas the theory of special relativity took Einstein only a few weeks to develop, he needed four years to extend the theory to all motion. In the process, he had to learn a whole new area of mathematics. When he was done, he'd produced what's considered to be the most beautiful scientific theory ever discovered. He called it the general theory of relativity.

General relativity says that a large object, like the Earth or the sun, warps the space around it, and gravity is nothing more than the result of that warping. The Earth itself doesn't keep you firmly on the ground. Instead, the space around the Earth is warped, and the slope of that warped space keeps you on the ground.

Because the sun warps space, a ray of light passing close to the sun will bend. General relativity also says that a clock runs more slowly in a stronger gravitational field. For example, a clock will run more slowly in your basement than in your attic. (However, the difference is so slight that you couldn't measure it even if you had the most precise atomic clock and extremely accurate equipment.)

Even before he was finished with it, Einstein wanted to test his theory, to make sure that he was on the right track. He knew that the motion of the planet Mercury hadn't been completely explained and that astronomers were puzzled by that problem. Einstein used his theory to calculate the correct orbit of Mercury, explaining that a small discrepancy in the observations was the result of the warping of space around the sun.

After Einstein published his theory, the English astronomer Arthur Eddington organized an expedition to Africa to measure the bending of light from a star during a total eclipse of the sun (the only time that the stars and the sun are visible at the same time). The results of the measurements confirmed Einstein's prediction. The confirmation thrilled the world, and Einstein became famous almost immediately. I devote Part IV of this book to explaining why this theory had such a profound impact.

Other contributions

As if relativity, $E = mc^2$, and quantum theory weren't enough, Einstein made other significant contributions to physics. Following is a sampling.

Proving molecules are real

In two of the five papers that Einstein published in 1905 (see Chapter 3), he showed that molecules are real and explained how you'd go about measuring them and studying their motions. At the time, not everyone was convinced that atoms existed. These two papers, in conjunction with two others that he'd published earlier, proved once and for all that molecules are real and measurable.

Stimulating radiation

Soon after he completed his general theory of relativity, Einstein began to think about the absorption and emission of radiation. He discovered a method for stimulating the emission of radiation from certain atoms. That discovery is the basis for the laser, invented 40 years later by Charles Townes.

Creating a model of the universe

Einstein decided to use his theory of relativity to build a model of the universe. The task turned out to be extremely difficult. When Einstein was done, he had a universe that was changing and moving, either expanding or collapsing. He didn't like the results. Observations of the time showed that the universe was static, so he introduced a term into his equations — a cosmological constant — that allowed the model to show a static universe as well.

Twelve years later, the astronomer Edwin Hubble discovered that the universe isn't static after all. It expands.

By making his model conform to what was believed at the time, Einstein missed the chance to predict the expansion of the universe. I discuss this apparent blunder in Chapter 18.

Many years after Einstein's death, scientists realized that his cosmological constant *does* belong in the equations for the universe. It's needed to explain the very accurate observations that the Hubble Space Telescope and other NASA spacecraft are currently making. Einstein was right after all, as I show you in Chapter 19.

Standing in Awe

The enormous progress in physics and astronomy that has taken place during the last century is due almost completely to the work that Einstein did between 1905 and 1917. If Einstein hadn't existed, most of his work would've been done eventually by other physicists. Some discoveries would've been made a few years after Einstein made them, while others would've taken decades longer. The general theory, his greatest achievement and the one with the greatest implications, wasn't on anybody's radar screen at the time Einstein developed it. Would scientists have discovered it by now? No one can tell.

But Einstein did live, and he did develop his revolutionary theories. To a great extent, the world is what it is today because of him. And it all started in a patent office in Bern, Switzerland, a century ago.

Chapter 2

Portrait of the Scientist as a Young Man

Albert Einstein had a fairly ordinary upbringing. He was born in the town of Ulm, Germany, in 1879 and grew up in Munich, where he attended a Catholic school (even though he was Jewish). His parents, Hermann and Pauline, worried that their child might be backward because he was late to speak. Clearly, their fears were unfounded; young Albert was among the best students in elementary school. In high school and college, however, Einstein was so independent that he often clashed with his teachers and professors.

In this chapter, I provide a quick overview of Einstein's life from birth to college graduation, dispelling some myths (he didn't have a learning disability, for example) and looking at the events that influenced his life.

Glimpsing Albert's Early Years

Albert Einstein was born at noon on Friday, March 14, 1879. In the summer of 1880, when Albert was a little over a year old, his family moved to Munich where his father and uncle opened an electrical engineering business (to replace an earlier business that had failed). At the end of 1881, when Albert was 2 and a half, his sister was born. She was named Marie, but everyone called her Maja.

Hermann Einstein's new business did well, and five years after their move to Munich, the Einsteins bought a nice house with a large garden where Albert and Maja spent many hours playing (see Figure 2-1).

Figure 2-1:
Albert
Einstein,
age 5, and
his sister
Maja, age 3.

Albert and Maja were very close as children, and they maintained a loving relationship throughout their lives. Most of what people know today about Einstein's childhood is due to Maja, who years later wrote a small book about her brother's early years. (See Chapter 21 for a brief biography of Maja.)

Being slow to speak

In her book, Maja described Albert at age 4 as a quiet child who kept to himself and didn't enjoy playing with other children. She wrote that her parents had worried that Albert might be backward because he learned to speak very late. Later in life, Einstein remembered his parents taking him to the doctor to see if his delayed speech development indicated that something was wrong.

The delay in Albert's speech may have been due to shyness and pride — even at the age of 2, he wanted to do things right and avoid mistakes. Albert said later that, at that young age, he made the decision to speak only in whole sentences. He would try the whole sentence out in his mind, sometimes even moving his lips, and when he thought he had it right, he spoke it out loud.

This little boy was already different from the rest of his peers.

Einstein's life during his early years was warm and stimulating. When he was about 4 or 5, lying ill in bed, his father gave him a magnetic compass to cheer him up. The motion of that needle, always returning to a very specific direction due to some mysterious cause unknown to him, left such a "deep and lasting impression" on the young boy that he wrote about it in his autobiographical notes some 60 years later.

Why did the compass needle behave in this way? This was something Albert wanted to understand. You can begin to see in this boy, marveling at the motion of a compass needle, the beginnings of the great genius that revolutionized our understanding of the world. Even at this early age, Einstein was attracted to what would become one of his favorite studies: electromagnetism (see Chapter 6).

Heading to the top of the class

Hermann and Pauline Einstein were not practicing Jews, and they were more concerned with their son's education than with religious practices. When Einstein was 5, his parents enrolled him at the local Catholic school, which had better standards, was closer to home, and was less expensive than the Jewish school.

We have no evidence that Einstein experienced any religious discrimination at school, in spite of being the only Jew enrolled. However, the young Einstein wasn't happy with the school's strict discipline. Granted, most children dislike discipline, but Einstein had an aversion to it throughout his life. (As I mention in Chapter 3, in college, this aversion helped cost him a recommendation for a graduate position.)

Inspired by Mozart

Einstein's mother, Pauline, was an accomplished pianist who wanted her children to be exposed to music at an early age. She enrolled Einstein in violin lessons and his sister in piano lessons. Einstein's lessons started when he was 6 and lasted until he was 14 years old. Most of the time, he hated the lessons because he disliked the mechanical and rote instruction methods of the instructors. When he was about 13, however, he fell in love with Mozart's sonatas, and his interest in playing music turned around. From then on, he strived to improve his technique to be able to reproduce the beauty and grace of Mozart's music.

Later, he taught himself to play the piano and enjoyed improvising occasionally. The violin remained with him throughout his life. He became a good amateur violinist and was fond of playing Mozart and Beethoven sonatas.

In spite of his distaste for the school, he got excellent reports. When Einstein was 7, for example, his mother Pauline wrote to her mother, "Yesterday Albert got his marks. Again he is at the top of his class and got a brilliant record." A year later his grandfather wrote, "Dear Albert has been back in school a week. I just love that boy, because you cannot imagine how good and intelligent he has become." (Do you know any grandparent who doesn't think his grandchild is "good and intelligent"?)

Many accounts of Einstein's life paint him as being slow as a child, perhaps having a learning disability. Einstein himself later wrote that he was able to develop the theory of relativity because his intellectual development had been retarded and, as a consequence, he began to think about space and time only as an adult, not as a child.

Was Einstein really slow as a child? He skipped first grade and was at the top of his class in a good school, so that label seems inaccurate. It's more likely that Einstein was a shy, very proud boy with an advanced mind that didn't particularly make itself known until his adolescence. He didn't enjoy elementary school but, due to his intelligence, could obviously perform very well. He kept to himself most of the time, coming up with his own unusual ways to solve the problems for his school work. Despite what some people have claimed, he didn't have a learning disability. He was smarter than any of his classmates but not a child prodigy.

Going backward in Greek

In October of 1888, when Einstein was 9 and a half, he entered secondary school (the equivalent of middle school and high school today) at the Luitpold Gymnasium. He would attend school there until he was 15. The Gymnasium was even more rigid than the elementary school he'd just left. Einstein once said that the teachers at his elementary school were like sergeants, while the teachers at the Gymnasium were like lieutenants.

The Gymnasium emphasized Greek and Latin. The curriculum also offered modern languages, geography, literature, and mathematics. Einstein liked the logical rigor of both Latin and mathematics and always got the highest grade in the class in those subjects. Greek was another matter. He hated the subject and often made his teacher angry. His Greek teacher didn't appreciate his independently minded student and stated clearly that Einstein would never amount to anything. Einstein's sister later wrote that perhaps the teacher had been right: Einstein never became a professor of Greek grammar.

When Einstein was in the seventh grade, he had the misfortune of having his Greek teacher as his homeroom teacher. This teacher once called him to his office and told him that he wished Einstein would leave the school. Einstein replied that he hadn't done anything wrong. "Your mere presence spoils the respect of the class for me," said the teacher.

However, not all was bad at the school. Another teacher there, Dr. Ferdinand Ruess, was different from the rest. Instead of emphasizing memorization and passive acceptance of facts, he made the students think for themselves. He inspired in them a love for German literature and for the study of ancient civilizations.

Einstein had a great appreciation for Dr. Ruess. Later in life, when Einstein was famous, he decided to pay his old teacher a visit. As often happens, Ruess didn't recognize his former student. Seeing Einstein in his usual baggy and worn-out clothes, Ruess mistook him for a beggar and had his maid throw him out.

Einstein kept his dislike for the Gymnasium and its methods of instruction from his family. He never complained about it until later in life.

Studying holy geometry

Although Einstein's parents were not religious, they followed an old Jewish tradition of sharing a meal with a needy student. For five years, starting when Einstein was 10, a poor medical student from Russia named Max Talmud joined the Einsteins for dinner once a week. Einstein enjoyed talking to the older college student, and Talmud soon realized that Einstein was not an ordinary boy. They talked about science, math, and even philosophy.

When Einstein was 13, Max Talmud brought him Immanuel Kant's *Critique of Pure Reason,* a dense book that even philosophy students find difficult. According to Talmud, Einstein was not daunted by it. From then on, the two friends discussed philosophy during the Thursday night visits. Einstein spent several years studying other philosophy texts, alongside his scientific readings. He continued to be interested in philosophy throughout his life, often discussing in his writings the views of well-known philosophers (see Chapter 20).

Talmud also brought Einstein several books on popular science, which the boy read enthusiastically. Einstein was particularly fond of a set of 21 books titled *Popular Books on Natural Science* by Aaron Bernstein. Einstein later said that he read five or six volumes in this series "with breathless attention." These books gave the young Einstein a basic understanding of physics and probably helped him develop his amazing ability to discover in his readings what was important and what wasn't.

One summer, Einstein became interested in a geometry textbook that he had received several months before the school year was to start. He began to work out the problems, showing his solutions to Talmud. By the end of the summer, Einstein not only had worked out all the problems in the book but had also attempted alternate proofs of the theorems.

Years later, Einstein said that this book — which he called his "holy geometry book" — was probably the reason he became a scientist.

Discovering religion

At the age of 11, Einstein began to attend religion classes, as was the custom among Jewish students. His parents were not practicing Jews, and Einstein grew resentful of them for not following religious traditions. He decided to set an example for his family by observing the Sabbath, eating only Kosher food, and even composing religious songs that he sang to himself as he walked to school.

Einstein's religious fervor didn't last. In his autobiographical notes, written when he was 67 years old, he said that what he was reading in the science books at age 12 clashed with many of the stories in the Bible. He then grew suspicious of every kind of authority and developed a skeptical attitude. This skepticism, he said, never left him, although it lost its original intensity.

From then on, he decided to understand the nature of the universe, which stood before him like a great riddle. Einstein didn't think that this quest was as comfortable and reassuring as the religious quest that he had briefly experienced, but he never regretted choosing it.

Later in life, Einstein developed a deep admiration for the beauty of nature and a belief in the simplicity of the order and harmony that he thought human beings can perceive only imperfectly. This admiration and belief formed his religion, which I discuss further in Chapter 20.

Learning on his own

Luckily, Einstein grew up with people who made up for the shortcomings of the schools he attended. His engineer uncle, Jakob, who lived next door and visited often, was one such influence. When Einstein was about 12, Jakob gave him an algebra book and told the boy that algebra was a merry science. "We go hunting for a little animal whose name we don't know, so we call it x," he explained. "When we bag our game, we pounce on it and give it its right name."

During the summer of 1891, Einstein decided to study the algebra book in detail and asked Uncle Jakob to give him problems to solve. Einstein worked out the solutions and gave them to Jakob to check. His uncle discovered that the 12-year-old Einstein could always find a solution to even the more challenging problems he gave him. That summer, Einstein even rediscovered the proof of the Pythagorean theorem.

From algebra and geometry, Einstein moved on to calculus. By the time he was 16 years old, he had taught himself differential and integral calculus, as well as analytical geometry. He enjoyed spending his early teen years learning on his own and found mathematics "truly fascinating."

For Einstein, studying calculus was like reading a mystery novel. The story for him reached climaxes when it got to the concepts of the differential, the integral, and the infinite series. These climaxes even compared with the immense joy he got while studying his holy geometry (see the preceding section).

Dropping Out of High School

In 1894, Einstein's father and his uncle Jakob closed the company that they had founded 14 years earlier. During the early years, the company had done well. However, in the early 1890s, the brothers expanded the company in order to market a dynamo that Jakob had invented. They hired more workers, bought equipment, and moved to a larger plant. Unfortunately, the business became too large to be managed well by the Einstein brothers but was still too small to compete against larger corporations. In 1894, it finally failed.

The two families decided to go to Italy and try their luck there. Hermann and Pauline thought that Albert should stay and finish his school year at the Gymnasium. Einstein was 15 years old and had three more years of high school to complete.

After six months alone in Munich, however, Einstein was depressed and nervous. He convinced his family physician, Dr. Bernard Talmud (Max's brother), to provide him with a certificate stating that, due to nervous disorders, he needed the company of his family. Einstein left the Gymnasium without informing his parents and joined them in Italy.

Although technically Einstein was a high school dropout, he didn't intend to abandon his education. He promised his upset parents that he would study on his own to prepare for the entrance examination at the prestigious Federal Polytechnic Institute (the Polytechnic) in Zurich. His father wanted him to study electrical engineering there, as his uncle had done. The Polytechnic did not require a high school diploma for admission. All Einstein needed was to pass the admission tests.

Hiking across Italy

Life in Italy was wonderful for Einstein. After his parents accepted the inevitable and agreed to his idea of studying on his own to prepare for the entrance exams at the Zurich Polytechnic, Einstein was free to do what he wanted. He combined studying with traveling around Italy, visiting museums and art galleries. He also hiked.

A man without a country

Einstein never liked the country of his birth. He detested Germany's militarism and regimentation. Shortly before his parents decided to move to Italy, he informed his father of his desire to give up his German citizenship because he wanted to become a Swiss citizen. Hermann reluctantly agreed and signed the necessary papers to allow his son to submit the request. On January 28, 1896, Einstein received the formal letter relieving him from his German citizenship, but he didn't become a Swiss citizen until 1901. For five years, he was stateless.

Einstein was never interested in sports or any other form of organized physical activity. However, while in Italy, he became an enthusiastic hiker and mountain climber. (One time, when he wanted to visit an uncle in Genoa, about 80 miles south of his parents' new home in Pavia, he hiked almost 60 miles across the Alps, taking the train for only part of the way.)

Failing the college admission test

As he had promised his parents, Einstein traveled to Zurich in early October of 1895 to take the admission test at the Polytechnic. He had been given special permission to take the test at the age of 16, even though the minimum required age was 18. Two letters — one from his math teacher at the Gymnasium (which Einstein had been clever enough to request before quitting) and one from his mother stating that Einstein was "gifted" — were apparently convincing.

Einstein's interest in philosophy had continued to blossom, and he considered studying philosophy in college. When his father heard about this idea, he told Einstein to study electrical engineering, like his uncle Jakob, and forget about this "philosophical nonsense." Einstein followed his father's advice and applied to study engineering.

Einstein was tested in political and literary history, German and French, drawing, mathematics, descriptive geometry, biology, chemistry, and physics, and he was required to write an essay. He failed the test. He did well in math and physics but poorly in the other subjects.

However, the director of the Polytechnic saw Einstein's potential and suggested that he obtain a diploma at a Swiss secondary school and reapply. One of the physics professors, Heinrich Weber, who was impressed with Einstein's performance in math and physics, told him that he could audit his class if he decided to stay in Zurich.

Spending a Great Year at a Swiss School

Einstein's parents agreed with the director of the Polytechnic and enrolled him in the Swiss Cantonal school in Aarau, in the German-speaking part of Switzerland. That year was perhaps one of the best of Einstein's youth. Located in a beautiful village some 20 miles west of Zurich, the school was ideal for Einstein. It was run by Jost Winteler, a respected and liberal-minded teacher who created a relaxed environment where the students were encouraged to think for themselves rather than being forced to accept "truths" from higher authorities. This approach suited the rebellious Einstein perfectly.

Einstein boarded with the Wintelers and quickly became part of their large family, calling Jost and Pauline Winteler "Papa" and "Mamma." Jost Winteler was a scholar himself, and Einstein admired him.

The Aarau school was the only school that Einstein ever liked. He made friends there and was quite popular. He also developed an attitude of self-assurance and, at times, appeared cocky. (This attitude remained with him through life, although it mellowed with age and fame.)

Falling into first love

The Wintelers were a large family. Pauline and Jost had three girls and four boys. Einstein's links to the Wintelers were to grow stronger in the years to come. One of the boys, Paul, would marry Einstein's sister, Maja. The oldest girl, Anna, would marry one of Einstein's closest friends.

Of the three girls, Marie was the prettiest. She was fun to be with and, like Einstein, loved music. She played the piano, and Einstein often joined her in duets. Einstein soon fell in love with her. Although Marie was two years older, Einstein was more mature. She admired his brilliance and, like other girls, thought that he was handsome. He liked her cheerful spirit and beauty, as well as the attention she bestowed upon him.

It wasn't easy for the two teenagers in love to enjoy their relationship in private, and soon even Maja was teasing her brother about his new girlfriend. Einstein's parents were extremely pleased to have their son under the guidance of such a respected family and approved enthusiastically of Einstein's relationship with Marie.

Jost Winteler was a bird-watcher and organized frequent field trips for his class, inviting friends and family to join in. On many occasions, Einstein and Marie went along on these trips, spending wonderful moments walking in the woods, a few steps behind the group.

Performing "thought experiments"

During this period, Einstein developed a method to logically think through a scientific idea by following the steps of an experiment in his mind. These were his famous "thought experiments" that were to be so useful to him when he later developed his theories. (As I explain in Chapter 4, Galileo had used thought experiments centuries before, with similar success.)

His first thought experiment planted the seed that became the special theory of relativity (see Part III). Einstein wanted to know what would happen if he were to ride alongside a beam of light. Would he be able to see the front of the light wave? The young Einstein realized that, in this case, the wave would disappear; it wouldn't oscillate.

To see why, you can perform your own thought experiment. Imagine that you are a surfer, riding a big wave in Hawaii on your surfboard. To you, the water doesn't move up and down. You stay at the top of the wave as it moves to shore, and you don't see it oscillate. The big wave disappears. For a "light surfer," light, which is an electromagnetic wave, would also stop oscillating.

Einstein wasn't satisfied with what his thought experiment was telling him and continued to think about it from time to time. Some nine years later, he combined this thought experiment with a better understanding of electromagnetism (see Chapter 6) to state that light travels at the same speed regardless of how the observer moves. Therefore, no one could catch up to a beam of light. As I explain in Chapter 9, that statement became one of the two pillars of his special theory of relativity.

Staying at the top of the class

Einstein passed his final exams at the Aarau school in the fall of 1896 with the top grades in the class. He obtained a 6 (out of 6) in physics, descriptive geometry, geometry, and history and near-perfect grades in everything else. His lowest grade was in French, and the French teacher actually wanted to challenge his graduation. (The French final consisted of an essay, and Einstein's essay was full of grammatical errors and misspellings.)

Einstein did graduate, however, and he was admitted to the Polytechnic in Zurich, even though he was six months short of the required age to enter college.

When Einstein first attempted to gain admission to the Polytechnic prior to attending the Aarau school, he applied to study engineering. The year in the Aarau school, however, rekindled his interest in science — particularly physics. In his ungrammatical essay for the French final exam, he wrote that his plans included entering the Polytechnic to study physics and mathematics. He was more adept at the theoretical sciences, he wrote, than at experimentation.

Accident in the mountains

Einstein had a close call during a field trip in the Swiss Alps with one of the teachers at the Aarau school. The class was climbing Mount Santis on a rainy day in June, and the ground was slippery. Einstein, who wasn't wearing hiking boots, slipped and started sliding down a slope when a classmate pulled him up with his walking cane. If it hadn't been for the quick reaction of his alert classmate, Einstein probably would've died, and we'd be living in a very different world today.

Becoming a College Rebel

About a thousand students entered the freshman class at the Zurich Polytechnic with Einstein, and most registered in the engineering schools. Einstein, however, opted for physics. Because the physics, astronomy, and math departments were in the College of Sciences, Einstein registered there.

Focusing on physics

Einstein's freshman class at the College of Sciences had five students. Three were math majors. Einstein and the only woman in the class, Mileva Maric (who would later become Einstein's love interest), were the only physics majors.

The physics department was in a large, modern building and was very well equipped. The faculty was world class. Adolf Hurwitz and Hermann Minkowski, two renowned mathematicians, were among Einstein's professors.

Einstein had been eagerly awaiting his first college physics class and was disappointed when his advisor scheduled him for math courses and some non-science electives during the first semester. In the second and third semesters, the physics majors took Newtonian mechanics. Engineering majors also took this course, which made Einstein unhappy because he didn't feel it was "real" physics.

His first "real" physics course was taught by Professor Heinrich Weber, the man who had seen Einstein's potential even when he failed his first attempt at entering the Polytechnic. Einstein wrote to a classmate that he eagerly anticipated Weber's masterful lectures on heat, thermodynamics, and the theory of gases. As I explain in the upcoming section "Butting heads," this mutual admiration wouldn't last forever.

Cramming for exams

Einstein's life was the typical life of a European college student at the time. He spent many hours at the local cafes and bars, drinking coffee and arguing with friends about science and philosophy. However, he was selective about what courses he gave his attention to, and he skipped classes if he disliked a course or a professor.

At the Polytechnic, students took two examinations during the four years: the intermediates and the finals. The rest of the time, they didn't have to worry about grades, tests, or even class attendance. Einstein, the rebel, did as he pleased. He studied books in areas that were not related to any of his classes just because he became interested in the subject, and he didn't bother with the courses he didn't like. But skipping classes didn't help when it came time to prepare for exams, because his class notes were full of holes.

Two or three months before the intermediate exams, Einstein started thinking about studying for them. Without good class notes, the task was impossible. The Polytechnic professors didn't simply follow textbooks. They were top researchers in their fields; many times their lectures were related to their work. Even when the material was already established, they presented it following their own approaches. The stuff wasn't in books.

Fortunately for Einstein, his friend Marcel Grossmann kept meticulous class notes. Grossmann was a math major and one of Einstein's lifelong friends. (He helped Einstein get a job in the patent office after graduation. Many years later, as professor of mathematics at the Polytechnic and dean of the Math-Physics College, Grossman provided Einstein with the advanced mathematical techniques needed for his general theory of relativity.)

Armed with Grossmann's notes, Einstein spent the summer of 1898 cramming for the exams, which took place in October. When the results came back, Einstein was happily surprised. He had received the highest grade. Grossman, a smart and conscientious student, was second.

Falling in Love Again

Einstein had lost interest in Marie Winteler soon after he left Aarau for the Polytechnic. They wrote letters to each other, but Einstein's initial enthusiasm faded. However, he still sent her his dirty laundry, which she dutifully washed and mailed back to him.

Einstein couldn't bring himself to tell Marie that he didn't love her anymore, so he simply stopped writing to her. However, he remained very close to the Wintelers and wrote to Marie's mother apologizing for causing her daughter such grief.

Meanwhile, Einstein met Mileva Maric when they both started college at the Polytechnic (see Figure 2-2). She was the daughter of Serbian farmers and was born in the region of Vojvodina, which belonged to Hungary at the time, later became part of Yugoslavia, and is now part of the Republic of Serbia. From an early age, Mileva decided to go to college even against the wishes of her family. Because the Swiss universities were the only German-speaking schools that would accept women, she entered the University of Zurich in 1896 to study medicine. After only one semester, she transferred to the Polytechnic to study physics.

Figure 2-2:
Einstein and Mileva Maric in 1911.

Mileva was three and a half years older than Einstein and the oldest student in the freshman class at the Polytechnic. In high school she had been good at math and physics, which is perhaps the reason for her switch from medical school to physics.

There is no evidence that Einstein and Mileva had any interest in each other until about the second semester, when they went out on a hike together. Like many of the women Einstein was interested in, Mileva liked music and played the piano. As he did with Marie Winteler, Einstein started playing duets with Mileva, who also had a beautiful singing voice.

Finding an intellectual companion

Although Mileva and Marie Winteler had music as a common interest, Mileva was different in every other aspect. She was plain-looking, moody, and had a temper. Einstein's friends often wondered what he saw in her. With her close friends, however, Mileva opened up, laughed, and had a good time.

That was the side that Einstein likely saw. To him, she was a serious, independent, and intellectual companion whom he considered to be his equal. His letters to her often dealt with his readings of the physics masters of the time, as well as his own research ideas. Although Mileva didn't comment on the physics that Einstein discussed in his letters, she was his companion in his program of self-study, reading physics along with him.

Unfortunately, after only one year at the Polytechnic, Mileva surprised Einstein by transferring to the University of Heidelberg (even though women couldn't enroll as regular students there, so she would be allowed only to audit classes).

Exchanging letters

During their separation, Einstein and Mileva exchanged several letters. After only one semester, however, Mileva decided to return to the Polytechnic. Einstein was delighted and offered to help her catch up in the courses she missed. Mileva was still planning on taking the intermediate exams with her classmates.

With Einstein's help and the use of his class notes, Mileva began to work on the courses she'd missed. Soon, however, she realized that she needed to postpone taking the exams until the following year.

Einstein and Mileva continued writing letters to each other when they traveled home during school vacations. These letters give people today a glimpse at how their relationship evolved. Unfortunately, while Mileva kept the letters that Einstein sent her, Einstein saved only a few.

Early in 1899, their letters changed from "Dear Mr. Einstein," or "Dear Madam," to "Dear Johnnie" and "Dear Dolly," the names they invented for each other. "I'll address you different next time," she wrote. "I've thought of a nicer way." From then on, the letters became love letters. She sent him "a thousand kisses from your Dollie." He sent her "a thousand wishes and the biggest kisses from your Johnnie."

Einstein and Mileva spent considerable time together in "their place," as Einstein called his own apartment in his letters to her. However, he and Mileva kept separate residences, so as not to "start any rumors."

During his final year in college, Einstein kept up his program of self-study, often reading with Mileva. They grew closer and, at some point during the year, decided to get married.

Justifiable jealousy

Even after Einstein broke up with Marie Winteler, Mileva appears to have been jealous of her. In 1899, Einstein's sister, Maja, entered the teachers college in Aarau and, like Einstein had done, roomed with the Wintelers. Einstein, who was always close to Maja, visited her often.

Einstein wrote to Mileva that she shouldn't worry about him seeing Marie. He assured her that his feelings for Marie were under control. "I feel quite secure in my fortress of calm," he told her. "But I know that if I saw her a few more times I would certainly go mad. Of that I am certain, and I feel it like fire." So much for reassuring Mileva.

Asserting His Independence

In his third year at the Polytechnic, Einstein took Professor Heinrich Weber's electrotechnical lab. He had been looking forward to taking this lab and spent a great deal of time in it, doing not only the experiments required for the class, but also some of his own design. He even began to skip lectures so that he could go to the lab and work there.

Butting heads

Although Einstein had been impressed with the introductory physics courses that Weber taught, he didn't feel the same about his more advanced theory courses. Einstein didn't like Weber's course in electricity and magnetism, for example, because Weber didn't present anything about James Clerk Maxwell's theory (see Chapter 6), which was "the most fascinating subject at the time that I was a student," Einstein later wrote.

Einstein became disrespectful and cocky, calling his teacher "Mr. Weber" rather than the polite and customary "Professor Weber." Weber hated Einstein's arrogance and classroom demeanor and became disappointed with him. "You are brilliant," Weber told Einstein at one point. "But you have a serious problem; nobody can tell you anything."

Einstein paid dearly for his arrogance with Weber after graduation. Weber succeeded in preventing Einstein from getting an academic position, and Einstein had to resign himself to becoming a patent reviewer in Bern (see Chapter 3).

"Physics is too difficult for you"

Einstein took several lab courses from Heinrich Weber during his last two years at the Polytechnic, earning top grades in all of them. In contrast, he failed a lab course he took with Professor Jean Pernet. This course was the only one Einstein ever flunked.

Einstein disliked Pernet from the beginning, and that was part of the problem. Characteristically, he skipped many classes, and when he showed up, he antagonized Pernet by not following the instructions handed out in class. Fed up, Pernet reported Einstein to the president of the university for neglect of duty. He said that Einstein was insolent and arrogant. When Einstein confronted him, Pernet told him to try some other field of study, because there wasn't any hope for him in physics. "Physics is too difficult for you," he told Einstein.

Pernet didn't just fail Einstein; he gave him a 1 in the course, the lowest possible grade. Einstein probably deserved it.

Getting his mind in shape

Disappointed at Weber's course in electricity and magnetism, Einstein decided to study the subject on his own. He obtained a copy of Paul Drude's *Physics of the Ether*, one of the first German books to use Maxwell's electromagnetism to explain electrical and optical phenomena. In his book, Drude, a professor of physics at the University of Leipzig, explained electrical conduction in metals, thermal conductivity, and the optical properties of metals in terms of interactions of electrical charges.

As he often did, Einstein immersed himself in the study of Drude's book with great intensity. Often, he read with Mileva, and she sometimes would also check out from the library a copy of the book they were studying. One day, when Einstein forgot his keys and found himself locked out of his room, he ran to Mileva's apartment and borrowed her copy of the book, leaving her a note asking that she not be angry with him for taking the book "in this emergency, in order to do some studying."

The emergency, of course, was his own compulsion to learn all he could about electromagnetism and about other areas of physics that interested him.

A few days later, Einstein told Mileva that he had read half the book already and found it stimulating and informative, but the book lacked clarity and precision in some places.

That year, Einstein's studies of the physics masters continued with books by Hermann von Helmholtz on atmospheric movements and by Heinrich Hertz on the propagation of the electric force. Einstein also studied Maxwell's electromagnetism from *Introduction to Maxwell's Theory of Electricity* by August Foppl, and he read Ernst Mach's *Mechanics*.

Spending time in Paradise

During the summer break before his fourth year at Polytechnic, Einstein traveled with his mother and sister to a resort town south of Zurich, where they stayed at the Hotel Paradise. Mileva went home to her family farm to study for her intermediate exams. Einstein wrote to her as soon as he got to the hotel, telling her that he was "completely bookless for a week" while the local libraries were taking inventory, but that this awful situation wouldn't last because the libraries were going to send him books by Helmholtz, Boltzmann, and Mach. He told her not to worry because he was going to review with her everything he read that summer.

He spent the mornings studying and the afternoons hiking with his sister or playing his violin. He was reading about the ether, a problem that had been on his mind since he was at Aarau (see the sidebar "A 16-year-old scientist"). As I explain in Chapter 3, the idea of the ether had been introduced in the 19th century to provide a medium for the transmission of light in space.

In a letter, he told Mileva about an idea he came up with in Aarau to investigate the motion of the Earth through the ether.

Einstein found the differing points of view about the motion of the Earth through the ether problematic. Hertz's interpretation, in particular, bothered him. Hertz had recently measured in his laboratory the electromagnetic waves predicted by Maxwell's theory, and this discovery took the world of physics by storm. In his book about the ether and electrodynamics, Hertz assumed that the ether traveled along with the Earth as the Earth moved in its orbit around the sun.

Einstein took issue with that assumption. In another letter to Mileva, he wrote that he was convinced that the current presentation of the electrodynamics of moving bodies did not correspond to reality. He thought that he could one day do it right and present it in a simper way.

Six years later, he would do just that, with his special theory of relativity (see Part III).

Measuring the ether wind

From the moment he arrived at the Polytechnic, Einstein wanted to perform an experiment to measure the Earth's movement against the ether. His disagreement with Hertz's interpretation of the motion of the Earth in the ether revived his interest in the experiment.

A 16-year-old scientist

Einstein first began thinking about the ether after he dropped out of high school and joined his parents in Italy at the age of 16. During the summer of 1895, he wrote a paper on the ether and sent it to his uncle Caesar Koch, his mother's brother, in Belgium. His uncle was in the grain business, and it's unlikely that he understood anything in Einstein's paper, so it's unclear why Einstein sent it to him. The title of his paper was "On the Examination of the State of the Ether in a Magnetic Field." It was never published.

For his experiment, Einstein wanted to set up two mirrors so that the light from a single source could be directed in two different directions, one along the motion of the Earth and the other in the opposite direction. Two *thermocouples* (devices to measure temperature) would detect differences in the amount of heat generated by the two beams. The difference would depend on the motion of the Earth with or against the ether "wind."

Einstein asked Weber for permission to do the experiment, but the professor would have none of it. Weber probably realized that this measurement was going to be almost impossible to detect.

Other scientists were proposing more sophisticated experiments to measure this velocity. Just a year earlier, for example, Albert Michelson and Edward Morley, two physicists at the Case School of Applied Science in Cleveland, Ohio (Case Western Reserve University today), had set up what became the landmark experiment to measure this phenomenon.

However, it's unlikely that Weber knew about the Michelson–Morley experiment. He had been disconnected from the forefront of physics research while he was in charge of building his new laboratory at the Polytechnic. (That's why his course on electromagnetism didn't include the recent discoveries of Maxwell and Hertz.)

At the time, Einstein didn't seem to know about the Michelson–Morley experiment either, and he said so several years later.

Writing his senior thesis

The Polytechnic required a senior thesis for graduation. Einstein and Mileva chose similar topics in heat conduction, with Weber as the thesis advisor. The thesis had to be completed in three months. However, Einstein didn't write his on regulation paper and Weber forced him to redo it. Einstein wasn't happy with this demand, since it shortened his studying time for the finals.

In contrast with the wonders to come (which I introduce in Chapter 3), Einstein's undergraduate thesis wasn't much more than a college paper written to fulfill a requirement. Years later, when Einstein was famous, he said that his and Mileva's theses were of no consequence and weren't even worth mentioning.

Taking final exams

Einstein and Mileva also prepared together for the final exams, but they weren't exactly in top form when exam time arrived. Einstein had spent a great deal of time reading other books and not enough time studying, plus he had played hooky in too many courses. Mileva hadn't done particularly well in her intermediates, which she had taken at the start of her senior year. And she had other concerns on her mind: She had heard that Einstein's parents were opposed to her relationship with Einstein. His mother, in particular, had said that Mileva was not good enough for her son and blamed Mileva for entrapping Einstein.

Although Einstein did well on his exams, he didn't repeat the feat of getting the top grades, as he had done in the intermediates. Mileva failed. She did fine in physics but poorly in math and astronomy. Three other physics and math majors graduated with Einstein. Mileva was devastated and thought of quitting, but Einstein talked her into trying again the following year.

Moving Forward

With his college degree at hand, Einstein was ready to start his adult, independent life. He planned on starting his academic career by becoming an assistant to a professor at the Polytechnic while at the same time working on a thesis for his PhD. As soon as he got a job, he and Mileva would get married.

He applied to Weber for an assistantship; however, his rude behavior had turned the professor's early good impression of Einstein around, and Weber wouldn't hire him.

Einstein didn't think that this first rejection was important. He submitted applications to other Polytechnic professors, confident that they would love to hire him. He told Mileva that after both of them obtained their PhD's, they would happily work together as professional physicists and "money will be as plentiful as manure."

However, life had some surprises in store for him.

Vacationing with mama

After graduating from the Polytechnic, Einstein joined his mother and sister in a resort town south of Lake Lucerne in central Switzerland, about 25 miles south of Zurich. The first days of the vacation were not pleasant. Although Maja hadn't dared to tell their mother anything about Mileva, the issue of Einstein's relationship with her inevitably came up. Einstein told his mother that he planned to marry Mileva. Pauline cried, implored, and argued in an effort to convince Einstein that Mileva was not right for him. Einstein wouldn't listen.

Soon Pauline realized that she wasn't getting anywhere and stopped her rant. When Einstein told her that they hadn't been intimate, Pauline saw some hope of eventually convincing her son of what she thought was a grave mistake.

With his mother appeased, Einstein could enjoy his vacation. He played the violin, went climbing at Mount Titlis with Maja, and read a book by the well-known physicist Gustav Kirkchhoff on the motion of the rigid body.

Chapter 3

1905: Einstein's Miracle Year

In This Chapter

▶ Working as an amateur scientist

▶ Entering the botched-up house of physics

▶ Writing the revolutionary papers

*I*n 1905, the year now recognized as Einstein's *year of miracles,* he was 26 years old, had a job as a technical expert at the Swiss Federal Patent Office, had been married for two years to Mileva Maric, and had a 1-year-old baby. In his spare time, he did research in physics.

Einstein did his scientific work at home or at the patent office library, not at a university or a research laboratory. He was what you would call today an amateur scientist. Yet, that year, he published five papers, three of which started the two most important revolutions in physics since Isaac Newton introduced his universal law of gravitation (see Chapter 4). One of the other two papers got him his doctorate. And one of these papers later earned him the Nobel Prize in physics.

In this chapter, I describe Einstein's professional situation in the years leading up to 1905. I briefly explain the dilemmas in the world of physics of Einstein's day (which I discuss in much more detail in Part II of this book). And finally, I introduce you to the revolutionary papers that Einstein published during this incredible year.

Searching for Work

As I explain in Chapter 2, Einstein graduated from college in 1900 with a degree in physics. He wanted to find a position as a graduate assistant so he could do research toward his doctorate degree.

However, as an undergraduate student, Einstein had angered some of his professors by openly contradicting them during their lectures. The professors also disliked him for skipping classes and studying only what he liked. Therefore, when faculty members were writing letters of recommendation, Einstein got what they felt he deserved: He ended up being the only person in his graduating class without a job. He sent applications to professors at different universities with copies of a research paper that he had published right after graduation, but no offer ever came. Finally, after 18 months of unsuccessful attempts, he gave up trying to get a university position and, with the help of one of his closest friends, got a job in a patent office in Bern, Switzerland.

As Einstein himself later said, the job at the patent office was not demanding and gave him time to pursue his scientific interests. During his first three years there, he published three papers in *Annalen der Physik,* a respected physics journal. This level of research activity was (and still is) unusual for someone who doesn't have connections to a university or a research laboratory.

The Botched-Up House of Physics

In the early 1900s, physics was in crisis. The two main branches of physics at the time were:

- **Electromagnetism:** James Clerk Maxwell's theory, which was finalized in 1873, explained the nature of light and magnetism (among other things). I explain this theory in detail in Chapter 6.
- **Mechanics:** Isaac Newton's laws about the science of motion, which I discuss in Chapter 4, dated back to 1666.

Although some scientists thought that physics was essentially complete with these two theories, by the time Einstein was a student some problems were becoming obvious. First, the theories contradicted each other on some points. Second, electromagnetism and mechanics couldn't explain several new observations that physicists had made.

Einstein said later that physics at that time was like a botched-up house, ready to collapse at any moment.

Considering the ultraviolet catastrophe

As I discuss in Chapter 15, one flaw in the house of physics was that current theories couldn't explain observations regarding heat radiating from objects. As you know, objects change colors as they get hotter. For example, if you turn on an electric stove, the burner initially glows red. As it gets hotter, the burner becomes orange, and later it's bright yellow.

Given this color progression, you would expect an object glowing in the ultra-violet part of the spectrum (which we can't really see except with special instruments) to have an even higher temperature. Physicists' equations certainly indicated this would be the case. But their observations showed quite the opposite: Hot objects emit *less* ultraviolet light and *more* light of other colors. Scientists called this problem the *ultraviolet catastrophe.*

The physicists were considering that the light emitted from the hot object moved from place to place like a wave. That's what Maxwell's theory said would happen and what famous experiments done by English physicist Thomas Young in the early 19th century said (see Chapter 7).

Enter German physicist Max Planck. In 1900, he noticed that if the light emitted by a hot object were somehow split into bundles or lumps, he could come up with a new equation that would describe what scientists were seeing: The radiated light would peak in other colors and would be almost nonexistent in the ultraviolet range.

Planck didn't think that the small lumps (he called them *quanta*) of radiated light were part of the nature of light itself. After all, as Young, Maxwell, and others had shown, light is continuous and moves like a wave. However, scientists knew that in certain instances, sound waves form lumps, or beats, when waves of slightly different frequencies overlap. Planck thought that perhaps something similar was happening with the hot bodies radiating light quanta. But he wasn't sure.

Struggling with absolute motion

A second major issue with the botched-up physics house was even more problematic, because it placed mechanics and electromagnetism in contradiction with each other: Newton and Maxwell disagreed about whether such a thing as absolute motion exists.

According to Newton, the laws of physics should be exactly the same whether you are at rest or moving with a constant velocity. In Newton's mechanics, motion has to be described in relation (relative) to some object. He thought that you couldn't come up with an experiment that would give you different results when you are moving than when you are at rest.

Consider a familiar example: If you're on an airplane, you can't tell whether you're moving or not (unless there is turbulence, of course). If you fall asleep before the plane takes off and wake up when the plane is flying steadily, you need to look outside to know that you are not still parked at the gate. That's because, according to Newton, the laws of physics are exactly the same in both instances: when the plane is at rest and when the plane is moving.

How did Maxwell's theory differ? Electromagnetism says that light is a wave. As such, light needs some sort of substance to propagate through (much like water waves need a body of water and sound waves need air). On Earth, light travels through air, water, and glass. But what happens in space? What substance does the light from the sun or a star travel through when it is on its way to the Earth?

Nineteenth-century physicists called this hypothetical substance *ether*. They said that the ether filled the entire universe, and planets, stars, and light would move through it. Therefore, the ether would provide a way for you to tell whether you are moving at a constant velocity or are at rest. You wouldn't need to look out the window when you are sitting in an airplane to find out if you are moving. All you'd need to do is to discover a way to measure your motion through the ether, which exists everywhere, even inside objects.

In other words, you could always measure motion in relation to the ether. The ether would be a fixed, standard reference place that would give you the unique or *absolute motion* of any object. With this standard, you would be able to distinguish between rest and motion, and the laws of physics would not give you the same measurements for each case.

Storming the Scientific World

As the previous section shows, when Einstein began his research as an amateur scientist, there were two major problems:

- ✔ Light was known to be a wave but had to be considered as made up of lumps — not waves — to explain the ultraviolet catastrophe.
- ✔ In mechanics, the results of experiments are identical in motion or at rest (all motion is relative, and there is no absolute motion). Not so in electromagnetism, because you can be at rest in the ether (there is absolute motion).

Scientists were struggling to make existing theories work, but more and more they were becoming aware of their inadequacies. The stage was set for Einstein to make history, and in 1905, he did just that.

What did Einstein achieve during his year of miracles? He wrote and published five scientific papers that would change physics forever:

1. **March 17:** "On a heuristic point of view concerning the production and transformation of light." This paper laid the foundation for quantum theory with the introduction of the concept of quanta of energy, or *photons*.

2. **April 30:** "A new determination of molecular dimensions." This was Einstein's PhD dissertation, which the University of Zurich accepted in July. Although not revolutionary, this paper helped establish the existence of molecules.

3. **May 11:** "On the motion of small particles suspended in a stationary liquid." This paper not only explained the zigzag motion of a speck in a liquid (called *Brownian motion*), which had puzzled scientists for a long time, but also showed the reality of molecules.

4. **June 30:** "On the electrodynamics of moving bodies." This was Einstein's first paper on the theory of relativity.

5. **September 27:** "Does an object's inertia depend on its energy content?" This second paper on the theory of relativity contained Einstein's most famous equation: $E = mc^2$.

Even before the first paper was published, Einstein suspected that what he was about to do was of great importance. In May of 1905, he wrote to one of his closest friends:

> *I promise you four papers . . . the first of which I might send you soon, since I will be receiving the free reprints. The paper deals with radiation and the energy properties of light and is very revolutionary, as you will see . . .*

The first paper of 1905 certainly was revolutionary. It laid the foundation for quantum theory, which I explain in Chapter 16. Einstein won the Nobel Prize in physics several years later for this work.

As if that weren't enough, the fourth paper and fifth papers that Einstein published that year were also revolutionary. In Part III of this book, I explain the impact that the special theory of relativity had.

The other two papers were also very important because they helped to establish the existence of atoms and molecules, which were not yet universally accepted. But unlike the other three, they didn't turn the scientific world upside down.

Einstein actually wrote a sixth paper that year, which he sent off to the *Annalen der Physik* on December 19. That paper also dealt with the sizes of molecules and with Brownian motion, and it was published in 1906. In that same year, the *Annalen* published his PhD dissertation.

Defining the nature of light

Einstein solved the first major problem in physics with the first paper of his miracle year, the paper on the light quantum.

The Nobel was not relative

You may have assumed that Einstein won the Nobel Prize for his theory of relativity, which he had developed fully by 1921. However, the Nobel committee thought that relativity was still too strange and controversial. The committee was afraid that relativity would later be seen as incorrect, and they didn't want to make a mistake. Therefore, they decided that of all the other work that Einstein had done by 1921, his first paper of 1905 with the light quantum idea was the one worthy of the Nobel Prize. Because this paper eventually led to quantum theory, the committee was correct in its decision.

Recall that Max Planck had used a mathematical trick to explain radiation in the ultraviolet part of the spectrum; he bundled light into quanta of energy. In the first paper of 1905, Einstein made Planck's quanta a property of light and of all electromagnetic radiation (radio waves, x-rays, ultraviolet and infrared light, and so on). It isn't that light is lumpy in some instances. Light is *always* lumpy, like a particle. It comes in bundles. The light emitted by hot objects isn't somehow split into these bundles. Light is made up of these bundles, these *photons* as they are called, that can't be split.

By making lumpiness a property of light, Einstein paved the way for the development of quantum theory that would take place in the 1920s. Quantum theory would later explain that light is both a wave and a particle. Light behaves like a wave under certain conditions, and under other conditions, it behaves like a particle. Quantum theory integrates both behaviors seamlessly.

Even though Einstein's first paper was read with a great deal of interest, most physicists didn't believe his idea of photons of light, including Planck himself initially. For the next 15 years, Einstein was almost the only one who believed in the light quantum idea. But quantum theory, developed by other physicists in the 1920s based on Einstein's work, would become the most successful physics theory ever.

In Chapter 16, I show you how Einstein's first paper of 1905 also explained a phenomenon called the *photoelectric effect* in a clever but simple way. In 1921, after Einstein had already become world famous, the Nobel committee awarded him the Nobel Prize in physics for this discovery.

Eliminating the ether

As I note earlier in the chapter, a key contradiction between mechanics and electromagnetism was the existence of absolute motion. According to Newton, all motion is relative — absolute motion can't exist. But according to Maxwell, it can.

Einstein sided with mechanics. In his fourth paper of 1905, commonly referred to as the *relativity paper* (even though the word *relativity* doesn't appear in the title), Einstein reformulated electromagnetism so that it would also remain unchanged whether the person observing was at rest or moving at a constant velocity. In other words, he modified electromagnetism so that its description would depend only on relative motion, without any need for the ether. Light does not need a substance to move through. It can move in the empty space between the stars.

With the publication of this paper, the ether was gone from physics. According to Einstein, absolute motion does not exist. When you are on an airplane, you have no way to tell, without looking out the window, whether you are moving or at rest. All the laws of physics, those of mechanics and those of electromagnetism, are the same everywhere in the universe, no matter how you move (provided that you don't accelerate; see Chapter 12 for more on that situation).

Einstein extended the idea of relative motion to light itself. Anybody, anywhere in the universe, whether at rest or in motion with a constant velocity, always measures the same speed of light.

All of the physics known at the time followed the simple principles that Einstein put forward in his relativity paper. And all the physics discoveries since then have followed those principles. Einstein's paper didn't just fix the problems with electromagnetism; it actually created a new way of looking at the world.

Introducing $E = mc^2$

Einstein's final paper of 1905, which was also the last of his revolutionary papers, contained the famous $E = mc^2$ equation. This paper was more of a follow-up to the first relativity paper (which I discuss in the previous section) than an introduction to a new equation.

In this beautiful three-page paper, Einstein used electromagnetic equations from his first relativity paper to explain that energy has mass. Two years later, he realized that the opposite should also be true, that mass of any kind must have energy. According to Einstein, mass and energy are equivalent. An object's mass is a form of energy, and energy is a form of mass.

Here are a few examples of how this tiny little equation has changed our lives in big ways:

- ✔ Scientists spent more than 40 years finding a way to demonstrate the reality of $E = mc^2$. World events made this demonstration very dramatic with the development of the nuclear bomb, which was first tried in the desert in Alamogordo, New Mexico, in July of 1945. One month later, the bomb was dropped for real on Hiroshima and Nagasaki, Japan. As I explain in Chapter 17, the energy released by the bomb comes from nuclear fission, the splitting of the uranium-235 nucleus.

✔ $E = mc^2$ gives the recipe for the conversion of part of the uranium nucleus into energy. The same recipe applies to a nuclear reactor, except that the production of energy is controlled with very precise procedures.

✔ Together with the later development of quantum physics (see Chapter 16), $E = mc^2$ helped explain another long-standing problem: understanding how the sun burns its fuel and generates the energy that makes possible life on earth.

For more information about how this equation changed the way we look at the world, don't miss Chapter 11.

Appreciating the two lesser papers

The three papers that I discuss in the preceding sections changed physics forever. That's why they are called revolutionary. The other two papers that Einstein published in 1905 paled by comparison. They didn't change physics, but they were still important contributions to science.

A spoonful of sugar

One day, perhaps as he was having tea, Einstein started thinking about the way in which sugar dissolves in water. He simplified the problem by considering the sugar molecules to be small, hard bodies swimming in a liquid. This simplification allowed him to perform calculations that had been impossible until then and that explained how the sugar molecules would diffuse in the water, making the liquid thicker, or (as scientists like to say) more *viscous*.

The c in $E = mc^2$

The quantity c in Einstein's equation refers to the speed of light. Why c-squared instead of just c or c-cubed (or c to some other power)? The answer dates back to the 17th century, when several scientists who were Newton's contemporaries were establishing the early ideas about energy. Christian Huygens, one of the most gifted of the group, showed that the energy of an object in motion is related to the square of the object's speed. Einstein's equation is also an energy equation and shows the same relationship to the speed.

In search of the PhD

The university that Einstein attended, the Federal Polytechnic Institute (Eidgenössische Technische Hochschule, or ETH) in Zurich was then one of the best technical colleges in Europe, with a small but extremely well-equipped physics department. At the time, the Polytechnic did not grant the PhD degree.

However, graduates could submit a thesis to the University of Zurich for approval. As I explain in Chapter 15, Einstein's first thesis submission to the university was not accepted. However, he later sent that thesis to the *Annalen der Physik* journal, where it was published as a research paper.

Einstein looked up actual values of viscosities of different solutions of sugar in water, put these numbers into his theory, and obtained from his equations the size of sugar molecules. He also found a value for the number of molecules in a certain mass of any substance (what scientists call *Avogadro's number*). With this number, he could calculate the mass of any atom. Einstein decided that this work should be worthy of a PhD and promptly sent it to the University of Zurich for consideration. The thesis was accepted very quickly, and he became Dr. Albert Einstein.

How smoke gets in your eyes

Three weeks after having his thesis approved, Einstein sent another important paper for publication. In this paper on molecular motion, he explained the erratic, zigzag motion of the individual particles of smoke (what's referred to as *Brownian motion*). Always seeking the fundamentals, Einstein was able to show that this chaotic motion gives direct evidence of the existence of molecules and atoms.

Einstein reasoned that the smoke particles would migrate in a way that was similar to how the sugar molecules dissolve in water, which he studied for his doctoral thesis. Comparing his calculations for the two processes, the zigzagging of the smoke specs and the diffusion of sugar in water, he came up with an equation that he then applied to the already developed molecular theory to obtain the sizes of atoms and molecules. Subsequent experiments confirmed his equation.

"My main aim," Einstein wrote later, "was to find facts that would guarantee as far as possible the existence of atoms of definite finite size."

The icing on the cake

Although not revolutionary, these two papers (his thesis and the Brownian motion paper) are among the most frequently cited Einstein papers. Their popularity is not surprising. They have practical applications in the mixing of sand in cement, the motion of certain important proteins in cow's milk, and the motion of aerosol particles in the atmosphere.

However, these papers didn't start a new physics, as did the relativity papers and the light quantum paper. The theory of relativity papers and the light quantum paper made 1905 Einstein's miracle year. The rest was icing on the cake.

Part I
A Genius Awakens

The 5th Wave   By Rich Tennant

1886 — 7-year-old Albert Einstein's genius begins to reveal itself.

In this part . . .

If you don't know much about Einstein, this part gives you an overview of who he was and what he did.

In this part, I discuss Einstein's life as a young boy growing up in Germany, as an independently minded young man keeping to himself in school, and as a rebellious college student getting in trouble with his professors. I also introduce you to the incredible explosion of ideas during his miracle year, when he made most of the discoveries that changed the science of physics forever.

Chapter 4

A Clockwork Universe

*B*y the time Einstein graduated from college, he had mastered the physics of his time. While in college, he took the standard rigorous program of study required for a physics major. But he also studied on his own, especially the new physics being developed at the time.

The physics that Einstein studied was based on the work of Galileo Galilei, Isaac Newton, James Clerk Maxwell, and many others. Their theories were in turn based on the advancement of science that started with the early civilizations. Einstein was familiar with the main ideas of science and used them as the basis of his own work.

In this chapter, I start at the beginning (almost) and look at the ideas of the ancient Greeks about matter, motion, and the universe that formed the foundation of the knowledge passed down to Einstein. I discuss Nicolaus Copernicus's revolution and Johannes Kepler's laws of planetary motion. I explain Galileo's development of the scientific method. These ideas made possible Newton's view of the universe "running like clockwork," with which Einstein was fully familiar. And finally, I show you how all these ideas set the stage for Einstein to turn Newton's clockwork universe into the "space and time are in the eye of the beholder" universe we know today.

Introducing the First Astronomers

In 1900, when Einstein graduated from the Polytechnic, physics was based on the work of Isaac Newton (mechanics) and James Clerk Maxwell (electromagnetism). But the ideas that led to the development of the science of physics had started with the ancient Greeks, 2,000 years earlier. What the Greeks discovered about matter, motion, and the universe formed the foundation of the scientific knowledge passed down to Einstein.

Inventing science

The ancient Greeks didn't invent science. That honor belongs to the Babylonians, some 5,000 years ago. The Babylonians, who lived in the region occupied today by Iraq, started a study of the sky motivated by their need to know the best harvesting times.

The Babylonians made gods out of the sun, the moon, and the five visible planets: Mercury, Venus, Mars, Jupiter, and Saturn. Their worship drove the Babylonians to follow closely their motions across the sky. They used their knowledge of the paths of the sun and moon to set up a calendar. They also observed that the planets, unlike the sun and moon, did not follow simple paths across the sky; the planets stopped their eastward motion now and again, retracing part of their paths, then stopping once more before resuming their eastward motions.

Getting it right: The ancient Greeks

Some of the knowledge acquired by the Babylonians was passed on to the Greeks who, in turn, made amazing advances in their understanding of the world. Through the study of the heavens, the Greeks were able to start on the long path toward the development of the ideas of physics.

For example, in the sixth century B.C., Pythagoras came up with the idea that the Earth was spherical and located at the center of the universe. Aristotle developed Pythagoras's view into a more complete theory, saying that the Earth was immovable and fixed at the center of the whirling heavens.

In the second century A.D., Claudius Ptolemy (who I discuss more in the section "Identifying 'The Greatest' patterns") expanded Aristotle's *geocentric,* or Earth-centered, model into an extremely complicated system that was accepted by nearly everybody for 18 centuries.

There were dissenters, like Aristarchus, who said that the sun was fixed at the center of the universe and that the Earth revolved around the sun in a circular orbit. He also said that the Earth rotated on its axis as it revolved and that this axis was inclined with respect to the plane of the orbit.

Aristarchus got it right. Today, we know that the sun is the center of our solar system, that Earth rotates around the sun *and* on its own axis, and that its axis is tilted.

Shifting their position, unfortunately

In spite of being correct, Aristarchus's view of the universe didn't prevail. The main reason was that the Earth seemed motionless. How could the Earth rotate around the sun if you couldn't detect any motion? What's more, if the Earth rotated around the sun, there should have been an apparent shift in the position of the stars as the Earth moved.

Consider an example closer to home. When you drive down a highway, the trees close to the road pass by quickly, while the ones far back seem to stay with you a little longer. (The moon, being much farther away than any trees, seems to move with you.) The shift in the position of the trees tells you that you are moving. With some measuring equipment, you could use the shift in position to figure out how far the trees are from you and how fast you are going. This apparent shift in position is called *parallax.*

At the time of the Greeks, nobody had yet observed or measured the apparent shift in the position of the stars relative to the Earth. As a result, the Greeks abandoned the sun-centered, or *heliocentric,* model of Aristarchus.

Aristarchus stayed with his theory, believing that he was correct. But the proof had to wait for western civilization to go through the long hiatus of the Dark and Middle Ages. We know today that the stars are so far away that none has a parallax that can be seen with the naked eye. During the Renaissance, instruments like the telescope were invented. By 1838, using a telescope, the German astronomer Friedrich Bessel was able to make the first observation of the parallax of a star.

Identifying "The Greatest" patterns

With the Earth appearing to be stationary in the middle of the universe, the ancient Greeks developed more sophisticated models to explain their astronomical observations. During the second century A.D., Claudius Ptolemy developed the definitive geocentric model, with the planets, the moon, and the sun moving about the Earth in circular orbits. The complicated motion of the planets in the sky required an elaborate model. (As we know today, this motion is the result of the combination of the Earth's motion around the sun and the planets' own motions.)

To explain the known planetary motions, Ptolemy had the planets moving in small circles that he called *epicycles.* The epicycles themselves moved around the Earth in circular orbits (see Figure 4-1). The combination of the motion of both these circles reproduced the observed pattern of the planets' motion.

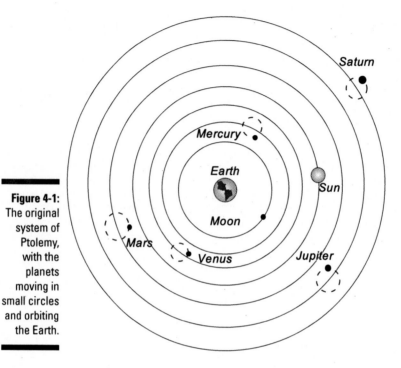

Figure 4-1:
The original
system of
Ptolemy,
with the
planets
moving in
small circles
and orbiting
the Earth.

The model grew in complication when newer and more accurate observations came in. Ptolemy added more circles that moved in circular orbits around other circles, with the planet moving on the last circle. He ended up with a system of 40 circles that reproduced very accurately the astronomical observations of his time.

Ptolemy published his model in *The Mathematical Collection,* a monumental work in 13 volumes. The Arabs took possession of Ptolemy's work after it survived the destruction of the library of Alexandria. They saved it for posterity, calling it *al Magiste,* meaning "The Greatest" in Arabic.

During their long occupation of Spain, the Arabs introduced the book in Europe where, known as the *Almagest,* it was studied for more than 1,000 years.

Sowing the Seeds of Physics

Besides astronomy, the ancient Greeks made advances in what we now call physics. In the following sections, I present two key examples.

Discovering buoyancy

The ancient Greeks' most important discoveries about physics were made by Archimedes, perhaps the greatest Greek scientist.

Born into a royal family in the third century B.C., Archimedes became a famous inventor, scientist, and mathematician. When the Romans laid siege to Syracuse, he invented machines that threw heavy stones at any Roman soldier attempting to climb up the walls. He also built powerful cranes that overturned the ships landing at the bottom of the cliffs around the city.

Archimedes didn't think that his accomplishments on behalf of the war were worthy of publication and wrote only about his numerous scientific achievements. The most important, and the one for which we remember him today, is the discovery of the principle of *buoyancy* (also called *Archimedes' Principle*). This principle says that a body submerged in water is buoyed up by a force equal to the weight of the water displaced by the object.

Imagining the atom

Living in the 21st century, we know that matter is made up of atoms. But 100 years ago, not even the physicists and chemists agreed that atoms existed. (The young Einstein began his scientific career with three important papers demonstrating that atoms existed.)

The development of our modern theories of matter began with John Dalton in the 19th century. However, the Greeks introduced the idea of the atom 23 centuries earlier. The Greek philosopher Democritus, who lived in the fifth century B.C., introduced the idea that all things are made up of small, indivisible particles called atoms, meaning "indivisible." In his writings, he credited his teacher Leucippus with the idea. (However, it isn't clear whether Leucippus really existed.)

According to Democritus, the atoms that make up matter have different sizes, masses, and even colors, and they combine to form all the substances that we see in the world. Democritus wasn't really a scientist, but a philosopher. He didn't know mathematics and couldn't make any calculations to show how the atoms might combine to make the different substances. In addition, laboratory experimentation didn't exist in ancient Greece. (That had to wait for Galileo to invent in the early 17th century.)

Without any mathematical model or laboratory measurements to show how viable atoms were, Democritus's idea remained just that — an idea.

Battling with Mars: Later Astronomers

Not long after Ptolemy died in the year 170 A.D., most of what the Greeks had discovered began to be forgotten. Western civilization took a different path during the Dark and Middle Ages. The sciences and the arts did not again reach the Greek standard until the 17th century, during the Renaissance.

Committing heresy: Copernicus

The long road back to a rational world started in the 15th century with Nicolaus Copernicus. Along with many astronomers of his time, Copernicus became dissatisfied with Ptolemy's model of the universe because it could not explain recent astronomical observations. Like Aristarchus 17 centuries before, Copernicus realized that astronomy could be more easily explained if the sun were at the center of the universe and the Earth rotated around it with all the other planets. He proceeded to build a new model of the universe with the sun at the center.

In the heliocentric model of Copernicus, the Earth, along with Venus, Mars, Jupiter, and Saturn, moved around the sun in circular orbits. After hearing of this model, Church authorities went ballistic. According to Church doctrine, the Earth had to be at the center of creation. Saying otherwise was heresy.

Scared, Copernicus decided not to publish anything on his theory. Many years later, when he was in his late 60s, some of his closest friends encouraged him to publish it. Copernicus gave in, and his book *On Revolutions* was published the day he died at age 70. (He did get to see his work in print: His publisher brought an advance copy to him a few days before his death.)

Discovering planetary laws: Kepler

Although Copernicus's model was much simpler and more elegant than the Ptolemaic system, the Earth still seemed motionless. Like the ancient Greeks, Copernicus's peers couldn't detect the motion of the Earth against the background of the distant stars. As a result, the Copernican model wasn't accepted.

A century later, during the early 1600s, a young and promising German astronomer by the name of Johannes Kepler joined the prestigious observatory of the Danish astronomer Tycho Brahe. (Scientists usually refer to Tycho Brahe by his first name; I follow that convention here.) Tycho's observatory was the best in the world and held the most precise astronomical data.

Tycho asked Kepler to work with a new and large set of unexplained observations of the motion of the planet Mars. Tycho believed in the Ptolemaic system. Kepler, on the other hand, had been converted to the Copernican model by one of his professors at the University of Tübingen, where he graduated in 1588.

Kepler used the precise measurements of Mars that Tycho and his assistants had made to show that the orbit of Mars was not a circle but a stretched-out circle, or oval, called an *ellipse.*

You can draw an ellipse by loosely threading a string around two tacks placed side-by-side on a board (see Figure 4-2). If you move a pencil around the two tacks while you keep the string taut, you can draw the ellipse. The location of each tack is called a *focus* of the ellipse. Kepler discovered that for Mars, the sun is located at one of these foci. (Note that in Figure 4-2, the ellipse representing the orbit of Mars is exaggerated; its actual orbit is a bit more circular.)

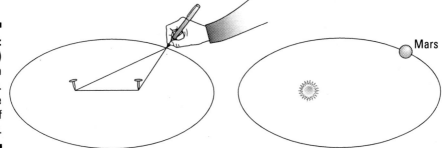

Figure 4-2:
(Left)
Drawing an
ellipse.
(Right) The
orbit of
Mars.

Mars

During the 16 years of his "battle with Mars," as he called it, Kepler discovered that in this elliptical orbit, the planet would move faster when it was closer to the sun and move at a slower speed when it was farther from the sun. He also found that the line joining the planet to the sun swept out the same area with equal intervals of time.

Kepler realized that he was actually discovering something bigger than how Mars orbits the sun; he was identifying the laws of motion of all the planets. After many years of complicated and tedious calculations, he found a mathematical relationship between each planet's own year or *period* (the time it takes for a planet to orbit the sun) and its distance to the sun.

With his discoveries, Kepler knew he had succeeded in discovering the planetary laws. He was immensely proud of his work, but especially so of the last law, called *harmonic law,* which identifies the relationship between the periods of revolution around the sun and the time that a planet is at a specific distance from the sun. He wrote a book describing this discovery, which he entitled *Harmony of the World.*

Here's a quick overview of Kepler's laws:

- ✔ **Law of orbits:** Each planet moves around the sun in an elliptical orbit, with the sun at one focus.

- ✔ **Law of areas:** A planet moves around the sun so that the line from the sun to the planet sweeps out equal areas in equal intervals of time. Take a look at Figure 4-3 to see this in graphic form; the planet moves faster from 1 to 2 than from 3 to 4, so that the line joining it to the sun sweeps out the same area in both cases.

- ✔ **Harmonic law:** The squares of the periods (or years) of any two planets are proportional to the cubes of their average distances from the sun.

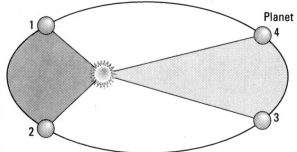

Figure 4-3: Kepler's law of areas.

With the three laws in place, the motion of the moon and the planets became predictable. The universe followed these laws. People could now understand why Venus's year was 225 days while a year on Mars was 687 days. These years or periods were known at the time, but no one had any idea why they were all different. Kepler demonstrated that the planets move around the sun in precise mathematical orbits and times, blindly following his laws.

Inventing Modern Science: Galileo

Kepler's approach to science was very close to that of a modern scientist. He started with the data that had been taken by astronomers in Tycho Brahe's observatory and used it to come up with a model. However, it was his contemporary, Galileo Galilei, who invented the methods followed by modern scientists.

Galileo was born in Pisa in 1564 to an old and distinguished Florentine family. He entered the University of Pisa at the age of 17 to study medicine, a career path he chose to please his father, who wanted his son to have a profession that would guarantee him financial security. Galileo switched to math and science after he started studying the work of Archimedes in one of his courses. (His father wasn't particularly happy with the decision.)

Playing the lute

Like Einstein 300 years later, Galileo enjoyed music. His father, Vincenzio, inspired in him this love for music, teaching him to play the organ and the lute. This interest lasted throughout Galileo's life. He often relaxed by playing the lute, an instrument that became his comfort later in life during his frustrating encounters with the Church.

Vincenzio also taught his son some music theory, introducing him to the musical ratios of the Pythagoreans. Pythagoras, in the sixth century B.C., had discovered that a set of strings vibrating together would produce a pleasant sound if their lengths, compared to the longest string, were in the ratio of one-half, one-third, one-fourth, and so on.

Using the tools at his disposal

A few years after graduating from university, Galileo started doing research in math and physics, giving papers at the Florentine Academy. His extraordinary abilities were soon noticed, and at the age of 26, he was offered a position as professor of mathematics at the University of Pisa.

Here, Galileo started his work in mechanics, clashing with Aristotle's simple and clear ideas about motion. Aristotle had taught that everything fell into its natural place, and the natural place of everything was determined by what the thing was made of. For example:

- A rock falls to the ground.
- Fire falls upward.
- A heavier rock, which contains more earth than a lighter one, falls to the ground faster because it has a greater tendency to fall to its natural place.

Things turned out to be even simpler than that, as Galileo proved. He published his work on mechanics in his book titled *Discourses and Mathematical Demonstrations Concerning Two New Sciences Pertaining to Mechanics and Local Motion,* which appeared in 1638. We know it today as *The Two New Sciences.*

Because Galileo was working in Pisa when he made his discoveries about the nature of motion and of falling bodies, it's not far-fetched to think that he dropped objects from the famous Tower of Pisa to prove his ideas. But he didn't. A stone falling to the ground from several floors high does so at a fairly high speed, so Galileo couldn't time it. He didn't have clocks that were accurate enough.

Galileo's "clocks" were rudimentary: wine bottles filled with water that each had a hole in the bottom and marks to show the water level as it emptied through the hole (see Figure 4-4). His tools weren't terrific, but Galileo was clever. He slowed down the motion of his falling bodies so that his clocks could time it. To slow down the motion, Galileo built a long, smooth, inclined track where he rolled down smooth wooden balls (see Figure 4-5).

Figure 4-4:
Galileo's
wine bottle
clock.

Figure 4-5:
Galileo with
his inclined
track.

Creating the modern scientific method

Galileo performed hundreds of experiments on his inclined plane, changing the inclination of the plane and using balls of different masses. All the balls rolled down at the same time, regardless of mass. Using steeper and steeper angles, he was able to show that in the extreme case of vertical fall, which he couldn't time, the balls should all fall to the ground at the same time, with the same acceleration. He is the first person in history to carefully set up experiments with the sole purpose of testing his theory of motion. He actually proved mathematically that all objects, regardless of mass, should accelerate to the ground with the same rate and, if dropped simultaneously, should hit the ground at the same time. With his experiments, he showed that his conclusions were correct.

With these experiments, Galileo created the modern scientific method. If you examine the way science is done today, you'll find that scientists use the method invented by Galileo:

- ✔ Modern scientists come up with theories or models of what they are observing in nature.
- ✔ They draw some conclusions about the behavior of the phenomenon that they are studying.
- ✔ Experiments are designed and performed to check the conclusions.

It sounds simple, but until Galileo came along, no one had thought of trying to explain the universe that way. His method made possible modern science.

Freeing his mind

Einstein used thought experiments (see Chapter 2) to seek answers to many of the questions that came up in the course of constructing his theories. Galileo invented the technique and also used it with great success.

One of Galileo's thought experiments had to do with his inclined tracks. First, he put together two tracks in such a way as to make a letter *V* (see Figure 4-6). A ball rolling down one incline speeds up until it reaches the bottom and then starts rolling up the second track. As it goes up, the ball slows down until it finally stops, reaching a height slightly lower than its original position on the first track.

Figure 4-6:
Galileo's inclined tracks to study motion at a steady speed.

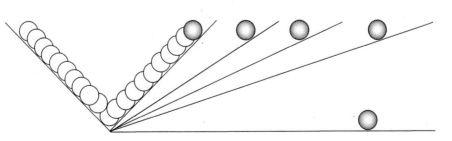

Moonlighting as an astronomer

Galileo's first important contribution to science was in astronomy, even though technically he wasn't an astronomer. News of the invention of the telescope in Holland reached Galileo, and he knew the physics principles on which it was based, so he was be able to make himself one. With it, Galileo studied the theory of *refraction* (the bending of light as it passes from air to glass that makes possible the images formed by a lens). More importantly from a practical point of view, he showed his telescope to the Venetian Senate and told them how useful it would be in spotting and counting enemy ships from the top of the Campanile before they could be seen with the naked eye.

Galileo also turned the telescope to the sky and discovered mountains on the moon and spots on the surface of the sun. When he observed the motion of the sunspots over many days, he discovered that the sun rotated on its axis once every 27 days.

He then turned his telescope to the planets, discovering that Jupiter has four moons (we call them *Galilean satellites* today) and measuring their periods of revolution around the planet. He also discovered that, like the moon, Venus has phases, which are formed by reflected sunlight as the planet rotates around the sun. With this discovery, Galileo obtained the first proof of the Copernican model. Not bad for someone who wasn't an astronomer.

Galileo quickly wrote a small book about his discovery and had it printed in a couple of weeks. The little book, which he called *The Starry Messenger,* was a bestseller all over Europe. (Like all learned books, it was written in Latin.) A Chinese translation of the book quickly appeared. Galileo became famous overnight, and he didn't dislike it at all.

Galileo then lowered the second incline but made it longer, so that the two ends of the more open *V* were leveled. This way, the ball had enough path to reach the same height as before. He kept lowering the incline while making it longer. Finally, when the second track was horizontal, the length had to extend an infinite length, because, in theory, the second ball should roll on, trying to reach the original height forever.

Galileo realized that, in reality, friction between the ball and the track slows the ball down and makes it stop. But he could do this experiment in his mind. In his thought experiment, he made the ball and the tracks perfectly smooth, with no friction whatsoever. In this case, with a perfectly smooth horizontal track, the perfectly smooth ball is free of any outside forces and rolls on forever.

This seemingly simple idea was not easy to come up with. The teachings of Aristotle, as well as our own perceptions, tell us that objects don't move forever. You must supply some force to keep them going. Horses pull on wagons to keep them going, and in still winds, sailing ships don't maintain their speeds. Everywhere you look, a force seems to be needed to keep an object in motion.

Galileo realized that real-life situations are complicated. Friction is every-where, and that is why objects in motion, when left on their own, always slow down and stop. He invented the thought experiment so he could rid himself of distractions and simplify the problem.

Marveling at Newton's Miracle Year

Kepler thought that the sun exerted some kind of influence or force on the planets to keep them in their orbits. Galileo, on the other hand, discovered that a force wasn't needed to keep an object in motion, as long as the object was moving at a constant speed along a straight line. In 1666, these two ideas were put together by Isaac Newton into a comprehensive model of the uni-verse. In that year, known today as Newton's year of miracles, Newton cre-ated what is now called *classical physics,* the physics that Einstein changed in 1905 during his own year of miracles (see Chapter 3).

Failing as a farmer

When he was just 11 years old, Newton's twice-widowed mother, Hannah, wanted her son to help run the properties she owned. Newton tried and failed. He didn't get along with the workers and wasn't interested in agricul-tural matters.

Fortunately for Newton, one of Hannah's brothers saved his nephew from life as a farmer. He talked Hannah into sending the boy to school so that he could eventually go to college. The world owes much to this smart uncle.

Although he didn't do well at first, Newton eventually became the best stu-dent. When he was ready to graduate, the school principal encouraged him to apply to college. But his mother had other plans. She was determined that her 16-year-old son take over the Woolsthorpe estate. Again, her brother (this time with some help from the school principal) convinced Hannah that her son was gifted and should go to college. Reluctantly, Hannah agreed.

Revealing his genius

Newton entered Trinity College in Cambridge in 1660. Five years later, he graduated with a B.A. degree. He wanted to go on and work on his master's degree, but the great plague broke out and the university was closed. Newton returned home in June of 1665. The university didn't reopen until April of 1667.

A mediocre college student

You may be surprised to know that Newton was not a good student in college. He was more interested in studying the works of Copernicus, Kepler, and Galileo than studying what was being taught in the regular courses. (The university taught the writings of Aristotle and Ptolemy.)

As I discuss in Chapter 2, over two centuries later, Einstein would also pay little attention to some of his college courses — showing much more interest in studying Maxwell's theories, which weren't taught in school.

During that one year and 10 months, Newton's mind revealed its full power. He set up experiments at home to investigate the nature of light, and he developed his theory of colors (see Chapter 7). He began his astronomical observations, tracking comets late into the night for many nights in a row. He also developed the main ideas of his law of universal gravitation, which became the basis for his celestial mechanics.

Newton found out that he needed a mathematical tool to be able to complete his calculations for his law of gravity. The mathematical tool didn't exist, so he invented it. Today, we call it calculus. All of this from a 22-year-old recent college graduate during his miracle year of 1666.

Developing Newtonian Physics

Newton took Galileo's revolutionary discoveries about the motion of bodies and expanded them to form a complete theory of the universe. Galileo had shown that an object moving at a constant speed along a straight line will continue moving forever, unless a force acts on it. Newton considered the effects of applying a force to an object. He soon realized that the only way to change the motion of an object is to apply an *unbalanced force* (the net force that's left after taking into account all the other forces acting on the object). To keep a planet moving in circles around the sun, you need to apply a force to the planet — precisely what Kepler had found in his observations of Mars.

Obeying the laws (of motion, that is)

Newton's analysis showed him that if he applied a force to an object, the object changed its state of motion. If the object wasn't moving, the force made it move. If the object was moving already, the force made it speed up, slow down, or change its direction, depending on how he applied the force.

Newton and the apple

Most people have heard the story of how Newton discovered the law of gravitation when an apple fell from a tree, perhaps hitting him on the head. But did it happen? Newton's friend William Stuckey writes that during one warm evening while drinking tea in the garden at Newton's house, under the shade of an apple tree, Newton said that the situation reminded him of "when the notion of gravitation came into his mind." He said that it was triggered by the fall of an apple, as he sat thinking.

The apple didn't fall on his head, but, unlike many such legends, the rest of the story is probably true. The fall of an apple from a tree started Newton thinking about gravity.

These two situations became Newton's first two laws of the motion of objects. Simply put, Newton's first law of motion says that with no forces acting, an object in motion stays in motion and an object at rest remains at rest. His second law of motion says that applying a force to an object changes its motion.

Here's how to visualize Newton's second law of motion. If you step on the gas pedal while driving, the car's engine supplies the force that accelerates the car, increasing the speed. If you step on the brakes, they provide the force to decrease the speed. Friction with the pavement provides the force that allows you to steer the car in a different direction. (And if friction isn't there, you get into accidents, as happens often when driving on icy or wet roads.)

The second law also says that you would need a larger force to move a more massive object. The two aspects of the second law combine into Newton's $F = ma$ equation (using F for force, m for mass, and a for acceleration), which is famous among scientists and engineers. It's not known as widely as Einstein's $E = mc^2$, but it's equally important. Newton's second law is the *equation of motion* of an object, and it's the starting point for any scientific analysis of the complicated motion of bodies.

Newton also came up with a third law of motion, the law of action and reaction. It says that forces always come in pairs and that applying a single force to an object is not possible. When you step on the gas pedal to accelerate your car, the engine makes the wheels turn. But if your car is on very slick ice, the wheels will spin and you won't go anywhere. When you are on dry pavement, the ground provides the frictional force that makes the car go. The car's wheels apply a force on the pavement, and the dry pavement applies an equal and opposite force (a reaction force) to the car that makes it accelerate.

Newton's three laws of motion read like this:

1. **An object remains in its current state of motion (at rest or moving at a constant speed along a straight path) until a force is applied to it.**

2. **A force applied to an object changes its state of motion.** If the object is at rest, it will start moving. If it is moving, it will speed up, slow down, or change direction. The change in motion depends on the mass of the object.

3. **Forces always come in pairs.** If you apply a force to an object, the object pushes back at you with an equal and opposite force.

It took Newton decades to actually write down the results of his research about the laws of motion. He finally did so only because his discoveries were being questioned by another scientist.

Revealing Newton's masterpiece

Newton's second law of motion told him that the motion of a planet in orbit around the sun requires a force that acts on the planet in the direction of the sun. Where does this force come from? He knew it had to be from the sun itself. But what keeps the moon in orbit around the Earth? In this case the force had to come from the Earth. And the Galilean satellites? Jupiter must be the culprit.

If the Earth pulls on the moon to keep it in its orbit, is that the same pull that makes an apple fall from a tree? Is the force of gravity responsible for keeping the moon in its orbit?

Newton remembered Kepler's third law, the relationship between the time it takes a planet to orbit the sun and its distance to the sun. He started trying to calculate the force the sun exerts on planets, and he came up with an equation showing that this force is inversely proportional to the square of the distance between the planet and the sun.

The moon is falling

If the moon is held in its orbit around the Earth by the gravitational force of attraction between the two bodies, the moon should fall toward the Earth. (Actually, they both fall toward each other, but since the Earth is much more massive, it doesn't fall as much.) Should you panic? I don't recommend it.

Think of it this way: If we could turn off the gravitational force on the Earth and the moon, the moon would move off in a straight line. A similar thing would happen if the string holding a ball that you're twirling around were to suddenly break — the ball would take off in a straight line. (It would soon curve down toward the ground due to its weight, but if you performed the experiment in space, that wouldn't happen.) Like the string holding the twirling ball, the gravitational force of the Earth on the moon makes it fall from the straight line into its circular orbit.

Trying to show that this force is the same force that makes an apple fall to the ground was another matter. Newton was a superb mathematician, but the mathematical tools to prove this correlation just didn't exist. He needed a new tool and set out to develop it. And he succeeded. He called his new tool the *theory of fluxions.* Today, we call it calculus.

With this new tool, Newton was able to show that the force that brings down an apple from the tree is the same force that keeps the moon in its orbit around the Earth. What's even more astonishing is that Newton was able to generalize his discovery from a force of attraction between a planet and the sun to that between the Earth and the moon, the Earth and an apple, or the Earth and you. He made it a universal law. That's the mark of genius.

Newton's *universal law of gravitation,* as we now call his greatest discovery, says that there is a force of attraction between all objects in the universe that is related to their masses and the distances of separation. It's the force that explains the workings of the universe. It shows how the planets move around the sun or how far and how fast each one of the moons of Jupiter must orbit the planet. It shows how the millions of small rocks and dust that make up the rings of Saturn must move and how fast you fall when you slip on a wet floor.

Newton's universal law of gravitation explains how the universe moves, like clockwork, in very predictable ways. Today, we use Newton's physics to calculate the orbits of the Earth, the moon, Venus, Jupiter, and Saturn. With Newtonian physics, we send out spacecraft that loop around Venus, come back, and allow the Earth to catapult them toward an empty spot in space where we know Saturn will be several years later when the spacecraft arrives with an array of instruments to show us how it looks up close (see Figure 4-7).

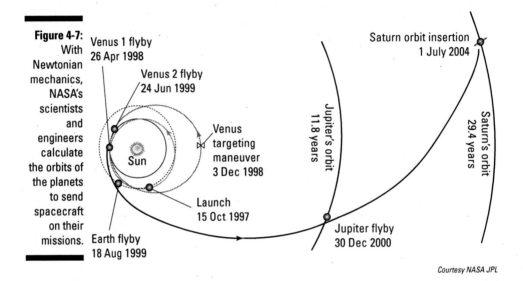

Figure 4-7: With Newtonian mechanics, NASA's scientists and engineers calculate the orbits of the planets to send spacecraft on their missions.

Venus 1 flyby
26 Apr 1998

Venus 2 flyby
24 Jun 1999

Venus targeting maneuver
3 Dec 1998

Sun

Launch
15 Oct 1997

Earth flyby
18 Aug 1999

Jupiter's orbit
11.8 years

Jupiter flyby
30 Dec 2000

Saturn orbit insertion
1 July 2004

Saturn's orbit
29.4 years

Courtesy NASA JPL

Sharing Genius: Newton and Einstein

Galileo, Newton, and Einstein are perhaps the greatest scientists that the world has ever seen. Galileo invented the modern scientific method and was an outstanding experimentalist. His studies on motion laid the foundation for the development of Newton's mechanics.

But Newton and Einstein changed science at its roots. Both Newton and Einstein laid the groundwork for their work right out of college and did so in a very short length of time, each during his own miracle year: 1666 for Newton and 1905 for Einstein.

In 1666, Newton came up with his theory of colors, discovered the law of gravity that laid the basis for his celestial mechanics (essentially explaining how the universe works), began his astronomical studies of comets, and developed the main ideas for calculus.

In 1905, Einstein developed his special theory of relativity, came up with his equivalence of mass and energy equation ($E = mc^2$), created a new method to measure the sizes of molecules, explained the zigzag motion of a speck (helping to establish the existence of atoms), and introduced the idea of the quantum of light, which started quantum theory. His explanation of how the universe at large works, essentially a complete rewrite of Newton's theory of gravity, had to wait a decade.

Both Newton and Einstein were *theoretical physicists,* which means that their work was done with calculations rather than by doing experiments, although they both dabbled in experiments. Actually, Newton's experimental work was a bit more than just dabbling. His landmark experiments with light alone, which I describe in Chapter 7, were enough to guarantee his appearance in the history books. But his theoretical work is so monumental, it dwarfs everything else he did.

A pair of loners

Newton and Einstein typically worked alone. During the development of his general theory of relativity, Einstein did work with a couple of physicists who helped him with the tedious and complicated mathematics. But Newton never worked with anyone.

Although Einstein twice married and enjoyed the company of women (getting into trouble with his wives for that reason), he really never committed himself to them or to his children. Newton never married and never even went near a woman. He remained celibate by choice, thinking that a relationship would distract him from his work.

Two views of the universe

In the system of the world that Newton developed, the universe runs like clockwork. The mathematical equations of motion in Newton's mechanics can tell us everything we would ever need to know about the universe. Given enough time and calculating power, you could take the present state of the universe, input all the variables you'd need into his equations, and run the clock backwards to unfold the entire history of the universe, all the way back to the beginning. You could also run the clock ahead and predict what would happen in the next second, year, or century. You could predict the future. You could discover the ultimate fate of the universe.

Einstein's universe is very different. The theory of relativity tells us that time and space aren't fixed. They change depending on how the observer moves. And the quantum that Einstein introduced to physics tells us that the world we observe is intimately linked to the observer — that even if we had all the computing power needed, we couldn't run the clock backwards to see the past history of the universe or run it forward and calculate its future state.

With these two revolutions, Einstein completely rewrote Newton's theories. Einstein's universe doesn't run like clockwork. The clocks depend on the motion of the observer.

Who was the greater genius? I don't think anyone can tell. Their revolutions in science were probably the greatest ever made. And each one was made by one human being alone. Einstein's genius can perhaps be remotely attributed to his family, his upbringing, and the time in which he lived. Newton's genius can't be explained. He came out of nowhere. In the history of the world, no one has equaled the genius of these two men.

Chapter 5

The Arrow of Time

*E*instein began his scientific career by studying problems related to the existence of atoms and molecules. Because molecules or atoms can't be seen, Einstein relied on a branch of physics called *statistical mechanics,* which uses statistical methods to study substances that are made up of a large number of components, like gases.

Statistical mechanics was developed in the 19th century in part to understand the laws ruling the way heat is transferred between objects. These laws came from another branch of physics called *thermodynamics,* which was also developed in the 19th century (and was fully developed by the time Einstein was in school).

Einstein's work later helped with the development of statistical mechanics. And his theories clarified the concept of time, which is intimately related to thermodynamics and statistical mechanics.

In this chapter, I introduce you to the laws of thermodynamics and to statistical mechanics, and I explain how each served as a springboard for Einstein's work.

Identifying the Laws of Thermodynamics

Why does time flow in only one direction? You grow older, never younger (unfortunately). Can this flow be reversed? All the laws of physics remain unchanged if the flow of time is reversed. They work equally well in either case. All the laws except for one, that is: The second law of thermodynamics spoils it for us. It appears that the flow of time originates in the second law. And it points the arrow of time firmly in one direction.

Thermodynamics is the study of heat and thermal effects. In this branch of physics, the world is divided into systems. A *system* can be a body or several bodies (like a gas). When you chose one system to study, all the others become part of the environment.

Thermodynamics can be summarized in four laws:

- ✔ **The first law:** The total sum of all forms of energy of a system, including its thermal energy, must always remain constant. In an isolated system, you cannot create or destroy energy; you can only change it from one kind to another. This law is also called the *principle of conservation of energy*. Check out the next section, "Conserving energy at all costs: The first law," for details.

- ✔ **The second law:** On its own, heat does not pass from cold to hot. Heat passes from hot to cold, but never the other way around without help in the form of some kind of energy. Take a look at the section "Mess, laws, and videotape: The second law" later in this chapter for more details.

- ✔ **The third law:** An absolute zero temperature cannot be reached. *Temperature* is a measurement of the average speed of the molecules of a substance. Try as we might, we can't get molecular motion to completely stop. Read the section "That's cold! The third law" later in this chapter for the story on why that is.

- ✔ **The zeroth law:** If two objects are each in *thermal equilibrium* (meaning they have the same temperature) with a third object (often a thermometer), they are in thermal equilibrium with one another. Because it seems so obvious, some people think this one's not really a law of thermodynamics. For more details, see the upcoming section "Getting picky: The zeroth law."

The second law was discovered first. The first was discovered second. The third was actually third, but it might not be a separate law of thermodynamics (because it can be viewed as an extension of the second law). And the zeroth law was described last, as an afterthought.

Conserving energy at all costs: The first law

What is energy anyway? Energy is one of those physics words that gets into the everyday language and loses the rigor of its meaning. In physics, *energy* means the ability to do work. If you have energy, you can do work. If you do work, you are using some form of energy.

Living force

In the 16th century, energy was called *living force,* because people thought that only living things could perform work. In the 18th century, the English physicist Thomas Young realized that nonliving things, like the wind, could also do work, such as by moving a windmill or a sail ship. He invented the word *energy* from Greek words that mean "work within."

Anything that changes anywhere in the universe requires energy. The explosion of a distant star, the roar of a tornado, the fall of a feather from a flying bird — all require the exchange of some form of energy.

Many kinds of energy exist, including thermal energy, mechanical energy, and nuclear energy. You can change one into another, but you can't destroy or create any of it. When you are done changing energy in some sort of process, you'd better come out even. What you end up with must equal what you started out with.

Physicists call this rule the principle of conservation of energy. And they defend it with their lives. They are not willing to violate it for any reason.

Einstein's famous equation, $E = mc^2$, actually extended the principle of conservation of energy to include *mass,* the m in the equation. (*Mass* is a measure of the resistance that you feel when you try to change the motion of an object. Unlike weight, it's not dependent on gravity.) His equation, which he published in the last paper of his miracle year as a follow-up to his special relativity paper (see Chapter 3), says that mass and energy are equivalent. Mass is a form of energy, and energy is a form of mass.

Consider this example: If you combine one kilogram of hydrogen with eight kilograms of oxygen to form water, you generate enough energy to run your hair drier for ten hours. If you had an extremely precise scale, you would discover that after running the hair drier that long, you would be missing five-billionths of a kilogram (out of the nine kilograms you originally put in). The missing mass is the energy that you used to run your hair drier.

This well-known chemical reaction is one example of the conversion of mass into energy. A nuclear reaction provides a more dramatic example. In this case, the same amount of hydrogen could produce 10 million times more energy, all of it coming from the conversion of mass into energy, according to Einstein's equation. This reaction generates the energy that powers the sun.

The one who dares, wins

In November 1929, the great German physicist Wolfgang Pauli wrote to his colleagues who were gathered at a scientific meeting that he wasn't able to attend, expressing some concern about discussions related to some missing energy that had been observed in certain processes. In his letter, he said that he'd discovered a "desperate way" to solve the problem of the missing energy. He proposed that there must be a new particle — later called the *neutrino* — that was taking away the missing energy.

He thought the idea was bold and didn't want to publish anything on it, since these neutrinos, if they existed, should've been detected already. "But only he who dares, wins," he said.

Pauli won. The neutrinos were discovered 25 years later. Today, we know that they play an important role in the mechanism that makes the sun work.

After Pauli's daring assumption, physicists adopted his approach of predicting the existence of new particles by measuring the missing energy in some process. The method works because of the principle of conservation of energy.

Technically, Einstein's extension of the principle of conservation of energy has universal validity. But in practice, physicists don't have to include it in their calculations unless they are dealing with nuclear processes, such as when they study the physics of the sun or the energies produced in nuclear reactors. Why don't they use it in all their calculations? Consider this example: The increase in the mass of the Space Shuttle due to its motion in orbit is so small that you couldn't measure it with the most accurate instruments. The uncertainties in the measurements would be larger than the energies that you would be trying to measure.

The first law of thermodynamics is actually a restatement of the principle of conservation of energy, with heat or thermal energy explicitly included for clarity.

Mess, laws, and videotape: The second law

The second law of thermodynamics is one of the most significant principles in all of physics. It can be stated very simply: On its own, heat does not pass from cold to hot. But the implications of this simple law are immense.

Dictating the flow of time

This law explains why a swimming pool doesn't suddenly freeze in the middle of a hot summer day, releasing heat to its surroundings and then solidifying into ice. No other law of physics prohibits this event from happening.

The second law is also the only law that forbids a baseball sitting on the ground from suddenly jumping across a field and hitting a baseball bat, forcing it to swing back in the batter's hands as the ball bounces back to the pitcher's glove.

You can actually see these and other similar "forbidden" phenomena if you record video of them and then run the video in reverse. In a very direct way, the second law sets a direction for the flow of time.

Moving toward disorder

The flow of time is related to disorder. Even when you're not bringing in new things, your home gets disorganized every day. You have to spend a good many hours to reverse this unstoppable trend. Apply that idea to a much larger space, the universe. It's been getting disorganized from the beginning, and there is no end in sight.

The term *entropy* measures the degree of disorder. All natural changes take place so that the entropy increases. As a result, the entropy of the universe is constantly increasing.

Why is entropy always increasing? The reason is actually simple: If there's one right way to put something together, there are many wrong ways to do it. For example, if you pick up all the pieces of a jigsaw puzzle that you accidentally dropped on the floor and quickly put them right side up on the table, you don't expect the puzzle to be put together the right way. There is only *one* correct way to put the pieces together and very many incorrect ways. Chances are you won't put them together the right way the first time.

Think about organizing your house. The number of ways you'd *like* to arrange things is probably fairly small. When things aren't set up the way you like them, they are in disorder. Nothing drives things into disorder. It's just that there are many possible ways of putting them together, and you only like a few.

The same idea is true for molecules. If you drink a can of soda that you left on the kitchen counter for a few hours, it tastes flat. That's because the carbon dioxide molecules that were trapped along with the air molecules above the liquid in the can have left. With time, additional carbon dioxide molecules that were inside the liquid found their way to the surface and also left. Eventually, little carbon dioxide is left in the liquid — the carbonation is gone. You can wait all you want, but the carbon dioxide molecules won't make it back to the open can to refresh the taste. They are now mixed with the air molecules in one of the many possible ways they can mix.

If you could somehow videotape the carbon dioxide molecules leaving the soda and then run the tape in reverse, you'd see that there is a directionality of time here too. It's the second law of thermodynamics at work.

The entropy of a black hole

In 1970, Jacob Bekenstein, then a graduate student at Princeton University, suggested that black holes have entropy and that their entropy increases as matter falls into them. (Black holes are objects so dense that not even light can escape.) At the time, the idea was a strange one, because entropy is the measure of the degree of disorder, and black holes didn't seem to have much in them that could be in a state of disorder.

But Bekenstein thought that as stars and other matter fall into a black hole, they bring their entropy with them, leaving the rest of the universe with less entropy. If you happened to be near a black hole, you could dump all your broken, messy things into it. Your spaceship would be very organized after that, and its entropy would decrease. The second law of thermodynamics requires that the black hole have entropy, which would increase by the same amount that yours decreases.

The famed British physicist Stephen Hawking had shown that the surface of no return in a black hole increases when stars fall into it. Bekenstein concluded that the value of the surface of no return in a black hole was a measure of the black hole's entropy.

This constant increase in entropy sets the direction of the flow of time. In real life, we never see what our videos running backwards show us. Time flows in the direction of increasing entropy.

That's cold! The third law

The third law of thermodynamics says that an absolute zero temperature cannot be reached. The *temperature* of an object is a measure of the average speeds of its molecules. When the object is warm, it has more molecular motion than when it's cold. When you place a thermometer in contact with a warm body, the molecules of that body collide with the thermometer, transmitting some of their motion. The thermometer then registers the temperature according to the calibration and the scale the thermometer uses.

At lower temperatures, the molecular speeds are slower, and a thermometer registers fewer and less energetic collisions. If you keep cooling the object, the molecules slow down even more. You can see that at some point, molecular motion and collisions *should* stop. If you could measure the temperature at which molecular collisions should stop, your thermometer would register –273°C or –480°F. In 1848, the English physicist William Thomson, known as Lord Kelvin, thought it would make more sense to have a scale with 0 for the lowest possible temperature, so he invented it. We call this temperature *absolute zero* or *zero Kelvin* (also 0 K or zero K).

How do we know that absolute zero is the correct value for the minimum temperature, since no thermometer can measure it? Measuring lower and lower values of the temperature, physicists can project what this value should be. Accurate and precise instrumentation at places like the National Institute for Standards has given us a very precise value for zero K.

You may notice that I've been careful to say that molecular motion *should* stop at absolute zero. It turns out that, in reality, molecular motion never stops. Molecules are small bodies whose motion can be studied only with *quantum mechanics,* the branch of physics that started with Einstein's introduction of the quantum of energy in 1905.

Quantum mechanics tells us that molecules always keep a minimum amount of energy, called the *zero point energy,* that can't ever be removed. As I explain in Chapter 16, there is an interplay between the speed of a molecule and its position in space. The more you try to fix one of these related quantities to a definite value, the larger the other becomes.

The more you slow down a molecule, the more room it needs for its position in space. Needing more room, it bumps into nearby molecules, gaining speed back from these collisions. If you try to stop a molecule completely, its position in space becomes infinite, meaning that it can be anywhere in the universe. But in this case, it can't avoid bumping into other molecules and regaining speed. So you really can't reach absolute zero.

Another way to look at this subject is from the point of view of entropy. At absolute zero, the molecules of a system would occupy the ultimate ordered state, where nothing moves and nothing gets out of place — a state where the entropy would actually decrease to zero. Seen this way, the third law is actually an extension of the second law.

Getting picky: The zeroth law

After the first three laws of thermodynamics were discovered, some picky physicists started thinking that there ought to be a law that told them when two objects were at the same temperature. The physicists wanted to formalize the process of determining when two objects are in thermal equilibrium with one another. *Thermal equilibrium* means that no heat is transferred between the objects; it also means they are at the same temperature.

The three other laws had been in use for some time, and people were used to calling them the first, second, and third laws. But this new law was so basic that it couldn't logically follow the other three; it had to precede them. So the scientists decided to call this new law the *zeroth law.* It simply states that if two objects are each in thermal equilibrium with a third object (the thermometer), they are in thermal equilibrium with one another.

Following the Arrow of Time

The only thing that stands in the way of reversing the arrow of time is entropy, the second law of thermodynamics. Nothing in electromagnetism or mechanics says that you can't reverse the flow of time.

Running the movie backwards

If you record a video of the collision of two billiard balls and show the video running backwards to your friends, they won't be able to tell the difference. If you had a special videotape that could see at the atomic level, you could do the same thing with two molecules bouncing around in a box (see Figure 5-1).

Figure 5-1: Which collision really took place? You can't tell. Both ways are possible.

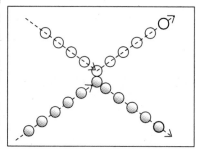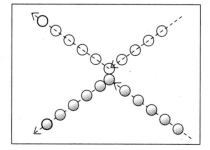

If you add a third molecule, your movie would also look the same when you run it in reverse. A fourth molecule won't give it away either. Or a fifth, and so on.

Now, imagine that you have a container with two compartments separated by a wall (see Figure 5-2). If you fill one compartment with a gas and then make a hole in the wall, the gas will begin to expand to the empty container.

Show your movie in reverse, and your friends will immediately tell you that you're running it backwards. They know that you can't start with a gas filling the two sides and eventually have the gas, on its own, empty one side and confine itself to the other side.

But your friends wouldn't be able to tell the difference if you had only two or three molecules. The molecules would bounce around and pass through the hole in either direction. At times, the three molecules would all be on one side. At other times, they'd be on the other side. And at other times, you'd have molecules on both sides. Either way you showed the movie, it'd look the same.

Figure 5-2:
Gas will
move from a
full to an
empty
compart-
ment, but
the reverse
isn't true.

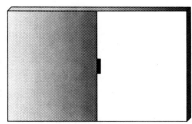 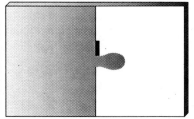

If you have ten molecules, you'd have to wait a longer time to find them all in one side only. With fifty, you'd better bring popcorn and maybe even a pillow; it'd take many hours for that to happen.

With a million molecules, you'd wait your entire life. And with a real gas . . . hell would freeze over.

You can see that there is a clear contradiction when you add molecules. With a few, you have a movie that you can show in reverse. With many, your movie is irreversible. Physicists actually call these situations *reversible* and *irreversible.*

Unpopping the cork: Statistical mechanics

Scientists originally discovered the laws of thermodynamics by studying the behavior of gases under different environmental conditions. These laws explained the observations, but no one knew exactly why they worked. The understanding came after scientists began to study the behavior of the atoms and molecules that make up these gases.

Because the number of molecules in a real gas is extremely large, and because molecules are extremely small, physicists realized that you can't possibly study the behavior of individual particles. But you can use statistical methods to discover their properties. That's what the Austrian physicist Ludwig Boltzmann did.

Boltzmann began thinking about the contradiction between the motion of a few molecules and the motion of the millions of molecules in a gas. After obtaining his doctorate in physics in 1866, Boltzmann became interested in *statistical mechanics.* This branch of physics was being developed by James Maxwell and others to use statistical methods in the study of substances that were made up of a large number of components, like gases, for example.

Boltzmann believed that the contradiction would be resolved if you could actually wait for an unimaginable length of time. Statistically, a huge number of other possible combinations of the many molecules take place before one particular combination — the one with all the molecules moving to one side — happens. When that combination occurs, you end up in the future with something you had in the past.

I realize that you probably don't care to wait an unimaginable length of time for a gas to move over to one side of a box. But what if you want recover the molecules that have escaped from that nice bottle of champagne that you left open? Or what if you want to relive a specific unforgettable afternoon, and to do so you need all the molecules of air and those that make up the trees and grass and the smell of the ocean breeze to come back to the same positions they had that day? (Of course, all the molecules in the nice configuration that made up your gorgeous date would need to return as well.)

If you could accomplish either scenario, you would be traveling back in time.

So, how long would it take to get back that nice bottle of champagne? A number of years so large that you would need 60 zeros to write it down. (In comparison, the universe has existed for 18 billion years — a number that needs only 9 zeros for you to write it down.)

Face it: Your champagne is gone. And your gorgeous date. They're things of the past. You are growing older by the minute, and there's nothing you can do about it. There is no traveling back in time. The second law of thermodynamics and statistical mechanics are the culprits.

But don't give up on time travel yet. Einstein will give us other opportunities.

Bringing Einstein into the Equation

So now you know something about thermodynamics, statistical mechanics, and the relationship between the two. What does all this have to do with Einstein?

Einstein's first foray into the scientific world had to do with both thermodynamics and statistical mechanics. In his first two professional papers, published soon after graduating from college, he used thermodynamic arguments to explain several effects observed in liquids. In his second paper, he dealt with the atomic foundations of thermodynamics.

In his Brownian motion paper of 1905 (see Chapter 3), Einstein used Boltzmann's statistical techniques to explain the zigzag motion of particles of smoke. The methods that he used in this paper paved the way for the further development of statistical mechanics.

In 1924, Einstein became interested in the work of the Indian physicist Saryendra Bose (see Chapter 16). Using a new way of counting particles that he invented, Bose was able to derive Max Planck's formula for the radiation of bodies (see Chapter 15). Einstein extended Bose's work and applied it to atoms and molecules. This new method became part of the modern development of quantum statistical mechanics. With their new method, Einstein and Bose predicted the existence of a new state of matter, the *Bose–Einstein condensate.* This new state of matter was discovered recently, as I explain in Chapter 16.

Chapter 6

Einstein's Most Fascinating Subject

"**C**onvert Magnetism into Electricity" — so wrote self-taught English scientist Michael Faraday in his lab book in the early 1800s. His work, and that of James Clerk Maxwell, made possible this conversion and produced the theory of electromagnetism.

Einstein considered this theory to be the "most fascinating subject" and skipped classes in college to read the original papers where the theory was presented. By the time Einstein graduated from college, he was an expert in this field, which was considered then to be at the frontier of physics. (He would later discover an inconsistency between electromagnetism and Isaac Newton's idea of absolute time and, to resolve it, introduce his theory of relativity.)

In this chapter, I show you the theories that Einstein read about in those early papers on electromagnetism. I also explain how those theories helped shape Einstein's (and our) understanding of the universe we live in.

Bringing Invisible Forces to Light

Newton's mechanics (see Chapter 4) took center stage in physics until the mid-19th century. Scientists developed elegant mathematical versions of Newtonian mechanics. Armed with these powerful mathematical techniques,

John Adams in England and Urbain Jean Joseph Le Verrier in France showed that small deviations in the orbit of Uranus were due to the existence of a planet orbiting beyond all the known planets. Neptune, the new planet, was discovered within a degree of where Adams and Le Verrier said it was going to be.

Successes like this made laypeople take an interest in science. They were excited to see that you could predict the existence of a planet by doing calculations on a piece of paper, using a scientific theory.

Other branches of physics, like optics, electricity, magnetism, and the studies on the nature of matter, continued developing at a much slower pace, away from the limelight. Luckily for Einstein, all of these branches reached maturity by the time he was in college. The most mature was *electromagnetism,* the very successful marriage between electricity and magnetism that had just been completed.

But Einstein's favorite subject wasn't just a 19th-century invention; it actually started with the ancient Greeks. In the next section, I tell you how their ideas developed into electromagnetism.

Feeling the sparks

Electricity and magnetism had been known from antiquity. The Greeks discovered that amber, a beautiful golden gem that's still used in jewelry, attracted seeds or feathers when rubbed with cloth. They called amber *elektron.* They also knew that lodestone, or magnetite, attracted iron.

The body of knowledge about electricity and magnetism stayed fairly stagnant until the end of the 16th century when William Gilbert, the court physician to Queen Elizabeth I and a contemporary of Galileo and Johannes Kepler, began carefully designed experiments with magnets. He also investigated the attractive properties of amber and coined the word *electric* for anything that attracts like amber. He published his work in a large book called *The Magnet.*

In spite of Gilbert's work, electricity and magnetism still remained curiosities — stuff used to entertain people at parties. Electric shows with sparks and tricks with magnets were not yet worth serious study.

The primary difficulty with understanding electricity and magnetism is that the sources of the attraction and repulsion of magnets and of electrified bodies aren't visible. (By contrast, in mechanics you can see objects moving faster or slower, speeding up or colliding. You can measure the masses, clock the motion of objects, and observe their collisions.)

What's the nature of these invisible forces? What makes amber attract pieces of straw? Why does a magnet attract iron regardless of which side of the magnet you use, when it either attracts or repels other magnets depending on which side you use? Studying electricity and magnetism seriously wasn't easy. Fortunately, a few people persevered.

Discovering opposing forces

One such scientist was Ben Franklin, America's renaissance man. He was aware of experiments done in France by the scientist Charles du Fay, who rubbed a glass rod with silk and then used it to touch a gold leaf (see Figure 6-1). The leaf was attracted to the glass rod before the rod touched it but moved away from it after touching. Du Fay thought that there were two kinds of electricity. He also thought that if two objects had the same kind, they would move away from each other, whereas if they had different kinds, they would move toward each other.

Figure 6-1:
A gold leaf
is attracted
to a glass
rod that you
rub with
silk — until
the leaf
touches
the rod.

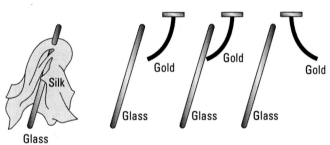

You can do a similar experiment at home. Simply take any plastic rod and rub it with silk. Instead of a gold foil, which is not easy to come by, cut a small strip of aluminum foil.

Franklin conducted similar experiments, as well as experiments with lightning, and saw that one kind of electricity could be neutralized by the other. He proposed that there was only one kind of electricity and that objects usually had a *normal* amount of it. Placing the objects together would allow some electricity to pass from one to the other.

After the transfer of electricity, Franklin thought that one of the objects would be left with an excess of electricity, which he indicated with a *positive* sign, while the other would be left with a deficiency, which he indicated with a *negative* sign.

In the experiments with the glass rod, which one was positive and which one was negative? Franklin had no way of knowing. He guessed that rubbing the glass rod with silk transferred electricity to the rod, leaving the rod positive and the silk negative (see Figure 6-2). He guessed wrong.

Figure 6-2:
If you rub a glass rod with silk and then move them apart, the silk gains negative electricity and the glass positive.

Silk

Glass

In the 20th century, scientists discovered that the carriers of electricity, or *electric charge* as we now call it, are electrons, which in Franklin's convention are negatively charged. Rubbing glass with silk transfers these negative electrons from the rod to the silk, which leaves molecules in the glass lacking electrons.

The silk ends up with an excess of electrons and becomes negatively charged. The glass ends up with a deficiency of these negative electrons, which creates a charge imbalance in some of the oxygen and silicon atoms that make up the glass molecules. Normally, atoms are electrically neutral. As I explain in Chapter 15, atoms have a core of positive charges and a cloud of negative electrons, and these charges balance out. If you remove one electron from an atom, the atom is left with a net positive charge. In the case of rubbing silk on a glass rod, the rod ends up positively charged.

Typically, if you rub a glass rod with silk a couple of times, you transfer about a billion electrons from the glass to the silk. That sounds like a large number, but even if you rub vigorously, you can expect to remove electrons from only about one in a million atoms (if you have the best possible conditions).

Franklin thought that the positive charges were the ones transferred. We now know that the negatively charged electrons transfer instead. But we still use Franklin's convention of positive and negative signs. Using Franklin's convention, we can say that two positive or two negative charges repel each other, while a negative charge and a positive charge attract each other (see Figure 6-3).

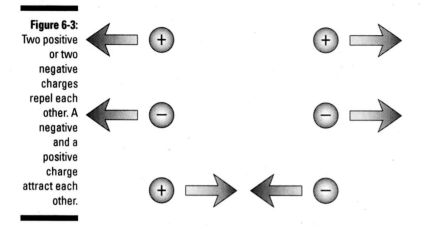

Figure 6-3:
Two positive or two negative charges repel each other. A negative and a positive charge attract each other.

Identifying Forces and Fields

Franklin taught us that electric charges attract or repel each other depending on their signs. But what is the nature of that attraction or repulsion? What is the force that makes them respond to the presence of the others?

There are two ways to look at this phenomenon, and both date back to the time before Einstein. One is the idea of the force acting between the charges that makes them move toward or away from each other. The second — the idea of fields — is more subtle but much more powerful.

Studying electric force

Before Franklin and Du Fay came onto the scene, Newton had already discovered that any two objects in the universe attract each other with a force that depends on the product of the objects' masses, as well as the square of their distance. As I explain in Chapter 4, this is Newton's powerful universal law of gravitation.

Newton's universal law of gravitation actually depends on the *inverse* of the square of the distance separating the two objects. The inverse of any number is 1 divided by the number. The universal law is then called an *inverse square law* (see the sidebar "Inverse square laws").

Franklin asked himself if the force between charges was also an inverse square law. But this force would have to be of two kinds, one attracting and the other one repelling. He asked his friend Joseph Priestley in England to look into this idea.

Inverse square laws

An inverse square law, like the electric force or Newton's universal law of gravitation, says that the strength of a force between objects decreases as the distance between the objects increases. Specifically, the strength of the force decreases in proportion to the square of the distance. For example, if you double the distance between objects, the force between them decreases to one-fourth of its original strength. If you triple the distance, the force decreases to one-ninth the original strength. And if you quadruple it, it decreases to one-sixteenth.

Priestley thought about the similarities between the electrical and gravitational cases, conducted some thought experiments, and proposed that this force was an inverse square law. Two years later, Charles Augustin de Coulomb, a French scientist, came up with a very clever method to measure this force and confirmed Franklin's and Priestley's insight (see the sidebar "Coulomb's torsion balance").

Like the gravitational force, the electric force between two charged objects depends on the inverse of the square of the distance. It also depends on the product of the charges of the two objects. Because there are both negative and positive charges, the product of these charges can also be positive or negative. A *positive force* is the force between two *like* charges (two positive or two negative charges). This force is *repulsive*; it pushes the charges apart. A *negative* force is the one between two *unlike* charges. This force is *attractive*; it tries to bring the charges together.

Defining electric fields

The second way to look at interaction between two electric charges is by using the idea of a field. The term *electric field* describes the property of the space around an electrically charged object. The presence of a charged object at some place changes or *distorts* the space around it so that every other charge in this field feels a force of attraction or repulsion toward the original charge.

Consider the following example. Suppose that you won tickets to the Super Bowl and are happily waiting for the game to start when a big pop star scheduled to perform during the halftime show enters the stadium. Quickly, everyone in the stadium knows about her presence. Some people see the singer directly, while others hear it from those who saw her. Most people just guess that she's there based on the unusual activity in the crowd and the knowledge that she is supposed to perform at halftime.

Coulomb's torsion balance

Calculating the force of gravity based on Newton's universal law of gravitation wasn't too difficult, because the masses and distances can be measured relatively easily. Not so with electrical charges. You can't even see them, so how are you going to measure how far apart they are or what their values (positive or negative) are?

French scientist Charles Augustin de Coulomb invented a device that measured the force needed to twist a pair of small electrically charged spheres. The two spheres were placed at the end of an electrically insulating rod held by a thin wire. As the charged spheres moved apart or closer together, depending on the sign of their charges, the wire became twisted. He calculated the repulsive force from the twisting angle and proved Priestley's insight: The force was an inverse square force.

Coulomb then placed uncharged spheres into contact with the original ones, transferring fractions of the original charge. With this procedure, he showed that the force depended on the product of the charges. The electric force between two bodies is now called the *Coulomb force*.

This knowledge of the singer's presence spreads through the stadium without everyone seeing her with their own eyes. The stadium then becomes a *field,* a region where the regular activity of the people waiting for a game changes as a result of the presence of a celebrity. This change affects everyone in the field. Their thoughts are focused momentarily on the singer, and her image pops into their minds.

Take a look at Figure 6-4. The electric field around a charge is represented by a set of lines. Because like charges repel each other and unlike charges attract, the field lines have arrows showing the direction that a small positive test charge would take if placed at each point. The field lines of a small positively charged sphere (on the left) point outward because the test charge always moves away from a positive charge. The field lines of a small negatively charged sphere (on the right) point inward because the test charge is attracted to it at every point where you place it.

If you place two small spheres with equal and opposite charges at a short distance from each other, their field lines bend and meet, as shown in Figure 6-5. The field lines always indicate the direction in which a positive charge will move if you place it in the field. A negative charge will move in the opposite direction.

Figure 6-4:
The electric field in the space around a positive charge (left) and around a negative charge (right).

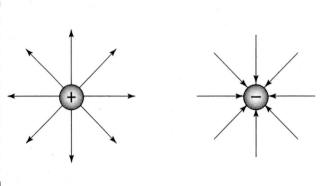

Figure 6-5:
The electric field near a positive and a negative charge that are close together.

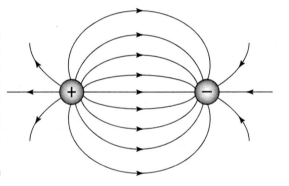

There are many other fields in physics. The gravitational field around the Earth, for example, is the property of the space around our planet where any object feels the Earth's gravitational attraction. Einstein used the gravitational field to show that what he called *spacetime,* the four-dimensional combination of space and time, is curved and that gravity is simply this curved spacetime. I explain what this means in Chapter 12.

Examining magnetic fields

Here is a field that you can see: If you sprinkle some iron filings on the back of a greeting card (or on any piece of heavy paper) and then place a small bar magnet under the card, you'll observe the iron filings aligning along curved paths from one end of the magnet to another (see Figure 6-6). The filings are showing you the shape of the magnetic field around the magnet.

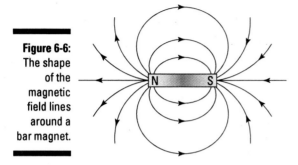

Figure 6-6: The shape of the magnetic field lines around a bar magnet.

Wherever you place a magnet, the space around the magnet changes. Any other magnetized body in the region senses this change and experiences a force. Like the gravitational force, the magnetic force is an inverse square law.

As you know from handling small magnets, every magnet has two distinct sides, usually called the *north* and *south* magnetic poles. If you hold two magnets with their north poles facing each other, they repel each other. The same thing happens if the two south poles face each other. When you flip one of the magnets so that the north pole of one magnet faces the south pole of the other, the two magnets attract each other and you can make them stick together.

Sensing the Attraction Between Electricity and Magnetism

Electricity and magnetism seem to have a lot in common. Here's how they're similar:

- ✔ Two kinds of electric charges exist, positive and negative. Two kinds of magnetic poles exist, north and south.

- ✔ Like charges repel each other, and unlike charges attract. Like poles repel each other, and unlike poles attract.

- ✔ The electric force is an inverse square-type force, and so is the magnetic force.

- ✔ The electric field lines around two equal and opposite charges have the same shape as those formed by the north and south magnetic poles in a magnet.

But there are differences. Positive and negative charges exist in isolation, while magnetic forces exist only in pairs.

Splitting magnets

In 1931, the renowned English physicist Paul Dirac proposed that single magnetic poles or *monopoles* should exist to complete the symmetry between electricity and magnetism. If the two electrical charges existed separately, why couldn't the same be true for the two magnetic poles?

Recent theories of particle physics and cosmology suggest that magnetic monopoles existed during the early universe. If they exist, they can't be obtained by splitting a magnet in two. Doing so produces two complete magnets, each with its own north and south poles.

Failing a Demo, and Changing Science

Encouraged by the similarities between electricity and magnetism, scientists looked for the connection between the two. One good place to start was with the possibility of electric currents generating magnetic fields. (An electric current is nothing more than the motion of electric charges, usually through some metal wire. Electric currents can exist in a vacuum or in some nonmetals, but the most common ones exist in metals.) Time after time, scientists tried and failed to demonstrate the connection.

In 1819, one professor in Denmark, Hans Christian Oersted, set up a demonstration to show his students that in spite of their similarities, electric and magnetic fields were *not* related and that you couldn't produce one from the other. He'd done this demonstration many times before. He laid wires on the table in front of him and passed a current through them. With a small magnetic compass, he showed his students that the compass needle always remained pointing north regardless of how close he placed the compass to the wires. When he finished, he picked up the compass and noticed that the needle twitched and pointed in a direction perpendicular to the wire (see Figure 6-7).

Professor Oersted continued experimenting. He reversed the current and saw that the compass needle reversed direction but remained perpendicular to the wire.

While trying to prove the opposite, Oersted accidentally proved that there was a connection, after all: Electric fields could generate magnetic fields. No one had noticed this connection before because they were all placing the compass right next to the wire, not above or below it. Oersted's experiment was the first documented instance of a force acting in a direction that was perpendicular to the motion of a body (in this case, the electrons that make up the electric current in the wire).

Figure 6-7:
Oersted
discovered
that a
magnetic
compass is
deflected if
placed
directly
above or
below an
electric wire
carrying a
current.

If you look at Figure 6-8, you'll get a better idea of Oersted's discovery. If you place several compasses right next to a current-carrying wire lying on a table, the compasses all point north (top left). If you pick one up, so that its magnetic needle is perpendicular to the wire, that compass is deflected (top right). The figure at the bottom shows how the magnetic field wraps around the wire.

Sloppy experimenter

Hans Christian Oersted made the discovery of the connection between electricity and magnetism for which he became famous somewhat accidentally. He might not have been a meticulous experimenter. One of his students wrote that Oersted was "a man of genius but . . . he could not manipulate instruments." If this description is true, his lack of skill as an experimenter might've helped him make his discovery. More skillful scientists probably turned the current off before taking apart the experiment and failed to see the movement of the compass

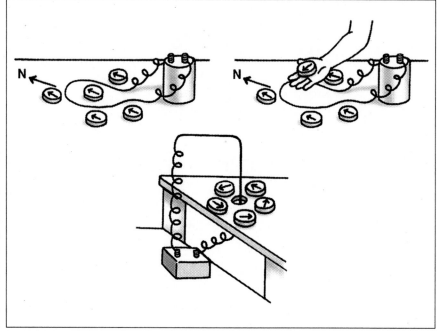

Figure 6-8:
Oersted's
discovery
of the
connection
between
electricity
and
magnetism.

Oersted published his discovery in 1820. Within a few months, scientists all over Europe were trying to reproduce his discovery. The young French physicist André Marie Ampère was able to extend Oersted's discovery, describing it mathematically and proving that all forms of magnetism are generated by small electric currents.

An electric current is nothing more than one or more electric charges moving across some space. Ampère's law, as we call this discovery today, can be stated as follows:

A moving electric charge generates a magnetic field.

Creating a Current

Oersted and Ampère had shown that an electric current produced a magnetic field. The obvious question now was: Would a magnetic field produce an electric current? Many scientists were trying to answer this question when, in 1821, a self-taught English scientist named Michael Faraday headed for his lab with several ideas in mind.

At first, none of Faraday's ideas worked, but nobody else's did either. Faraday didn't give up. He tried intermittently and unsuccessfully for ten years to show that a magnetic field could produce an electric current. Finally, in 1832, he wound an insulated copper wire around one side of an iron ring and connected the two ends of that wire to a battery (see Figure 6-9). He then wound a second insulated wire around the other side of the ring and monitored any currents that might be generated in this coil.

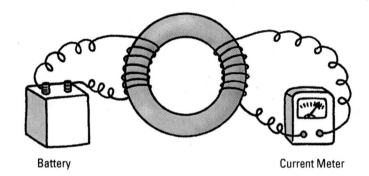

Figure 6-9:
Faraday's
experiment.

Battery   Current Meter

Faraday knew that the electric current in the first wire would produce a magnetic field. That was Ampère's law. That was what Oersted had seen and what got everyone excited.

Faraday also expected the magnetic field created in the first coil to propagate through the iron ring all the way to the other side, where the separate coil was. That propagation of the magnetic field had already been proven.

What Faraday was looking for was for this magnetic field to produce a current in the separate wire coil. The second coil was not connected to a source of electricity and was insulated from the iron ring on which it was wound. Faraday connected his battery and checked to see if any current was flowing through his second wire. Nothing.

He kept trying. Still no current in the second loop. But he noticed that every time he connected or disconnected the battery, the current meter on the separate loop tweaked. He was puzzled. Was it perhaps the *change* in the magnetic field in the ring that made the current meter register? He then tried to change the current on the first loop to see if that was the case.

It worked. He had his discovery. Actually, he had one of the major discoveries of the century. He had produced electricity from magnetism.

What's this invention good for?

After discovering his law of induction, Michael Faraday invented the electric generator. When he was already a famous scientist, the British prime minister is said to have asked him what his invention was good for. Supposedly, Faraday told the prime minister that one day he could tax it.

This story is very likely fictional, but the statement ended up being true. An electric generator is nothing more than several loops of wire that are made to rotate inside a magnet. A paddlewheel turned by a waterfall or by a river can be the source of energy to move the wire loops. As the wire loops rotate, the magnetic field lines that thread through the loops change from none (when the loops are oriented along the field lines) to a maximum (when the loops are at right angles to the field lines). The changing magnetic field generates the electric current in the wire. You now use this current in your home. And you can bet that the current prime minister is taxing this utility.

So it was a changing magnetic field that generated a current. For the next several months, Faraday tried other ways to produce a current in an isolated wire. He showed that the iron ring wasn't needed. A changing current in one coil generated a changing magnetic field that in turn produced a current in a second separate coil sitting nearby. Even a moving magnet did the trick, because the isolated coil sensed an approaching or receding field (see Figure 6-10).

Figure 6-10:
If you move a magnet toward a metal ring, you can create a current in the ring.

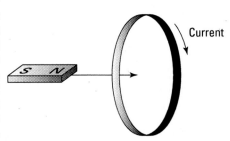

Current

Faraday's *induction law,* as we call his discovery today, is stated as follows:

A changing magnetic field generates an electric current.

The Great Scot: Appreciating Maxwell

The discoveries of Oersted, Ampère, and Faraday showed to the scientific world that electricity and magnetism were closely related. Faraday showed us the complete connection between the two. But because he had no grasp of mathematics, he couldn't give us the complete picture. He couldn't understand a word of Ampère's highly mathematical papers. He had to go by the descriptions of Oersted's experiments and presentations of Ampère's papers at meetings.

Enter James Clerk Maxwell (1831–1879), a highly trained Scottish scientist with a remarkable mathematical ability. In his first two papers on electromagnetism, he came up with a mathematical model for Faraday's induction law. When he applied his model, he noticed that in addition to reproducing Faraday's law (where a changing magnetic field produces a changing electric current), the model suggested that a changing electric field would also produce a magnetic field. That was close to what Ampère had said.

Ampère had discovered that a moving charge produced a magnetic field. If you use Faraday's idea of electric field, Ampère's law actually says that the electric field of the moving charge produces a magnetic field. Maxwell's model was more general than that. It said that any changing electric field produced a magnetic field. A changing electric field between two metal plates, for example, where no charge was moving, should produce a magnetic field.

Maxwell decided to modify and extend Ampère's law to include this possibility. This extension (which we now call the Ampère–Maxwell law) says

A changing electric field produces a changing magnetic field.

With this extension, Maxwell had one of the major scientific discoveries of all time. His was the stroke of genius that unified electricity and magnetism into one single theory that we now call *electromagnetism*.

Creating T-shirt Equations

The marriage between electricity and magnetism was now complete. One field generates the other. And Maxwell put it all in mathematical form — Maxwell's famous equations. Today, you can buy a T-shirt with these equations on it (and some people even think it looks cool).

What Maxwell did was to take the work of Coulomb, Ampère, Faraday, and others and put it together into a complete and beautiful theory. The whole story is described in four equations. (Trust me, you don't want to see them; they're an eyeful.) The first one is a more elegant version of Coulomb's law and gives a relationship between an electric charge and its electric field. The second equation describes magnetic field lines and shows the differences with electric field lines.

The beauty comes in the last two equations. The third equation is Faraday's law of induction, and the fourth is the Ampère–Maxwell law.

You've seen what these laws say and do. I'll show you why they are beautiful.

According to the third equation, a changing magnetic field creates an electric field that's also changing. But the fourth equation says that this changing electric field in turn produces a changing magnetic field. This last changing electric field now creates a new changing magnetic field. You get the idea. Back and forth with the two equations.

When you set up the first changing field (either one of the two — it doesn't matter which comes first), the other one is created right away, and the whole thing takes on a life of its own. The two interlocked fields become one single *electromagnetic* field that begins to expand in space.

Maxwell combined his equations into a single one to show that this electromagnetic field moves through space like a wave at 288,000 kilometers per second (kps). That number was very close to the speed of light, which had been measured at the time to be 311,000 kps.

Nine years after Maxwell died, Heinrich Hertz used Maxwell's theory to generate electromagnetic waves in his lab. Today, of course, you are surrounded by electromagnetic waves generated by your hometown radio stations, your remote controls, or your cellphone. These waves all travel at 300,000 kps, the value that scientists have measured for them (which is very close to what had been measured a century and a half ago when Maxwell was discovering them).

We also send these electromagnetic waves to our spacecraft on the surface of Mars with instructions to climb up that intriguing hill we're able to see because of the electromagnetic waves that the craft sent us 20 minutes ago.

Pretty exciting stuff. No wonder Einstein cut classes to go read up on Maxwell's theories.

Chapter 7

And There Was Light

* *

* *

*W*hat is light? Scientists have been trying to understand the nature of light for centuries. The Greeks thought that light was made up of small particles traveling in straight lines that entered our eyes and stimulated our sense of vision. Isaac Newton also thought that light was made up of little particles. But the English scientist Thomas Young thought that light was a wave, and he came up with a clever experiment to prove it.

In Chapter 16, I discuss Einstein's view on the nature of light. But before I can delve into how Einstein revolutionized our understanding of light, I need to explain what Einstein learned about light from his teachers and his own studies. In this chapter, I present a quick overview of the study of light from the time of Galileo, and I discuss Newton's and Young's contributions to the field.

Trying to Measure the Speed of Light

As I explain in Chapter 6, James Clerk Maxwell's theory of electromagnetism tells us that light is an electromagnetic wave traveling at 300,000 kilometers per second (kps). Maxwell's equations tell us that changing electric and magnetic fields create and sustain each other even in regions where there are no electric charges to accelerate or magnets to move. Maxwell showed how these two fields, interlocked in a dance, create their own light show. The fields spread out through space as light or as any other electromagnetic wave.

But before Maxwell, other scientists made their own attempts to identify the nature of light and to calculate its speed. In this section, I discuss two such attempts that Einstein learned about in school.

Galileo: Hanging lanterns

How fast does light travel through space? The modern value for the speed of light is 300,000 kps (186,000 mps). Actually, it's 299,792.458 kps, but that's a tough number to remember. The circumference of the earth is about 40,000 km (25,000 mi), so it would take light slightly longer than a tenth of a second to travel around the world.

With modern instruments, the extremely large value of the speed of light can be measured. But how did anyone measure it before those instruments were created?

Galileo was the first person who tried. He had two people stand on distant hills flashing lanterns. Clearly, Galileo's experiment didn't work — he couldn't even measure seconds accurately, much less the tiny fraction of a second that it took for light to travel between the two hills.

But Galileo was Galileo, and with his crude approach to this very difficult experiment, he was still able to show that the speed of light is finite. His contemporary, French philosopher René Descartes, had been saying that it was infinite.

Roemer: Timing a satellite

Some 70 years after Galileo's experiment, the young Danish astronomer Olaus Roemer was able to get the first value of the speed of light. But he had to go farther than a distant hill to get it. He used the satellites of Jupiter instead. And he also had to fight with his boss — the famous astronomer Jean-Dominique Cassini, for whom the Saturn rings are now named.

Tackling an inconsistency

Roemer was a bright 21 year old who was hired by one of Cassini's assistants to help at the Paris Observatory, which was headed by Cassini. But Roemer didn't just help; he tackled one of the observatory's major problems.

Cassini's observations were showing a problem with the motion of one of Jupiter's satellites, the one named *Io* (after one of the many lovers of Zeus, who is called Jupiter in Roman mythology). It seemed as if Io's orbit was a bit unpredictable. The times when the satellite came out from behind the planet changed inexplicably. Cassini ordered his assistants to make better observations and to do more calculations.

Roemer doubted that the observations or calculations were the problem. The problem was that no one had taken into account the relative distance of the Earth and Jupiter as the two planets went around the sun. At different places in their orbits, the planets are sometimes closer and sometimes farther apart. When Io comes out from behind Jupiter, the distance that light travels from the satellite to the Earth depends on the separation of the planets at that time.

Cassini didn't agree with his assistant. He believed that light traveled from place to place instantaneously, without delays. It didn't matter how far Jupiter was.

Roemer stuck with his idea. He went back and reviewed many years' worth of data taken in Cassini's observatory. With this data, he was able to calculate the changes in the eclipsing times for Io as it went around in its orbit. He was sure that he was right and wanted to go public.

Going around the boss

What to do? Normally, the lab director would make the public presentation of new findings, along with the researcher who made the discovery. But Cassini didn't agree with Roemer's work, so Roemer decided to go alone. He'd been in Cassini's observatory for five years and felt cocky. He appeared before the Academy of Sciences in Paris and announced that Io was going to come out from behind Jupiter exactly ten minutes after Cassini said it would.

Cassini had calculated that Io was going to come out of the eclipse on November 9, 1676, at 5:25:45. The astronomers went out to look that night. 5:25:45 came and went, and Io wasn't there. At 5:30, there were still no signs of it. But at 5:35:45, Io reappeared. Roemer had been right.

Roemer's friend Christian Huygens used this data to come up with the first measured value for the speed of light. His number was 227,000 km (140,000 mi) per second, which is about 24 percent lower than the modern value.

Cassini never admitted his error. Most European astronomers followed Cassini and didn't believe that the speed of light was finite. Some 50 years later, other methods to measure the speed of light showed that Roemer had been correct.

By the time Einstein was in school, the speed of light had been measured with fairly good accuracy. This speed, represented in Einstein's work by the letter c, ended up at the very foundation of his special theory of relativity.

How long does it take?

You can get a feel for the speed of light and for the distances in the universe with the examples shown in the following table. Einstein said that nothing can travel at the speed of light except for light itself, so you would take much, much longer to get to these destinations. But maybe not as long as you'd think. In Chapter 10, I discuss how Einstein's special theory of relativity helps us get around the slow pace of travel we're used to.

Traveling at the Speed of Light

Location	Time for Light to Get There
Across the room	0.02 millionths of a second
Moon	A bit over 1 second
Sun	8 minutes
Edge of the solar system	5½ hours
Nearest star (Alpha Centauri)	4 years
Center of the galaxy	30,000 years
Across the Milky Way galaxy	100,000 years
Nearest galaxy (Andromeda)	1 million years

Proving Maxwell Right

James Clerk Maxwell died of cancer at the age of 48. Because he died so young, he never saw the confirmation of his discovery that light was an electromagnetic wave that could be generated by moving a charge back and forth. If he'd lived just eight more years, he would've seen the proof.

It fell to Heinrich Hertz to produce Maxwell's electromagnetic waves and measure their speed. Hertz was a bright German physicist who had obtained his PhD at age 23 from the University of Berlin. Three years later, in 1883, he decided to study Maxwell's papers so he could understand the theory of electromagnetism, which wasn't yet taught in college or graduate school. (It was too new, and few professors knew enough about it to teach it.)

Jumping sparks

Hertz learned electromagnetism on his own, and in two years, he was an expert. He decided to generate the electromagnetic waves Maxwell had described and to measure their speed.

He built a replica of the setup that Michael Faraday had used to discover his famous induction law (see Chapter 6), which became one of Maxwell's equations. But Hertz modified it a bit. Faraday had wrapped two separate insulated wires around a metal ring: One wire was connected to a battery, and the other was a closed loop. Hertz decided to open the closed loop and place two small metal balls at the ends of the wire (see Figure 7-1). The two balls were separated by a small gap.

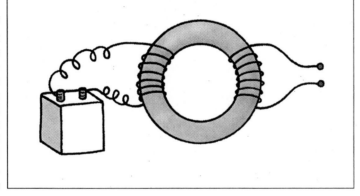

Figure 7-1:
Hertz's
experimen-
tal setup
with two
small metal
balls
separated
by a small
gap.

From Maxwell's theory of electromagnetism, Hertz knew that when he connected or disconnected the battery in the first coil, the fast change in current would produce a changing magnetic field that in turn would generate a voltage in the second separate coil. In other words,

Changing electric current → changing magnetic field → voltage in second coil

When the voltage generated in the open coil was large enough, a spark jumped across the two balls. According to Maxwell's theory, these sparks sent changing electric and magnetic fields across the gap, which should take off and move across the surrounding space as an electromagnetic wave.

Inventing the first radio

Hertz realized that if he had a second open loop with balls at the ends forming a small gap, the electromagnetic field would reach it and produce a voltage in that new loop (see Figure 7-2).

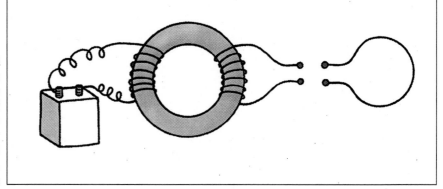

Figure 7-2:
Hertz's
invention of
the radio
transmitter
and
receiver.

Hertz had just invented a radio *transmitter* (the first set of loops) and a radio *receiver* (the second loop). He was then able to measure the speed of electromagnetic waves generated with this spark setup. He got the same value as the speed of light, exactly as Maxwell had said.

Making light

Hertz's experiment showed that light was an electromagnetic wave. Hertz had essentially made light by running an electric current through a wire. This light, which was invisible, was actually a radio wave. What do radio waves and light have to do with each other? Radio waves, light, and other waves that were discovered later are all electromagnetic waves generated in a similar way — by accelerating electric charges. The only difference among them is how fast the waves wave, or *oscillate*.

Once generated, all electromagnetic waves spread out through space in all directions at the speed of light, 300,000 kps. You can imagine them as a pulsating bubble rapidly expanding, as shown in Figure 7-3.

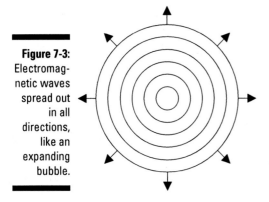

Figure 7-3:
Electromagnetic waves spread out in all directions, like an expanding bubble.

If you examine an electromagnetic wave with some instruments, you detect the electric and magnetic fields pulsating or oscillating in step (see Figure 7-4). This oscillation is what travels through space. The wave doesn't deform as it travels; the length of each oscillation, or *wavelength,* stays the same for a particular electromagnetic wave. But the wavelength is different for different waves. Radio waves, like the ones generated by Hertz, have wavelengths that range from about 1 meter to thousands of kilometers. Hertz's was a short one, about 1 meter in length.

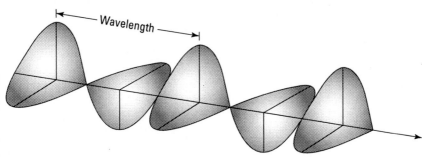

Figure 7-4:
The pulsating electric and magnetic fields that make an electromagnetic wave oscillate in step.

Wavelength

The electromagnetic waves that heat up your food in your microwave are measured in centimeters, and x-rays are much, much smaller. That's why they can penetrate through your skin and muscles and give physicians a picture of your bones.

Identifying the electromagnetic spectrum

Visible light has wavelengths larger than x-rays but smaller than those for radio and TV. Because of the small size of the wavelengths, scientists use *nanometers* to designate their length — a nanometer (nm) is a millionth of a millimeter. Visible light ranges from 400 nm for the color red to 700 nm for violet.

In Figure 7-5, which shows the *electromagnetic spectrum* (as Newton called it), I list the names we've given to the different ranges of wavelengths discovered. Each wavelength has a different energy; the shorter wavelengths are more energetic. Scientists have invented instruments to detect different ranges, like x-rays, gamma rays, or radio.

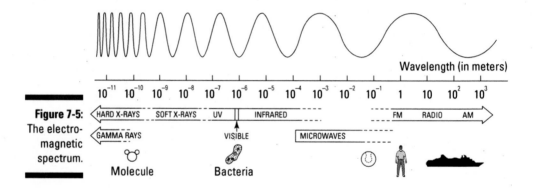

Figure 7-5:
The electro-
magnetic
spectrum.

Creating a Theory of Colors

During his miracle year of 1666 (see Chapter 4), Newton started experiments on what later became his theory of colors. This work was of great impor-tance; what we know today about color started with the experiments he did in that marvelous year.

Newton knew that a beam of light passing through a prism broke up into a splash of the colors of the rainbow: violet, blue, green, yellow, orange, and red. This knowledge was commonplace even at the time of Aristotle. But no one knew why light could be broken up into colors until Newton came along.

Drilling a hole in the shutters

Early in 1666, Newton wanted to try the "celebrated phenomena of colors." He bought a glass prism, brought it home to his mother's farm, went into his room, closed the doors and windows, and made a small hole in the shutters to let a narrow beam of light come into the room.

Red curtains

Newton's favorite color was red. When he died, people were surprised to find that this serious, conservative man was surrounded in his home by a sea of red. His bed was covered with a red bedspread, and red drapes with matching red valances covered the windows. In his dining room, he had a special red chair for the occasional guest. In his parlor, he had a red easy chair and six red cushions where he sat to read or rest after he returned home from work.

Newton didn't grow up in a very colorful environment. The clothes that he wore growing up were gray, brown, or tan. But every once in a while, someone would gather some bright berries and roots to dye clothes for special occasions. Newton was very interested in these dyes, especially the red ones. In one of the notebooks that he kept about things that interested him, Newton had different recipes for preparing painters' colors, with many more formulas for making red than for any other color.

This early interest in color appears in contrast with Newton's lack of interest in the beauty of nature. Unlike many scientists, Newton rarely showed any interest in anything other than the abstract concepts of physics and mathematics.

Did Newton's interest in mixing colors and pigments as a young boy influence his scientific interest in them later? There is no evidence to support this idea. But there is no question that he had an intense scientific interest in color.

He placed his prism in the path of the light beam. The beam broke out into colors on the opposite wall. People had seen this happen many times — it was nothing new, but it was beautiful.

Newton noticed something peculiar. He had carefully made a circular hole, but the shape of the spot on the wall was oval, not circular.

Before Newton, people thought that a prism changed the color of light. The theory was that sunlight passing through the thick end of a prism was darkened more, so it became blue, while light passing through the thin end was darkened less and became red. But the prevailing theory didn't explain why the round hole made an oval shape on the wall.

Newton wanted to known why. He made the hole bigger, then smaller. He changed the location of the prism and the place where the beam entered the prism. The spectrum never changed.

Newton placed a second prism a few yards away so that the light beam would pass through both prisms. Then, he noticed something remarkable. The blue end of the rainbow was bent even farther than the red, but no additional colors appeared. The second prism didn't change the color of light at all: Red was still red, and blue was still blue.

Millions of colors

White light is made up of the colors of the rainbow. How many colors are there? You may hear people say that there are only seven colors in the rainbow, but you know that there are many other colors. You can set up your computer monitor to display "millions of colors," for example. Where do these colors come from?

A prism actually breaks light up into an infinite number of colors. The problem is that our eyes aren't sensitive enough to see them all. The eye has only three kinds of cone cells that distinguish colored light. These cones contain three types of molecules that change shape with light of wavelengths in the red, green, or blue areas of the spectrum. You really see only red, green, and blue. The rest are combinations of these three colors.

So, we actually see only three pure colors among the infinite pure colors in nature. You knew your eyes weren't perfect, but did you know they were this bad? At least we've been able to invent instruments that can detect the rest of the colors.

This experiment was key because Newton discovered that light isn't changed by the prisms. It is, instead, separated into different colors. After these colors are separated by one prism, they can't be separated any further.

Mixing colors

Newton didn't stop with this discovery. He wanted to know more about light. He'd seen that white light from the sun was made up of many colors and that you could separate them with a prism. Could that process somehow be reversed? Could the colors be mixed back together to make white light?

You probably know the answer already. Perhaps you've seen a wheel with all the colors of the rainbow printed on it that becomes white when set to spin. But that wheel was created after Newton answered the question.

Newton added a third prism to his experiment and passed a separate beam of light through it by making a second hole in the shutters. Then, he overlapped the two rainbows from the two prisms and formed white light.

Years later, when he was a famous scientist, Newton went back to this experiment and used a lens to converge the spectrum from a single prism into a spot. The spectrum disappeared into white light at that spot but, as it continued its path beyond that point, spread out and separated into its component colors.

Pitting Particles Against Waves

Newton thought that light was made up of particles. However, he accepted that light showed some aspects of wave behavior. He thought, for example, that the different colors of light had different wavelengths.

What's the big deal about wave versus particle?

It turns out that the properties of waves and the properties of particles are exclusive. It's like day and night, fast and slow, rich and poor. If you have one, you can't have the other. You can't have both particles and waves at the same time.

Exhibiting distinct behaviors

The best way to observe the properties of waves is with water waves, because you can see them. If you throw a pebble in a lake, you see the circular ripples spreading out. If you throw two pebbles, two sets of ripples spread out and, at places, run into each other. These ripples don't bounce off each other — instead, they pass through. And when they overlap, there are areas on the surface of the water that are higher and regions where the water is flat. If you observe carefully, you can see a pattern.

Sound is also a wave. It's formed by pushing molecules of air (or water or a solid) together. When you speak, your vocal cords vibrate and push the air molecules away. These molecules bump into neighbor molecules, and the whole thing spreads until the vibrations get to your friend's ear and cause her ear membranes to vibrate. Then she can hear you.

If your friend is out in the hallway and you are in a room where you can't see her, she still can hear you. Sound waves bend around corners. In fact, all waves bend around corners.

Particles, on the other hand, don't have the same behavior. They bounce off each other when they collide, and they don't bend around corners.

Believing that light doesn't bend

Newton didn't fully accept the idea that light was a wave because light doesn't seem to bend around corners. You can see sharp shadows, which would seem to be evidence that light travels in straight lines.

However, even in Newton's time, there was some evidence that light bends around corners. An Italian scientist named Francesco Maria Grimaldi had passed a light beam through two narrow slits, one behind the other. The beam then fell on a black surface. He noticed that the band of light on that surface was a tad wider than the slits, and he concluded (correctly) that the beam had been bent slightly at the edges of the slits. He named this phenomenon *diffraction*.

Newton knew of Grimaldi's experiments but thought that the bending was due to the light particles bumping into the edges of the slit. Without further studies, both ways of looking at this phenomenon were equally valid. Because of Newton's great standing in the scientific world, his view was accepted more widely.

Young: Showing that light is a wave

A century after Newton, in 1802, an English scientist by the name of Thomas Young improved Grimaldi's experiments. Young passed a beam of light through a pinhole that he punched on a screen. This light spread out from the hole and passed through a set of two pinholes that he had punched side-by-side on a second screen. He used a third screen to observe the pattern of dark and bright regions that he had made.

Young knew very well that what he was seeing was telling him that light was a wave. The light behaved like water ripples that run into each other; it made similar patterns.

Creating coherent beams

Young's *interference experiment,* as we call it today, was very clever. It turns out that you can't get these interference patterns with a regular source of light. The reason is that the light beams from a regular source don't vibrate in lockstep, and when they run into each other, they don't form these patterns. You need two beams that vibrate in step — what we now call *coherent* beams — for the experiment to work.

How did Young manage to make coherent beams? The holes in the screens did it. The light beams from the two holes in the second screen had the same origin; they both came from the light passing through the first hole. Because Young placed the two holes in the second screen at equal distances from the first hole, the two light beams that came out of the holes in the second screen were coherent.

Calculating wavelengths

Young did more experiments, replacing the two pinholes in the second screen with slits (see Figure 7-6). The pattern of bright and dark regions became parallel bands. Using simple geometry, he calculated the wavelength of the light he used from the distances between the lines.

A Young prodigy

Young had been a child prodigy. When he was 4 years old, he read the Bible twice. He spoke eight languages by the time he was 14. He studied medicine at the universities of Edinburgh and Göttingen, where he graduated in 1796. He practiced medicine all his life but was not a very good doctor because of his poor bedside manner. He was more interested in science than in medicine and didn't pay enough attention to his patients.

While in medical school, Young discovered how the lens of the eye changes shape when focusing at different distances. He later discovered that astigmatism was due to imperfections in the curvature of the cornea. From studying the eye, Young moved to the nature of light.

Figure 7-6:
Young showed that light formed an interference pattern, the signature of a wave.

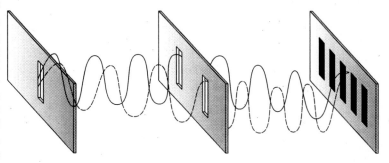

From his calculations, Young found out that the value for the wavelength of light was much smaller that Newton thought. The longest wavelength in the visible spectrum is the one for red light, which is less than one-thousandth of a millimeter. That's why light casts sharp shadows and doesn't appear to bend around corners. You need tiny objects, like Young's pinholes, to detect the bending.

Meeting resistance

Young's experiment is what we call a *landmark* experiment. It's now repeated in schools around the world to demonstrate to students the wave nature of light.

His experiment showed, without any doubt, that light is a wave. The interference pattern that Young saw with his setup is the mark of a wave. You can't get that pattern with particles bouncing off the edges of the pinhole. The particles would have to have a coordinated motion to be able to form such a symmetric pattern.

You'd think that with this irrefutable proof, the wave nature of light would become well-established right away. But it didn't happen that way. Young's experiment went against the teachings of the great Newton, and the English physicists were not going to have any of it.

Young tried to tell people that Newton himself was really not against the wave nature of light. Newton accepted the idea that the different colors of light had different wavelengths. But sometimes when people have strong beliefs, arguments are not enough to persuade them.

It wasn't until 1818, when two French physicists came up with a complete wave theory based on mathematics, that the wave theory was finally accepted. It hasn't been challenged since.

Oh, except that Einstein later said that light was made up of particles. More on that subject in Chapter 16.

Part II

On the Shoulders of Giants: What Einstein Learned in School

The 5th Wave   By Rich Tennant

THE 4th LAW OF THERMODYNAMICS:
Don't try to explain the first 3 on a blind date.

In this part . . .

To appreciate Einstein's greatness, you need to understand the state of physics at the time he developed
his revolutionary theories. This part offers an overview
of what Einstein learned from his college professors and
from his own studies.

The science that Einstein learned in school began with the
ancient Greeks' ideas about the universe. But most of the
Greek thinkers weren't scientists; they were philosophers.
Some of their ideas were crucial to the development of
modern physics, but they didn't have the means to conduct experiments to test an idea's merit.

Galileo Galilei was actually the first scientist; in the late
16th century, he invented the method that today's scientists still use (more or less). In this part, I show you what
Galileo did and how Isaac Newton was able to expand
Galileo's ideas into the first complete view of the universe.
Newton's theory explains how the planets move around
the sun and how a cannonball flies across a field. It includes
the laws that objects in motion follow.

Not long before Einstein's time, James Clerk Maxwell
developed his theory of electrical and magnetic effects —
what he called *electromagnetism*. Maxwell's theory not only
explained the behavior of electricity and magnets but
showed us how light behaves as well.

Galileo, Newton, and Maxwell all set the stage for Einstein's
great leaps forward. In this part, I show you how.

Chapter 8

Relativity Before Einstein

Contrary to popular belief, Einstein did not invent relativity. The honor belongs to Galileo Galilei. His ideas shaped the theories that flourished and floundered in the centuries between his own and Einstein's. And they set the stage for Einstein to establish one of the most revolutionary theories of our time.

In this chapter, I discuss the origins of relativity. Galileo came up with the idea well before Isaac Newton started work on his laws of motion in the 17th century, and Newton used Galileo's idea of relative motion in his mechanics.

Conducting the First Motion Experiments

As I discuss in Chapter 4, Galileo began his studies on the motion of objects in Pisa in the early 17th century. Lacking a good clock, he timed the swinging of church chandeliers with his pulse. Later, he rigged a simple timer by measuring the water draining out of a wine bottle with a hole in the bottom. He used this clock to time the motion of a falling object so that he could understand how it changed its speed as it fell.

Galileo noticed that as an object fell to the ground, its speed increased by the same amount during equal time intervals. With his experiments, Galileo discovered that the steady increase in speed — or *acceleration* — of an object falling to the ground is always the same. We call it the *acceleration due to gravity* and, as Newton taught us, it's caused by the attraction between the Earth and the object. (Check out Chapter 4 for more on Newton's theories.)

Experiencing movement on board a ship

Galileo didn't stop with experiments at rest. He also wanted to know what would happen if he dropped the object while he was moving.

Dropping a ball from the crow's nest

As the left side of Figure 8-1 shows, if you are in a sailboat moving steadily dead ahead and drop a ball from the crow's nest, the ball falls straight down and lands at the foot of the mast, not behind. But if a friend is watching your sailboat from shore, the ball seems to move in a curved path, as the right side of Figure 8-1 shows.

Figure 8-1:
The falling ball hits the deck at the foot of the mast (left), but someone looking at the boat from shore sees a curved path (right).

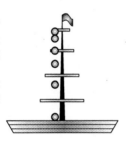 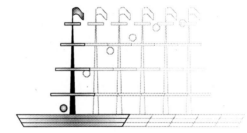

Before you drop the ball, your friend on shore sees it being carried along by the ship's motion. When you drop it, the ball begins to fall but also continues with the horizontal motion that it had when you held it. Like you, your friend sees the ball fall alongside the mast, but the mast and the ball continue moving along with the ship. You see the ball fall straight down, while she sees a curved path.

If you go inside a cabin in the ship and drop the ball there, it again falls straight down to the floor. When you're inside the cabin traveling on smooth water, you can't tell if your ship is moving steadily ahead or if it's docked at port. Everything behaves exactly the same in either case. If you throw a ball straight up, it comes right back down into your hand.

You can even play pool inside the ship. You won't be any better or worse than you are when you play on your pool table at home. The balls behave in the same way, as long as the ship maintains a constant speed on even seas.

Observing uniform motion

Galileo actually described a thought experiment like the scenario I just described in his bestselling book, *Discourses and Mathematical Demonstrations Concerning Two New Sciences Pertaining to Mechanics and Local Motion*, familiarly called *The Two New Sciences.* This is an interesting book. At the time, scholarly books dealing with philosophy or science were written in Latin. Galileo wrote *The Two New Sciences* in Italian. And he wrote it as a play, a dialogue among three characters. It isn't dry or difficult; it's actually entertaining.

In his book, Galileo encourages you to gather some friends and head for the cargo hold of a large ship. He tells you to bring some gnats, flies, and other winged insects, as well as a few fish that you'll place in a tub. And don't forget two bottles: one for you to hang upside down so that it drips into the second bottle right underneath.

Before the ship sails, he asks you to carefully observe how the insects fly, how the fish swim, and how the water drips into the bottle below. Galileo also wants you to throw a ball to your friends and to look at its motion.

When the ship sets sail and is moving smoothly, not tossing or lurching, you'll find out that there is no change in the way the insects fly, the fish swim, the water drips, and the ball moves. You won't be able to tell if the ship is moving by watching any of these events. Galileo writes that this is because the ship's motion is shared by all the things in it, including the air.

According to Galileo,

> *Uniform motion (motion along a straight line at constant speed) cannot be discovered without a reference point.*

Bringing his ideas to Earth

In *The Two New Sciences,* Galileo also discussed the problem of the behavior of falling objects on the moving Earth. If the Earth is moving, why does a ball thrown straight up into the air fall back to the same spot from which it was thrown? Many of Galileo's contemporaries used this argument to deny that the Earth moved.

Based on his thought experiments, Galileo concluded that if the Earth were moving, a ball would fall to the ground exactly as it would appear to do if the Earth weren't moving. Galileo said that you can't tell whether the Earth is moving by watching an object fall, just as you can't tell whether a ship is moving by watching an insect fly.

Finding uniform motion on a train

Einstein liked to use trains to illustrate his own theory of relativity. Trains were the main means of transportation during his time, and Einstein was very familiar with them. Trains offered a smoother ride than horse-drawn carriages. They offered one of the few ways people had to experience what Galileo called *uniform motion*: motion along a straight line at a steady speed.

Establishing the Principle of Relativity

According to Galileo, you can't distinguish steady motion in a straight line from rest. If you can't distinguish the two, they are the same. Uniform motion (as Galileo called it) and rest are the same thing.

That concept may sound a bit strange. You may not know when you're moving, but you certainly know when you're not moving. When you're sitting at home watching television, you aren't going anywhere. Or are you?

Let's say some astronauts are on their way to Mars. They have a powerful telescope and, for some reason, become interested in you. Through their telescope they see you sitting by the window in your living room, *moving* around the sun (along with the Earth) at 30 kilometers per second (kps). And that's without taking into account the motion of the sun and the entire solar system moving around the Milky Way galaxy, or the galaxy's motion within the Local Galactic Cluster.

Understanding that motion is relative

We usually refer to motion in everyday situations relative to the Earth. Earth is our reference point, or *reference frame* (as physicists say). Relative to the Earth, you are clearly at rest while you watch television in your home. At the same time, you are moving at 30 kps relative to the sun.

Imagine astronauts of the future, traveling in interplanetary space, away from any solar system. If they encounter another ship returning from an expedition, heading in the opposite direction, the astronauts won't be able to determine how fast the other ship is moving or how fast they are moving without checking their instruments, calibrated to read speeds relative to the Earth.

Are we there yet?

Sitting in an airplane, anxiously waiting to take off, you may be fooled into thinking that you are finally moving only to discover that the airplane taxiing next to yours is moving in the opposite direction. Unless you look outside and see the ground or the terminal, you can't tell who is moving.

You've also probably experienced a momentary confusion when driving on a multilane road during a traffic jam. The slow motion of the cars around you may make you look carefully to figure out who is moving.

Riding the bullet train

Consider another example. The bullet train between Madrid and Seville reaches speeds of up to 300 kilometers per hour (kph), or 188 mph, taking about two hours to travel the 470-km (293-mi) route through Spain's country-side. When the train travels at 230 kph, your camera is at rest relative to the train but moves with you and all the passengers at 230 kph relative to the ground.

A train attendant pushing a food cart toward the front of the train at 2 kph while the train travels at 230 kph has a speed relative to the ground of 232 kph. (His speed relative to the train is, of course, 2 kph.) If he boards the rear door of the last car and steps down at the end of the trip from the front door of the first car, he shaves off a few minutes of travel time.

If the train attendant walks toward the rear of the train at 3 kph to get some decaf for a passenger, his speed relative to the ground is 227 kph. What is the train attendant's real speed? Is it 3 kph or 227 kph? Both. It depends on the reference frame. As long as you're careful in its description, each is equally valid. There are no fixed or absolute speeds.

Nothing strange or new here. Galileo's relativity agrees with our common sense. However, Einstein will disagree with what we are saying. His relativity will be strange, as I show you in the next chapter.

Stating Galileo's principle of relativity

According to Galileo, then, all motion along a straight line at a constant speed is relative. It's the same as saying that you don't have fixed, absolute speeds, that you can't distinguish between rest and uniform motion.

Galileo believed that no experiment in mechanics could reveal whether you are in uniform motion or at rest; all mechanics experiments work the same way regardless of your motion. This is the *Galilean principle of relativity.* Simply put, it says

> *The laws of mechanics are the same in all frames of reference in uniform motion.*

Not being able to distinguish uniform motion from rest means that all reference frames are equivalent. No reference frame is special or *absolute,* as scientists call it. There is no absolute standard of rest, and uniform motion has to be always referred to a frame of reference. Uniform motion is relative.

If you measure the speed of your boat at 30 kph relative to the water you're navigating in, someone else may measure it to be 20 kph relative to shore. And someone else on another boat wanting to catch up to you may measure it to be 5 kph relative to his boat. Which is correct? All are. It depends on the reference frame.

Creating Another Relativity

For Galileo, physics was mechanics. In reality, in Galileo's time, not much was known about mechanics. And what was known had been discovered by him, like the motion of falling objects and the ideas of uniform motion and accelerated motion. Newton came along and developed all of mechanics. In doing so, he built a system of the world, a way to look at the universe that worked like clockwork.

In Newton's mechanical universe, objects move in predictable ways that can be calculated precisely using the three laws of motion and the universal law of gravitation (see Chapter 4). In Newton's world, space and time are fixed, absolute. A sailor walking on the deck along the centerline toward the bow of his boat at 4 kph while his boat sails at 20 kph relative to land can easily figure out that he is moving at 24 kph past the land. When he returns toward the stern at the same speed, he moves at 16 kph past the land.

Newton adopted Galileo's principle of relativity and used it when he developed his mechanics. He even stated it clearly in his *Principia,* the masterpiece he wrote to describe his mechanics. It was clear to Newton that uniform motion made no difference to the laws of mechanics.

Integrating the laws of motion with the speed of light

All was going well for Galileo's relativity until James Clerk Maxwell came up with his theory of electromagnetism in the 19th century. His four equations (which I discuss in Chapter 6) taught us that light is an electromagnetic wave. But if it's a wave, it needs some sort of substance to move through. Sound waves move through the air or water, or even through solids.

The mysterious substance that light supposedly traveled through was called the *ether*. The commonly held belief after Maxwell developed his theory was that light traveled like a wave at about 300,000 km (186,000 mi) per second through the ether. (By 1882, the measured value of the speed of light was very close to the modern value of 299,792.458 kps or 186,282.397 mps.)

If light traveled through the ether, the Earth did as well. And if Earth were moving through the ether, the speed of light would change. When the Earth moved in the same direction as the ether, it would gain some ground on the light beam, and you would measure a smaller value. When the Earth moved in the opposite direction in its orbit around the sun, you'd measure a larger value for the speed of light, because you'd be losing ground.

At the end of the 19th century, two physicists at what is today called Case Western Reserve University, Albert Michelson and Edward Morley, set up a delicate experiment to measure the change in the speed of light as the Earth moved through the ether. I discuss this experiment in detail in Chapter 9. But strangely enough, the experiment measured the same speed for light no matter how the Earth moved.

That result was difficult to understand. It was like trying to measure from shore the speed of a boat that's moving in the water at 20 kph and coming up with the same speed whether it goes upstream or downstream. The water is going to carry the boat faster when it travels downstream.

Didn't light follow the principle of relativity? Perhaps you can't add up the speeds of the Earth and light, like you do with boats and trains. The results of the Michelson–Morley experiment created a new problem for scientists.

Expressing the idea of contraction

The ether experiment of Michelson and Morley was very carefully done, and scientists were puzzled by its results. After the results were published, two physicists came up with an explanation. And by coincidence, they did so independently of one another. The explanation wasn't what anybody was expecting.

George FitzGerald at Trinity College in Dublin, Ireland and Hendrik Antoon Lorentz of the University of Leyden in the Netherlands said at about the same time that the reason the speed of light is independent from the motion of the Earth is that objects shrink when they move, and the shrinking is along the direction of motion. The faster the object moves, the more it shrinks. What's more, the shrinking is exactly in the amount needed to keep the speed of light measurements unchanged.

That was some strange idea. Objects shrink when they move?

Lorentz provided an explanation for it. He had developed a theory of matter based on electrons. According to Lorentz, all matter is composed of electrons, and properties such as elasticity or hardness are due to the way these electrons interact. When a body moves through the ether, these electrons flatten out, producing an overall reduction in the size of the object.

Lorentz modified the simple rule in Galileo's principle of relativity and came out with an equation that could be used to compute the length reduction with speed. We know this equation today as the *Lorentz–FitzGerald contraction*.

In the end, the length contraction idea of Lorentz and FitzGerald wasn't taken seriously. It was too much of a coincidence that the shortening of lengths was what was needed to make the Michelson–Morley experiment work.

Lorentz published his paper in 1895. That year, the 16-year-old Einstein was thinking about what he would see if he could travel at the speed of light. Ten years later, he provided the final explanation for this puzzle. Einstein used the Lorentz–FitzGerald equation in his theory of relativity, but with a different interpretation. I cover Einstein's version in Chapter 9.

Identifying the Man Who Almost Discovered Relativity

Jules Henri Poincaré in France had a different approach to explain the strange results of the Michelson–Morley experiment. He sympathized with Lorentz but was unhappy with introducing the idea of length contraction only to explain the result of the experiment.

Thinking about elastic time

Poincaré was unhappy that Lorentz had abandoned the principle of relativity. The laws of physics appeared to be the same in all frames of reference, which told him there must be some more general principle of relativity. He asked Lorentz to work on an extension to his length contraction equation.

Lorentz went back to the drawing board. He came back with a new set of transformation equations that included his length contraction but added time dilation to the mix. What his new theory said was that if you're moving relative to the Earth, for example, not only do objects change in length, but your clock ticks at a different rate. Time has a sort of elastic property that stretches and contracts depending on how you move.

Of course, no one — not even Lorentz himself — thought that these equations applied to the real world. They just helped in the calculations; they were a math tool with no connection to reality.

If the Lorentz transformations were correct (mathematically), how do you measure time? Poincaré suggested that clocks in different moving frames could be synchronized with light signals. But he said that these clocks don't show "true time," and some clocks are slower and some faster. The only true time is the one measured relative to the ether.

Expressing an unrealized hope

At the International Congress of Arts and Sciences in St. Louis in 1904, Poincaré delivered an invited lecture where he gave a clear and simple description of the principle of relativity. It was an extension of Galileo's principle, to include all the laws of physics. He said that the laws of physical phenomena should be the same whether you are in uniform motion or at rest so that you couldn't have any way of knowing if you are moving or not.

As I show you in Chapter 9, Poincaré's version of the principle of relativity is essentially the same as Einstein's. And Poincaré stated it one year before Einstein's own relativity paper was published. It's surprising that Poincaré didn't take the last step and discover the correct version of relativity.

In his lecture, Poincaré mentioned the experiments of Michelson and Morley, who had "pushed precision to its last limits." He also included Lorentz's transformations, which gave the formula to change length and time so that the speed of light remains the same when you measure it while in motion through the ether.

Poincaré said that the principle of relativity needed to be explained, so that we can perhaps build a whole new mechanics where the speed of light can't be exceeded. Poincaré, the experienced and respected scientist, who had made original and significant contributions in mathematics and physics (and continued to do so), ended his lecture by saying that this new mechanics was an "unrealized hope and conjecture."

Just a year later, the 26-year-old inexperienced and unknown Albert Einstein would make this unrealized hope a reality.

Chapter 9

Riding on a Beam of Light

*E*instein's brand of relativity rests on two ideas:

✔ The laws of physics are the same in all nonaccelerated frames of reference.

✔ The speed of light is always constant.

These ideas began growing in Einstein when, as a 16 year old, he tried to imagine what he would see were he to ride alongside a beam of light, moving at its same speed. Would he be able to see the edge of the beam? Would the light beam stop at some point (looking like a light saber from *Star Wars*)?

In this chapter, I show you the developments that helped Einstein continue to think about this problem for the next ten years. I explain the "failed" experiment by Albert Michelson and Edward Morley that attempted to measure the speed of the Earth in the *ether,* the stuff that supposedly filled space. I show how Einstein used Galilean relativity to help solve the problems with mechanics and electromagnetism. And, finally, I show you how his answer to these problems came in the form of his special theory of relativity.

Accounting for the Ether

During his junior year in college, Einstein wanted to set up an experiment to detect the motion of the Earth through the *ether,* the stuff that supposedly filled the entire universe and allowed light to travel. By the time he was a senior, he had designed the experiment. But (as I explain in Chapter 2) Professor Heinrich Weber, the physics department chair at the Zurich Polytechnic, wouldn't let him set up the experiment in the school's lab.

At the time, neither Weber nor Einstein knew that Michelson and Morley had performed a landmark experiment in 1886 to try to accomplish the same goal. Michelson and Morley had come up with a clever way to measure the motion of the Earth through the ether by measuring the speed of light at different times during the Earth's orbit around the sun.

Michelson had invented the instrument to perform this experiment when he worked in Hermann von Helmholtz's laboratory in Germany. The method that he had in mind was actually proposed by James Clerk Maxwell in 1875. It was simple. Because the ether fills space, the motion of the Earth in its orbit around the sun must create a wind (as shown in Figure 9-1). It's not too different from when you stick your hand out the window when you're riding in a car down the highway.

Figure 9-1:
The Earth moving through the ether as it orbits around the sun.

To see how you'd conduct such an experiment, think about how you'd measure your speed when swimming upstream and downstream in a river. If you know that you swim at 2 meters per second (m/s), about 120 yards a minute, in calm waters and are now swimming downstream in a river that's running at 1 m/s, you really are advancing at 3 m/s relative to shore. When you turn around, you'll be swimming upstream, advancing at only 1 m/s relative to the shore.

Michelson and Morley believed you could do essentially the same thing to measure the speed of light in the ether:

✔ If you measured the speed of light in the direction of motion of the Earth around the sun, you'd be going against the ether wind and get a speed equal to the speed of light in the ether minus the speed of the ether wind.

✔ If you measured the speed of light in the opposite direction, you'd get a value equal to the speed of light relative to the ether plus the speed of the ether wind.

Michelson did his experiment in Germany in 1881. He knew that his *interferometer* — as his instrument is called — was sensitive enough to measure the difference between the speed of light in the ether (300,000 kilometers per second [kps]) and the speed of light relative to the Earth moving upstream in the ether wind. The speed of the ether wind was the speed of the Earth in its orbit around the sun, which he knew to be 30 kps. He expected to measure the speed of light at 299,970 kps. He got 300,000 kps, as if there were no ether wind.

Some time later, Michelson accepted an offer to be a professor at the Case School of Applied Science in Cleveland, Ohio (now Case Western Reserve University). There, he met Edward Morley, a chemistry professor. The two redesigned Michelson's experiment with increased accuracy.

Michelson and Morley measured the speed of light in the direction of the ether wind (opposite to the direction of motion of the Earth in its orbit) and across the ether wind simultaneously. Using a two-way mirror, they split a light beam so that it could travel along those two directions (see Figure 9-2). The two beams met and fell on a screen where they were superimposed. Because the two beams came from a single beam, they were in lockstep, or *coherent*. (I discuss the importance of this fact in Chapter 7, where I describe Thomas Young's experiment.) Therefore, when they met, they formed an interference pattern that the scientists used to calculate the speed of light with extreme precision (see Figure 9-3).

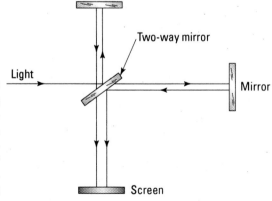

Figure 9-2:
The setup of the Michelson–Morley experiment.

Figure 9-3:
An inter-
ference
pattern
obtained
with a
modern
Michelson
and Morley
interfer-
ometer.

Courtesy E. Arens, NASA

The two scientists believed that their experiment failed, because they didn't see any difference in the measurements in the two directions. They believed that the interference pattern should've shifted.

The negative results of the Michelson–Morley experiment puzzled scientists all over the world. According to their experiment, the speed of light didn't change regardless of how fast you moved.

Einstein was 7 years old when Michelson and Morley first did their experiment. He learned about it only after he graduated from college. His special theory of relativity would provide the final solution to the puzzle. But he didn't develop it with their experiment in mind. He was more concerned with electromagnetism and with Galileo's principle of relativity.

Struggling with an Inconsistency

Einstein developed his special theory of relativity during a few weeks in 1905, his miracle year, when he was 26 years old. The word "special" wasn't origi- nally part of the theory's name; Einstein added it later to distinguish this early theory from an important extension that he developed (which he called the *general* theory of relativity). The relativity paper was the fourth of five incredi- ble papers he published in 1905. With these papers, he changed physics at its roots. Check out Chapter 3 for the details about what he accomplished during this extraordinary time period.

What led Einstein to develop the special theory of relativity? As I explain in Chapters 3 and 6, Einstein was fascinated by electromagnetism and studied it on his own throughout college. He continued his studies after graduation.

In doing so, he discovered that Galileo's principle of relativity (which I explain in Chapter 8) worked for mechanics but not for electromagnetism. He set out to figure out why.

Discovering that you're moving

Isaac Newton had adopted Galileo's principle of relativity when he formulated his mechanics (see Chapter 4). The principle of relativity says that the laws of mechanics don't change just because you're moving. According to Newton and Galileo, if you are inside the cabin of a ship moving at a constant speed on smooth waters, for example, you can't tell if you are moving or docked at port. Things behave the same in either case.

In 1905, Einstein found out that electromagnetism, as presented by Maxwell, gives you a way to discover if you are in uniform motion or at rest, without stepping out of your cabin or looking out the window. He started his special relativity paper by pointing out this inconsistency.

Focusing on electric fields

If you take a magnet and move it toward or away from a stationary wire, the moving magnet produces an electric field in the wire that generates a current (see Figure 9-4). That's Faraday's law — and one of Maxwell's four equations, as I explain in Chapter 6. With his experiments (which I also explain in Chapter 6), Michael Faraday showed that to produce an electric field in the wire, the magnetic field has to change. In this case, the field from the moving magnet changes at the location of the wire. It becomes stronger and stronger if the magnet is approaching, or weaker and weaker if the magnet is moving away.

Figure 9-4:
Move a magnet toward a wire (or away from it), and you can detect a current in the wire.

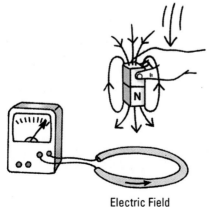

Electric Field

The law in Betelgeuse

What difference does it make if the laws of physics are the same everywhere? Why all the fuss about whether all motion is relative or whether absolute motion exists?

The big deal is that if things don't work the same everywhere, the universe is unpredictable. You couldn't discover anything, because the laws here wouldn't apply somewhere like Betelgeuse, the red supergiant star in the constellation of Orion. If the laws of physics change when you change locations, for all we know the apples on Betelgeuse might fall up.

If, on the other hand, you agree with Einstein that the laws of physics are the same everywhere, you can discover something on Earth (like the way objects heat up) and then look at the sun and use your discovery to study it. Eventually, a satellite is sent there, and you find out that the sun works the way you predicted. You can then start to make predictions about solar flares and other phenomena that disturb communications and climate here on Earth.

Now, what happens if you keep the magnet at rest and move the wire? According to Maxwell, because the magnetic field in the area around the magnet isn't changing, there is no electric field that can create a current in the wire — see Figure 9-5. (The current still appears in the wire, but according to Maxwell, that occurs for an entirely different reason.)

Figure 9-5:
There is no electric field in the wire when you move it toward a magnet.

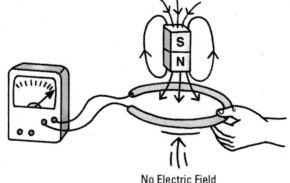

No Electric Field
In Wire

In one case, when the magnet moves, there is an electric field. In the other case, when the magnet is at rest, there is no electric field. So, according to Maxwell's electromagnetism, you have a way to tell if you're moving or not. Just bring a magnet along. And an electric field sensor.

Being at rest in the universe

If you can distinguish motion, if you can tell when you are at rest, then motion is not relative. You could take your motion-detector device into space and slow down until your device tells you that you are at rest. Or you could use it on the ground and start moving in the direction opposite to the Earth's rotation and revolution around the sun, trying to balance all the possible motions of the Earth and the solar system until your meter indicator showed zero. Then you would be at rest in the universe.

From this vantage point, you could see everything else moving around you with their true motions, their *absolute* motions, as scientists call them.

Siding with Galileo

Einstein didn't like the implications of this aspect of electromagnetism. As formulated by Maxwell, electromagnetism applied only to objects that didn't move relative to the ether. That was actually the reason why no electric field appeared in the moving wire; the wire wasn't at rest in the ether.

Einstein didn't believe that absolute motion existed. He thought that Galileo was right in believing that all motion was relative, that the laws of mechanics were the same everywhere. But he wanted to go beyond mechanics. Einstein believed that the laws of physics were the same everywhere in the universe.

Laying the Cornerstones of Relativity

In his 1905 paper, Einstein made Galileo's principle of relativity universal. Galileo and Newton had applied it to mechanics (the only physics they ever knew), and Einstein extended it to the rest of physics.

Dispelling absolute motion

Einstein made his extended principle one of the cornerstones of his new theory. He called it a postulate, and it reads as follows:

The principle of relativity: The laws of physics are the same in all nonaccelerated frames of reference.

His extended principle of relativity means that

- ✔ The laws of physics are the same everywhere; everything works the same regardless of how fast you're moving.
- ✔ You can't distinguish rest from motion; this means that all reference frames are the same, and there is no absolute motion.
- ✔ Without a reference point at rest, all uniform motion is relative.

Armed with his postulate, Einstein was able to reformulate electromagnetism. In the second part of his 1905 paper, he showed that all electric and magnetic effects remain unchanged in all reference frames in uniform motion. In his paper, Einstein fixed electromagnetism so that it would depend on relative motion.

What about the moving wire and the stationary magnet? According to Einstein, there is only relative motion between the magnet and the wire. If you stay with the wire, the magnet moves toward you, and if you stay with the magnet, the wire moves toward you. The situation is identical, and everything you measure should be identical. If you measure an electric field in one case, you should also measure it in the other case.

I mention in the "Focusing on electric fields" section that Maxwell's electromagnetism indicated that an effect other than an electric field causes a current when you move a wire toward a magnet that's at rest. But Einstein showed that Maxwell was wrong; an electric field creates the current in that situation as well.

A modern physicist will not even bother to decide what's moving. She will simply consider the magnet and the wire to be in relative motion. For today's physicists, there is no confusion. But that's because Einstein proved that there is no absolute motion.

Thanks to Einstein's correction, electromagnetism and mechanics are on equal footing. The principle of relativity applies to both. The motion-detection device based on the absence of an electric field in one case doesn't work. There is no difference in what you measure in either case. You really can't distinguish rest from motion.

But Einstein didn't just solve the inconsistency with electromagnetism and mechanics. He extended the principle of relativity to all of physics.

Struggling with the speed of light

According to Maxwell's equations, light moves at a fixed speed relative to the ether. But Einstein didn't have a need for the ether. With his principle of relativity, he did away with an absolute standard of rest. He believed that light moves as independent electric and magnetic fields vibrating through empty space.

Without an ether, with respect to *what* is light moving? Einstein's answer was unexpected: *Light travels at the same speed with respect to everything.*

That simple answer contained the key to relativity. But Einstein didn't just arrive at this conclusion one day. He struggled with it.

Why should light be different?

Einstein was saying that light travels at the same speed — 300,000 kps, or c (the letter Einstein used for the speed of light), regardless of how you move. The problem was, this idea is crazy.

Think of it this way: If you ran at 10 kilometers per hour (kph) after a bus that's moving at 30 kph, you'd clock the bus moving at 20 kph. And if you sped up, you could match the bus's speed and hop on. So, if you run up to a beam of light at one-third of c — at 100,000 kps — and measure its speed from your moving vehicle, shouldn't you get 200,000 kps? Why can't you use the same type of calculation for the speed of light that you use for the speed of the bus?

The Olympic Academy

As I explain in Chapter 3, Einstein struggled to find a job after he graduated from the Zurich Polytechnic. He finally secured a job as a patent examiner in the Bern patent office, but he found out that the position wasn't going to be available for several months. He had a temporary job as a math tutor at an institute but was extremely unhappy about the institute's militaristic director and his meager salary. To make ends meet, he placed an ad in the paper offering tutoring in physics and math.

Two people called in, Maurice Solovine and Conrad Habicht. Solovine was a philosophy and physics major at the University of Bern. Habicht was an old friend of Einstein's who had studied physics and math and was now getting his PhD in math at the University of Bern.

Einstein didn't lecture to the two men. Instead, the three of them held discussions; Solovine and Habicht would ask questions that Einstein would answer and explain. They also discussed physics and philosophy books. The three became good friends, and they often held discussions while hiking to a nearby village, climbing a mountain, or going on a trip to a lake. They decided to call their group the "Olympic Academy," partly as a joke, but also because they felt that during their discussions, they learned more that they ever did in any formal class.

The discussions with his two friends helped Einstein figure out things in his own mind. Solovine and Habicht (as well as Einstein's other friends) were sounding boards for the ideas that he was developing.

The meetings of the Olympic Academy continued even after Einstein married Mileva Maric (see Chapter 2). Mileva joined in but, according to Solovine, was not a very active participant and never joined them when the discussions took place outdoors.

The Olympic Academy lasted for a few years until Solovine and Habicht left to accept job offers. The men continued their friendship throughout their lives.

Einstein had extended the principle of relativity to include all the laws of physics. But by doing this he was creating a problem. He'd opened a new hole by trying to plug another.

Plugging the new hole

At the time Einstein was formulating many of his famous theories, he worked at the Bern patent office with his old friend Michelangelo (Michele) Besso. Besso was an engineer with a good grasp of physics. Einstein talked to Besso about his ideas regarding the principle of relativity. On their daily walks to and from work, they discussed Einstein's struggle with the conflict between the speed of light and the speeds of ordinary objects.

The nagging conflict kept bothering Einstein. One day, he went to visit Besso to see if he could help him think the problem through. They talked late into the night, but Einstein got no closer to solving the problem. However, when he woke up the next morning, the answer came to him. He greeted Besso on their way to work by saying, "I've completely solved the problem."

"My solution was really for the very concept of time," Einstein said some time later. What Einstein realized is that time is relative. And space is relative. Time and space aren't fixed, like Newton believed they were. For Einstein, time and space change when you move, but they adjust themselves so that the speed of light stays the same, regardless of how you move.

After Einstein made this startling discovery, he was ready to finish his theory. "Five weeks after my recognition of this, the present theory of special relativity was completed," he later said. Einstein made his discovery that light always travels at the same speed into the second cornerstone of his theory, his second postulate. This postulate says:

> *The principle of light: The speed of light is a universal constant. All observers in uniform (nonaccelerated) motion measure the same value c for the speed of light.*

The two postulates were the cornerstones upon which he built his theory.

From here on, space stopped being the stage where things happen, and time no longer flowed at the same rate for everyone. Space and time became *relative,* but the speed of light was absolute. (I expand on this strange idea in the next chapter.)

You See, Light Always Travels at c

Einstein developed his special theory of relativity from beginning to end in five weeks. He submitted it for publication in June of 1905, and it was received at the offices of the prestigious journal *Annalen der Physik* on June 30th.

Finally, Einstein had his answer to the question about what he would see if he rode alongside a beam of light. The answer was that he couldn't ever catch up to it. Light would always be traveling at c, no matter how fast he moved. There is a front of the wave, an edge to the beam, but no one can ever move along with it. Light moves at c with respect to anything.

This remarkable and completely unexpected idea was the key to relativity, the stroke of genius. This idea was what differentiated Einstein's relativity from Poincaré's (see Chapter 8). Einstein took the crucial step. That step didn't even cross Poincaré's mind, or anybody else's. Einstein's step changed our ideas of space and time.

With his special theory of relativity, Einstein also solved the problem of the Michelson–Morley experiment. The problem had bothered physicists for almost 20 years. As I explain in Chapter 8, Hendrik Antoon Lorentz and George FitzGerald had proposed the strange idea of length contraction so that objects would shrink as they moved, with the shrinking matching exactly what was needed to make the Michelson–Morley experiment work. Scientists were not happy with this too-convenient idea. Lorentz had also added the idea of time stretching and contracting as you moved. But to him and to everyone else, his equations didn't apply to the real world. They were tools to explain the Michelson–Morley experiment.

Einstein's solution was even stranger. As with Lorentz and FitzGerald's solution, time and lengths change as you move. But for Einstein, these changes are *real*, not just mathematical tools. Einstein's equations represent the real world.

But, if time and space change when you move, as Einstein said, why hadn't anyone noticed? Why don't we notice it now? Because the changes are extremely small at ordinary speeds. They become noticeable only if you move at speeds close to the speed of light.

In his 1905 paper, Einstein gave us equations to correctly calculate the relative speeds of objects in motion, and they're slightly different than the speeds you would normally measure. For example, say you're driving down the highway at 90 kph in a 90 kph zone and a car passes you at 97 kph. Wouldn't you clock the other car going 7 kph faster than you? Not exactly. If you had a very precise instrument, you'd clock it going 7.0000000000001 kph faster than you. Obviously, the difference is tiny at such a speed.

When you apply Einstein's equations to spaceships moving at speeds close to the speed of light, the correction becomes important. Say you're on a spaceship traveling at $0.97c$ relative to the Earth in a mission to the center of the galaxy. You pass the slower *Expedition One* ship that left earlier and is traveling at $0.90c$ relative to Earth. Will the *Expedition One* crew see you pulling past it at $0.07c$? No. The crew will see you speeding away at $0.5c$ (see Figure 9-6).

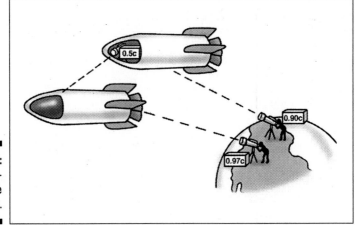

Figure 9-6:
· The space-
ships are
relativistic.

It you try to measure the speed of a ray of light moving at c relative to Earth from your spaceship that's moving at $0.97c$ relative to Earth, you won't measure it at $0.07c$ relative to you, but at c relative to you. Light travels at c as measured from anywhere.

Making Physics Beautiful

Einstein came up with the equations that I used to calculate the speeds in this thought experiment. He worked them out from his theory. What's remarkable is that they came out to be the same as the Lorentz transformations that had been introduced to make the Michelson–Morley experiment work.

Einstein wasn't trying to make the Michelson–Morley experiment work. Extending the principle of relativity beyond mechanics, he was looking to make physics simpler, more beautiful.

Although the equations that he obtained were the same as the Lorentz–FitzGerald transformations, Einstein's interpretation was different. I discuss the implications of the special theory in Chapter 10.

Chapter 10

Clocks, Trains, and Automobiles: Exploring Space and Time

* * *

* * *

Switch your brain to science fiction mode for a minute. Consider a universe where clocks keep different time depending on how fast they're moving. (A clock in a spaceship might run at a different pace than a clock on land, for example.) Or a universe where people age faster if they're standing still than they do if they're moving. (See all those Hollywood stars running for dear life?) Or a universe where distances and shapes change depending on how fast you're moving when you observe them.

Sound like a fascinating place? It is, and it just so happens to be the universe you're living in.

In this chapter, I show you how Einstein's special theory of relativity changed the way we think about space and time.

Your Time Is Not My Time

As I explain in Chapter 9, Einstein developed his special theory of relativity from one simple but powerful idea: The laws of physics are the same for all observers in uniform motion (without acceleration). This statement is Galileo's principle of relativity, which Einstein extended to apply to all of physics rather than just to Newton's mechanics. When Einstein adopted this principle, the need for an ether disappeared, along with the idea of absolute motion. All uniform motion is relative. Einstein's principle of relativity also required him to make the speed of light a fundamental constant.

Casting doubt on simultaneity

Einstein's beautiful special relativity paper was the fourth paper that he published in 1905, his year of miracles (see Chapter 3). In that paper, Einstein discussed the implications of his theory on simultaneous events. "We see that we cannot ascribe *absolute* meaning to the concept of simultaneity," he wrote.

He explained that two events that are simultaneous in some particular moving frame aren't simultaneous when observed from a reference frame that is moving relative to the first one. Einstein's conclusions regarding the simultaneity of events led to unexpected situations.

Conducting a thought experiment

Consider the following thought experiment involving two spaceships.

You're traveling on a spaceship on an interstellar expedition. A crew member turns on a light bulb in the middle of the crew quarters (see Figure 10-1). You notice that the light reaches the front and back of the cabin at the same time (as it should, because the speed of light is the same whether you are moving or not, and the distance from the light bulb to each wall is the same). The two events are simultaneous. Or are they?

An astronomer named Ellie is watching your transparent spaceship through a powerful telescope from her own spaceship, and her version of events is different. Ellie sees that your ship is heading toward the star Sirius at half *c*. She then sees the crew member turning on the light bulb in the middle of the spaceship. From Ellie's perspective, the light going toward the front of the spaceship, traveling at *c*, has a slightly larger distance to cover than the one going to the back of the spaceship. That's because the front wall has moved a bit farther away from the light bulb since it emitted the light. The back wall, however, has moved a little closer and meets the light going there a little sooner, as shown in Figure 10-2.

Figure 10-1:
You see that the light from the light bulb reaches the front and back of the spaceship at the same time.

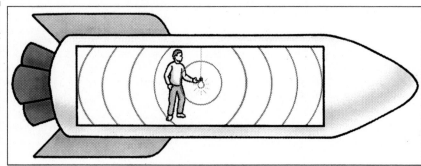

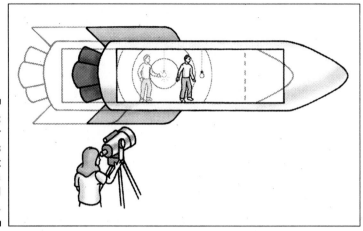

Figure 10-2:
Astronomer
Ellie sees
that the light
reaching the
back wall
arrives first.

To Ellie, the light doesn't reach the front and back of the ship at the same time. These two events are not simultaneous.

Who is right? Ellie is right. And you are right. Both are right at the same time. As Einstein said,

> *Events that are simultaneous in one moving frame are not simultaneous in another.*

Dilating Time

According to Einstein, you and Ellie disagree on the timing of what you both see because you are moving relative to each other. Suppose now that for a second experiment, you send one laser pulse straight up to a mirror in the ceiling of the spaceship's cabin. From the spaceship, you see the pulse go up, bounce off the mirror, and come straight back down (as shown at the top of Figure 10-3).

Ellie sees the pulse travel up along a diagonal, because the light travels up and then across with the moving spaceship. She then sees the pulse bounce off and head down along another diagonal, because now the pulse travels down and also across with the ship (as shown at the bottom of Figure 10-3).

According to Einstein, both you and Ellie, in motion relative to each other, measure the same speed for the light pulse. However, Ellie sees the pulse traveling through a *longer* path than you do. The same event, the light pulse going up and down, takes longer to happen from her perspective than from yours.

Figure 10-3:
(Top) You see the light beam go up, bounce off, and come straight back down. (Bottom) Ellie sees the beam go up along a diagonal, bounce off, and move down along another diagonal.

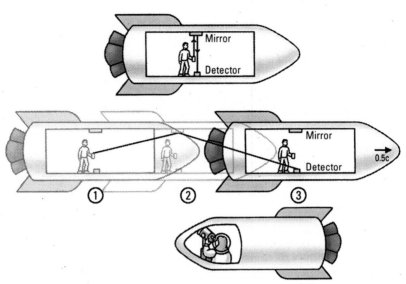

You could arrange for this experiment to repeat over and over, with the light pulse going up and down in your spaceship. That would be a kind of clock. You could count the number of return trips for the light pulse in a day, and from there on you could say that when you count so many of these returns, a day has passed. To make it easier, you could adjust the height of the mirror so that 50 million return trips equals a second on your regular watch. Your device could tick every time it counts 50 million, so you know it ticks every second, like your regular clock.

Ellie is still on her spaceship as well, and she also builds the same kind of clock to keep track of the time on your ship. Will her clock and your clock keep the same time? No. Ellie finds out that her light clock takes longer to tick than the regular clock on the wall. Remember, her new clock is keeping the time on *your* ship, and it's taking longer to count up to a second than her regular clock. She concludes that time on your ship flows more slowly than on hers.

You disagree. From your perspective, your ship isn't the one moving. To you, Ellie's ship is moving at half *c*. If you ask her to set up the same experiment with the laser pulse and the mirror on her ship, you'll be able to monitor the flow of time on her ship. And when you do, you'll observe that time on her ship is running more slowly than on yours.

From your ship, it appears that Ellie's ship is moving, and time in her frame runs more slowly than in yours. From Ellie's ship, your ship seems to be moving, and your time flows more slowly than hers. How do you explain the differences? All you can say is that, according to Einstein,

Time in the moving frame always runs more slowly.

Shortening Space

According to Einstein, time is relative. It changes depending on how the person measuring it moves. But time isn't the only thing that changes with the motion of the observer. Space also changes.

Conducting a repair mission

Ready for another thought experiment? Imagine that you are on a spaceship that has docked at a large space station for maintenance. While you are there, you receive news that a sister ship was disabled at a point 360 million kilometers (km) from the space station. A service runabout out on a short trip is rerouted to assist the ship. While on its way, the pilot of the runabout realizes that he has fuel for only 320 million km, at the most, and radios back to the station that he is returning to base. The station commander does a quick calculation and orders the runabout to continue on its service mission to the disabled ship.

Reluctantly, the pilot obeys orders and keeps his course. Thirty-four minutes later, he arrives at the disabled ship, and he still has enough fuel left to go another 10 million km. His instruments tell him that he's traveled only 310 million km. How can that be?

The station commander had calculated the shortened distance, which is why he sent the pilot ahead with the mission. The commander used Einstein's equation for the shortening of space from the perspective of the moving runabout. At the one-half c that the runabout could travel, Einstein's special theory of relativity says that the distance is shortened by 13 percent — enough for the runabout to make it to the disabled ship. (Once fixed, the ship can carry the runabout back to the station.)

According to Einstein's special theory of relativity,

Space is shortened in the moving frame.

Having more time than you thought

Another way to look at why the runabout makes it with the fuel it has is to consider the lengthening of time for the runabout. Einstein said that time flows more slowly in the moving frame. If you're in the station comparing the clock on the wall with the clock in the runabout, you'll see that the runabout's clock moves more slowly. Using the clock on your wall, you'll measure a longer time for the trip than if you used the pilot's clock.

Because the clock in the moving runabout runs more slowly (as it's viewed from the frame of the station), the pilot's time is expanded or dilated, and his fuel lasts longer. The longer distance that you measure in your frame is shortened in his. There is an interplay between space and time here, which I discuss more later in the chapter.

Understanding length contraction

The runabout made it to the disabled ship with the fuel it had because it was moving relative to the station, and space in the moving frame is shortened or contracted. However, you could say that the space station was moving relative to the runabout, and its space is the one that should've been shortened. According to relativity, both statements are equally valid.

If you're moving relative to me, I see your space contracted, and anything that you're carrying, including yourself, will be shortened in the direction of motion (see Figure 10-4). If your ship measures 300 meters and is moving at half *c*, I measure it as being only 260 meters long — a 13-percent contraction. I see a yard stick laying down in the direction of motion in your moving ship to be 31 inches long instead of 36. You look 13 percent thinner, but your height hasn't changed (see Figure 10-4).

From your perspective, everything is normal: The yardstick is still 36 inches long, and you don't look any skinnier than normal. For you, however, I am the one moving at half *c*, and when you observe my surroundings, everything is shortened by 13 percent in the direction of motion. Remember: According to Einstein, space is relative.

Figure 10-4:
If you move relative to me, I see your space shortened in the direction of your motion.

This shortening of space is linked to the lengthening of time for the moving observer. Both space and time are relative. Einstein was forced to reach this conclusion after he decided that the speed of light is a universal constant. This way of thinking was completely opposite to what Newton had done. For Newton, both space and time were fixed, absolutes, but the speed of light could change depending on how fast you were moving.

Deciding If It's All Real

How can it be possible that I see your space contracted and, at the same time, you see mine contracted? I see your time running slow, and when you measure my time, you see it running slow. Are these effects real, or are they simply illusions? Does your time *appear* to me to be running slow when you and I are in relative motion, or is your time actually running slow?

You're a muon!

The effects are real and have been measured many times with modern instruments. The first observation was with *muons,* elementary particles that are created in cosmic rays at an altitude of 6,000 meters (20,000 feet) and that reach the ground in abundance.

The average lifetime of a muon is 2.2 microseconds. Physicists measure this lifetime with precision instruments in their laboratories. Cosmic ray muons travel at 0.998c, very close to the speed of light. At this speed, they could travel only 660 meters (2,200 feet) in the atmosphere. Because they start their journeys 6,000 meters above the Earth, you should never detect one.

However, because they are moving relative to us, their lifetimes are extended in our frame of reference from 2.2 microseconds to 34.8 microseconds. Because they last longer, they can cover a distance of 10,000 meters (33,000 feet), more than enough to reach the ground (see Figure 10-5). A muon passes each square centimeter of the Earth's surface about every minute.

If you are a muon, you know that you will live only 2.2 microseconds. In your reference frame, you aren't moving, and that's what your life expectancy is. Yet you make it to the ground below. And most of your neighbors do, too. The reason is that the distance from your birthplace to the ground isn't 6,000 meters, as the Earthlings say, but 380 meters (1,200 feet), and you know you have time to travel that far.

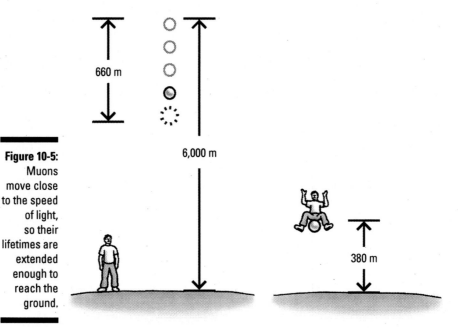

Figure 10-5:
Muons
move close
to the speed
of light,
so their
lifetimes are
extended
enough to
reach the
ground.

Slowing it down

Biological processes are also slowed down as you move faster and faster. Your heartbeat and the rate of cell division in your body, for example, are slowed down when you move relative to the Earth. How does this happen?

If you take off on a spaceship and eventually reach a speed of $0.9c$ relative to the Earth, your heart will continue to beat normally, and the cells in your body will continue splitting at their normal rate. But to me, here on Earth, your ship's clock runs more slowly than mine (because you're moving at $0.9c$ relative to the Earth). For every hour that passes on my clock, your clock marks only 26 minutes (see Figure 10-6). When a day passes for me, it's only been ten and a half hours for you. A year later, you'll be seven months younger than me. In ten years, you'll age only four years and four months. I'm talking about real age here, not an illusion, because all your biological processes have slowed down. You will honestly age more slowly than the rest of us here on Earth.

Speeding it up

But wait. Didn't I say that this type of motion is relative? Couldn't you just as well describe the situation by saying that when you are on your spaceship, the Earth and the entire solar system are traveling at $0.9c$ while you are at rest? This is true.

Figure 10-6:
When my clock registers an hour, only 26 minutes have passed for you on the spaceship.

For you, then, all of us staying here on Earth are aging more slowly, and when you return in ten years, you should find that everyone has aged almost six years less than you.

Uh oh, our usual drill won't work. We can't say that both situations are equivalent because you can clearly see who's younger. What went wrong here?

Don't worry, relativity hasn't failed. If you look at the situation more closely, you'll see that the two frames of reference are not equivalent. Relativity applies to *uniform* motion — motion that you can't distinguish. For example, if two spaceships are moving in interstellar space, either one can say that the other is moving. Or both can agree that they're both moving. You can even say that while you are around the solar system, the solar system is moving past you, and you're standing still. As long as you don't accelerate, you're fine.

However, when you take off in your spaceship, you must accelerate for some time to reach the constant speed that you'll be traveling at. When you get to your destination, you have to slow down, stop, turn around, and then accelerate to reach the speed that's going to bring you back home. And when you get here, you need to slow down and finally stop to meet your younger old friends.

All those accelerations are not uniform motion where special relativity is valid. You can certainly feel accelerations. You don't have to look outside to know that you're moving. When you are accelerating and you meet another spaceship, you won't doubt that you are moving.

Back on Earth, we can clearly say that you're the one accelerating away from us, and you won't disagree. The two situations are not interchangeable, so special relativity doesn't apply.

Einstein was bothered by the fact that his special theory wasn't general enough and spent many years extending it. The result was the general theory of relativity, which I discuss in Part IV.

Mixing Space and Time

Einstein derived his theory of relativity from one simple idea: that the speed of light is the same everywhere in the universe, regardless of where you are or how you move. But the implications of this idea are anything but simple.

If you think the information in this chapter has been heady so far, hang on!

If you and I are not moving relative to each other, your clock and mine keep the same time. Both of us are moving through time at the same rate. Our clocks tell us how fast the minutes, the hours, and the days go by. We both wake up the next morning and agree that a day has passed. So far, so good.

But here's where Einstein's theory takes us for an exciting mental ride. As soon as you start moving relative to me, part of your motion through time changes into motion through space. If I don't move, I keep all of my motion through time. The faster you move, the more part of your motion through time gets converted into motion in space. You give up moving through time so that you can move in space, and so your motion through time is not as fast as mine. That's why your time flows more slowly than mine.

The mathematical origins of spacetime

Einstein's professor of mathematics at the Polytechnic, Hermann Minkowski, didn't like Einstein when he was his student. Minkowski once said that he thought Einstein was "a lazy dog." In 1907, Minkowski was planning a seminar on the electrodynamics of moving bodies with the famous mathematician David Hilbert in Göttingen, and he inevitably came across Einstein's special relativity paper. The two men were very impressed with the paper, but Minkowski couldn't believe that Einstein was the author. He told a colleague that he wouldn't have thought Einstein was capable of that.

Minkowski went on to develop an elegant mathematical formulation of special relativity in which the three dimensions of space and the one dimension of time were joined into what he called *spacetime*. "From here on," he wrote, "space by itself and time by itself are doomed to fade away into mere shadows, and only a kind of union of the two will preserve an independent reality."

If you could convert all of your motion through time into motion through space, you'll be moving at the speed of light. Time would stand still for you. This is one way of seeing why Einstein said that nothing, except light, can move at the speed of light. The reason is that you can't completely stop the flow of time. But you can come very close, when you move close to the speed of light. For light, time stands still.

According to relativity, the combination of your motion through time and your motion through space equals exactly the speed of light. This combination of the three dimensions of space and the one of time became what was later called *spacetime,* a four-dimensional entity that shows that space and time are not separate, like Newton thought, but intermixed.

No one had noticed this connection before Einstein because these effects can be observed only at speeds close to the speed of light. Even today, the highest speeds that we can achieve are a tiny fraction of the speed of light. NASA's New Horizons spacecraft to study Pluto and its moon, Charon, moves at 80,000 kilometers per hour (kph), or 50,000 mph. This speed is only one ten-thousandth of the speed of light. At this speed, New Horizons will take ten years to reach Pluto.

And at these slower speeds, only a tiny amount of motion though time is converted into motion through space. This small amount exists but is hard to detect.

Making Interstellar Travel Possible

For those of us who keep our eyes fixed to the heavens, Einstein's theory of special relativity has thrilling implications. Namely, the relativity of time and space allows for the possibility of human interstellar travel.

The nearest stars to Earth, the binary stars Proxima and Alpha Centauri, are about four light-years away. In other words, light from these stars, traveling at 300,000 km (186,000 mi) per second, takes four years to reach us. And there are other interesting stars for us to visit beyond our closest neighbors. Over the past ten years, astronomers have discovered more than 125 planets orbiting around stars similar to our sun. They've been able to "see" them by studying the tiny motions that these planets cause on their suns as they move around them.

Among these newly discovered planets, there is a very young one — a planet in orbit around the star CoKu Tau 4, about 420 light-years from Earth. There is even one that astronomers have actually seen directly with the European Southern Observatory Very Large Telescope in Chile. It orbits its sun at some 230 light-years from us.

We may also want to visit the center of our galaxy, which is hidden from our eyes by interstellar dust but visible to our x-ray, infrared, and radio telescopes. Scientists have discovered a super massive black hole there. In the future, human beings may also want to tour our entire galaxy and even visit other galaxies.

However, even if we design a spaceship that can travel at $0.99c$, interstellar travel beyond the nearest stars seems impossible for the foreseeable future. Crossing our own galaxy will take more than 100,000 years, and a trip to Andromeda, the nearest galaxy, will take more than 2 million years.

That timeline is accurate for those of us staying behind. But, on the moving ship, time will be dilated. A future spacecraft, using technologies that we haven't even dreamed of, may use an engine that could sustain a constant acceleration of 1 g until the ship reaches relativistic speeds. With such an engine, a trip even to Andromeda may be possible within a human lifetime. For those astronauts, however, returning back home is out of the question. Back on Earth, entire civilizations would've come and gone, while the astronauts who left in their 20s would be only in their 80s.

Table 10-1 shows several possible trips on a ship constantly accelerating at 1 g. The figure for "Distance in Light-Years" is also the time that would pass on Earth while the ship traveled to its destination.

Table 10-1	Ship Time for Interstellar Travel at 1 g	
Destination	*Distance in Light-Years*	*Ship Time in Years*
Alpha Centauri	4	3
Sirius	9	5
Epsilon Eridani	10	5
2M1207: Star with first visible planet	230	11
CoKu Tau 4	420	12
Galactic center	30,000	20
Andromeda galaxy	2,000,000	28

Chapter 11

The Equation

*I*n September of 1905, only three months after he published his paper on special relativity, Einstein sent off the last paper of his miracle year. This paper, only three pages long, was published in November.

In his beautiful paper, which Einstein titled "Does the inertia of a body depend on its energy content?", Einstein says that the results of his previous investigation "led to a very interesting conclusion, which will be derived here." What this technical expert third class at the Bern patent office deduced was that mass and energy are equivalent. Einstein condensed his deduction into one simple and powerful equation, $E = mc^2$.

In this chapter, I show you how Einstein used ideas that were commonly known at the time to get to his uncommon conclusion. I show you how this paper (along with the other contributions Einstein made during his miracle year) led to him finally getting a professorship that allowed him to have more time to work on his amazing ideas, thought experiments, and theories.

Bringing Mass into the Equation

When physicists use the word *energy* (the big E in the equation), they mean the ability to do work. The c stands for the speed of light, which is constant throughout the universe, regardless of how you move or where you are. (I discuss this fact in detail in Chapters 9 and 10.) What about the m in the equation? We know it stands for *mass,* but what exactly does that mean? Like the word energy, *mass* entered our everyday language and lost some of its initial meaning. We tend to use the word interchangeably with *weight,* which is not entirely accurate.

Measuring our laziness

Mass measures the resistance that you feel when you try to change the motion of an object. This resistance is called *inertia*.

We use the word *inertia* in our everyday language to indicate sluggishness or inaction. To overcome it, you need to get up and get going. As I explain in Chapter 4, Isaac Newton's first law of motion is that objects have a tendency to stay where they are, either resting or in uniform motion. His second law of motion states that to overcome inertia — to get objects to change their motion — you need to apply a force.

Mass is a measure of inertia, a measure of an object's laziness, if you like — its desire to maintain the way it is moving (or staying still).

But keep in mind that there is a second way to measure mass — according to *weight,* the gravitational attraction of an object to the Earth. Physicists distinguish between the two measurements of mass, calling the first one *inertial mass* and the second one *gravitational mass.* In Chapter 12, I tell you more about this distinction and show you that these two masses are actually the same. (Einstein used this fact as the basis for his general theory of relativity.)

The name *inertial mass* is very descriptive. A massive object is one with a large inertial mass, presenting a large resistance to any attempts to change its motion. It's more difficult to move than an object with small inertial mass, and, if it's already moving, it's more difficult to stop than a light object. We're all familiar with this idea. However, sometimes the rough surfaces objects move on or the rubbing of their internal components complicates their motions. It's easier to see the differences between large and small inertial mass in space, where objects have no drag or friction.

For example, during the Hubble Space Telescope servicing mission in 2002, astronauts had to install the Advanced Camera for Surveys, a large new camera with a mass about the same as that of a golf cart. During the mission, the astronauts had a difficult time moving it and positioning it correctly because of the camera's large inertial mass. Pushing it was about as difficult as pushing a golf cart on smooth level ground on Earth if the wheels are well-lubricated.

Gravity doesn't affect an object's inertial mass. The camera's inertial mass is a property of the camera, which stays the same regardless of where it is. You'd have a hard time moving a cart carrying a massive satellite that's being readied for launch from Earth. And an astronaut in the cargo bay of the Space Shuttle would have the same difficulty moving it in space (see Figure 11-1). The satellite's large inertial mass is the same here on the ground or up in space.

Figure 11-1:
An astronaut in the cargo bay of the Space Shuttle has the same difficulty maneuvering a massive object as we do here on the ground.

Courtesy NASA

The title of Einstein's $E = mc^2$ paper — "Does the inertia of a body depend on its energy content?" — makes more sense when you know the meaning of inertial mass. He is asking the reader if the inertial mass of an object changes with the amount of energy in the body. He shows in his paper that it does.

Realizing that mass is relative

Einstein discovered that the mass of an object is relative. In Chapter 10, I discuss how space and time are interconnected. In a nutshell, when you and I are standing still, we are moving together through time. If you start moving relative to me, I see that you are converting part of your motion through time into motion through space. If you keep moving faster and faster, you'll be converting more of your motion through time into motion through space.

If you could convert *all* your motion through time into motion through space, you'll be moving at the speed of light, in essence stopping time. But you can't completely stop time. Which means that you can't move at the speed of light. Nothing, except light, can. For light, there is no motion through time; all its motion is through space, at the speed of light *(c),* of course.

Suppose that you are traveling in a very advanced interstellar spaceship that has already reached 0.99*c*. What happens when your skipper wants to get even closer to *c*? To accelerate, his engine has to supply the force that overcomes the ship's inertia and increases the speed. That's how the skipper reached his current speed. But now the ship doesn't respond as easily. It has more inertia, and he needs to supply a large force to achieve a small increase.

The ship's inertial mass, its resistance to being accelerated, increases as the speed increases, making it more and more difficult to accelerate the ship to a speed closer to the speed of light. If the ship could somehow reach the speed of light, its inertial mass would be infinite.

According to Einstein's special relativity, then,

> *The inertial mass of an object in motion relative to us increases with the speed, becoming infinitely large at the speed of light.*

Because an infinite mass would require an infinite force to accelerate, which means that you would need an infinite amount of energy to supply this force, we conclude that

> *No object can travel at the speed of light.*

Choosing c^2

Einstein's famous equation, $E = mc^2$, involves the square of the speed of light, c. Why did he choose c-squared and not c-cubed? Einstein's equation is an energy equation, and it must have the general properties of energy.

The properties of energy began to be discovered during Newton's lifetime, starting when his contemporary, Christian Huygens, was preparing a paper to present before the Royal Society of London in January of 1669.

Christian Huygens

The Dutch scientist Christian Huygens was one of the most famous scientists in Europe and certainly the pride of his homeland. He came from good stock: His father was Constantin Huygens, a towering figure in Dutch literature.

The young Huygens was influenced by the ideas on space of his friend, the French philosopher and mathematician René Descartes. Huygens published several important mathematical papers that made him well known before he was 30 years old.

While helping his brother build a telescope, Huygens became interested in optics and invented new methods to grind lenses. He also became interested in astronomy and discovered the Orion Nebula, a large cloud of interstellar dust that still fascinates amateur astronomers all over the world. (Today, we know that this cloud is one of many birthplaces of stars.) Using a telescope that was 7 meters (23 feet) long, he discovered the rings of Saturn and its largest moon, which he named Titan.

In the paper, Huygens talked about the collisions of objects and tried to clarify confusion that existed at the time about the physics of these collisions. Specifically, physicists were arguing about the motion of two small metal balls that swing and collide repeatedly. (You've no doubt seen a modern version of such a device in novelty shops, similar to the one shown in Figure 11-2.) The scientists couldn't understand why, after one such collision, the incoming ball stops completely while the struck ball swings back to the same height that the first ball had before the collision. Nothing in their existing body of knowledge about energy and speed explained why, for example, the first ball would not bounce back at half the speed as before the collision, while the second one would take off with the other half of the speed.

Figure 11-2:
The total energy of the swinging steel balls colliding with each other stays unchanged.

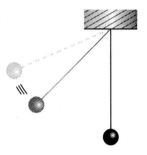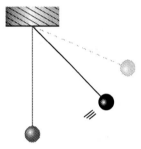

Huygens clarified the behavior of the balls in his paper. He explained that if you take the product of the mass of each ball, multiply it by the *square* of the speed, and add these two quantities, the sum is always the same before and after each collision. The product of the mass times the square of the velocity of each ball gives you the energy of motion of the ball.

The energy of each ball changes when the balls collide, but at each collision, the energy is exchanged between the balls so that the total amount stays the same. This idea became the powerful principle of conservation of energy, which I discuss in Chapter 5. The constant exchange of energy back and forth, while keeping the total amount fixed, explains why the struck ball has to always take off and reach the same height, time after time.

According to Huygens, the mass of an object times the square of the speed at which it is moving gives you the object's energy of motion. (Actually, it gives you one-half of that value, but that fact isn't important at this point.) Einstein's energy equation is also the product of the mass of the object times the square of the speed, but in this case, it's not the *object's* speed but the speed of *light*. Why the speed of light and not the speed of the object? Read on to find out.

Formulating $E = mc^2$

In the short paper that features Einstein's most famous equation, he showed that if an object at rest in the laboratory emits light (such as an atom undergoing radioactive decay), its energy changes, because part of the energy is carried away by the emitted light.

From the conservation of energy principle, Einstein knew that the energy the emitted light carried away came from the object itself. The total energy of the object decreased. That much was known. But Einstein took an additional step. He used his special relativity equations to calculate the energy difference of an atom emitting light while at rest in the laboratory and while the body is moving relative to the laboratory. His calculations showed him that the *mass* of the atom decreased after the emission of light.

At this point Einstein did what he did better than anyone else: He extended his statement. He analyzed the emission of light by an atom, saying that its mass decreases every time it gives off light.

Then he made the big step: the generalization. He was not simply making a statement about an atom emitting light. He said that his discovery applied to all matter. Einstein stated that the mass of a body is a measure of its energy content, and that this fact is always true. According to Einstein,

> *An object's mass is a form of energy, and energy carries mass. Mass and energy are two forms of the same thing.*

These two sentences are the meaning of $E = mc^2$.

In 1905, when this patent clerk was making his bold statement, scientists were only beginning to accept the existence of atoms. Radioactive decay, the spontaneous emission of light and charged particles from atoms, had been discovered only five years earlier.

Questioning his own conclusions

Einstein ends his short paper with the statement that perhaps it would be possible to test his theory using bodies with an energy content that changes dramatically, like radium salts. "If the theory agrees with the facts," he wrote in his paper, "then radiation carries mass between emitting and absorbing bodies."

Why c^2?

Einstein's $E = mc^2$ tells us that energy and mass are equivalent. You can change one into the other. And c^2 is the conversion factor telling you how they are linked. When you convert inches to centimeters, both measuring length, the conversion factor is 2.5. When you convert mass into energy or energy into mass, the conversion factor is the square of the speed of light. Because c is so large (about 300,000 kilometers per second) and its square much larger (90,000,000,000 kilometers^2 per second^2), a tiny amount of mass can be converted into a huge amount of energy.

A few weeks later, he wrote to his friend Conrad Habicht about the paper, expressing some doubts. He told him that his conclusion about light carrying mass with it was a seductive idea, but that for all he knew, the Lord might be playing a trick on him and laughing about it.

The Lord wasn't playing tricks. What Einstein discovered not only explained the workings of the sun but also made possible technological advances ranging from smoke alarms to PET scanners. It's hard to think of an area of physics developed over the last 100 years where $E = mc^2$ didn't play an important role. Forty years after Einstein proposed the equation, World War II precipitated a dramatic demonstration of $E = mc^2$ with the development of the nuclear bomb and its use over two cities in Japan.

But all that technology had to wait until the correct understanding of the atom was in place, which was decades after Einstein wrote his paper. In 1905, scientists had only a very primitive idea of what an atom was. Just a couple years earlier, Einstein himself provided several irrefutable proofs of the existence of the atom for the diehards that weren't accepting its existence.

Running to gain mass

As Einstein said, the mass of an object is a form of energy, and energy is a form of mass. A bird standing on a tree branch has less energy than when it is flying. If you could measure the bird's mass with extreme precision, you'd find that it's very slightly larger when flying than when sitting still. But a single feather from the bird's wing has a mass billions of times larger than the mass increase due to the energy of motion. Similarly, when you run, your mass increases because of your motion. However, you lose more mass by radiating heat and sweat than you gain by running.

Consider this example: Take two small balls and join them with a spring. Pull them apart until the spring breaks. If you had a super-precise balance, you could measure the mass before and after you break the spring (see Figure 11-3). You'd find that the mass of the two balls is smaller when they're pulled together by the spring than it is after you break the spring and pull them apart. If you're using marbles with a mass of 100 grams (3.5 ounces), the mass increase is about one-billionth of a gram. A balance with the precision to measure this small increase doesn't exist.

Figure 11-3:
The total mass of the balls and the spring is smaller when the balls are together than when they are apart.

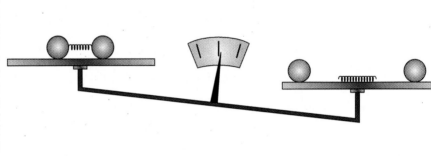

Cutting a strong thread

During the 1920s, physicists discovered the correct composition of the atom: a tiny nucleus made up of two types of particles — the positively charged *protons* and the electrically neutral *neutrons* — which is surrounded by a cloud of negative *electrons*. During this decade, they also developed *quantum physics,* the physics of the atom, which had started with Einstein's 1905 paper on the photoelectric effect. (For the details on these developments, see Chapters 15 and 16.)

Physicists found that the particles that form the nucleus — the positive protons and the neutral neutrons — are held together by a very strong force, *the nuclear force.* This nuclear force is the thread that keeps them together. If you could cut this thread, they would fly apart, because the positive protons repel each other.

Much like the two balls held together by a spring, the mass of an atom's nucleus is smaller than the mass of its neutrons and protons. Einstein's $E = mc^2$ says that mass is a form of energy. The nucleus, with less mass, has less energy than its component particles when they are apart.

Here's how this energy difference comes about. The nuclear force provides a very strong thread tying these particles together in the nucleus. You'd need to do a great deal of work (use a large amount of energy) to pull them apart. This situation is similar to the case of two powerful magnets sticking together with their north and south poles facing each other. You have to work hard to separate them (see Figure 11-4).

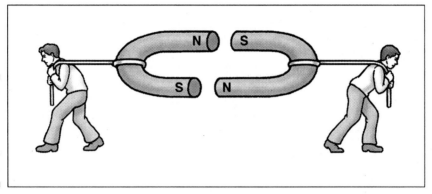

Figure 11-4:
You need to
work hard to
pull these
magnets
apart.

After you manage to separate the two powerful magnets, it's easy to bring them together again. They actually do the work for you. Not only do they come together on their own, but they pull you along. To do that, they must use their own energy. So when they are together, they have less energy than when they are apart.

Did anyone read it?

Einstein knew that his work on relativity was "revolutionary." He said so in a letter he wrote to his friend Conrad Habicht in May of 1905, which became one of the most famous letters of all time. At the time, Einstein was working on four papers on the existence of atoms and molecules (which he later sent to the *Annalen der Physik*), and on the special theory of relativity. The $E = mc^2$ paper wasn't on his mind. He thought of it only after he'd submitted his relativity paper.

Einstein's sister, Maja, wrote in her book about her brother's early years that after the publication of his papers of 1905, Einstein was anxious to see the response of the physics community to his work. He didn't have to wait long. In May of 1906, Einstein said that his papers were receiving much acknowledgment and generating new investigations, and that he had even received a letter about the relativity papers from the great Max Planck.

Weighing a speck of soot

The smallest mass ever measured with a scale is that of a speck of soot. The "scale" was made with miniature tubes of carbon (called *carbon nanotubes*) as springs. The scientists who made the measurement at Georgia Tech placed the speck on one of the tiny tubes and started vibrating the tube by applying an electric charge to a nanotube placed near a probe with the opposite charge. The speck weighed down the vibrating nanotube, and the researchers were able to calculate the mass of the speck. The mass of the speck of soot was 22 femtograms, or 22 millionths of a billionth of a gram. However, measuring a mass *difference* that small is still not possible.

Like the magnets sticking together, the protons and neutrons sticking together to form the nucleus have less energy than the separate particles. The "missing" energy is the energy that keeps the nucleus together, which is called the *binding energy* of the nucleus.

According to Einstein's $E = mc^2$, then,

Things sticking together have less mass than when you pull these same things apart.

Introducing Professor Einstein

After 1905, Einstein's isolated and quiet life as a lone scientist working as a clerk in a patent office came to an end. Max Planck, the well-known German physicist who had introduced the idea of the quantum of energy only five years earlier, became very interested in Einstein's relativity. In 1906, he became the next scientist to write a paper on relativity.

Soon, and largely because of Planck, other scientists took notice. Well-known physicists and recent PhD's came to Bern, wanting to meet Einstein and to work with him for a couple of months. Einstein's sister, Maja, wrote that soon after the papers of 1905, he started receiving letters that were addressed to "Professor Einstein at the University of Bern."

Einstein was quite proud of his growing recognition. In May of 1906, he wrote to his friend Maurice Solovine telling him how his work was becoming highly regarded and that even Professor Planck had written to him about his theories.

Looking for a job again

Encouraged by his growing fame, Einstein decided to try again for an academic career. Things would surely be different than they were when he first graduated, he thought, with all these important papers generating excitement in the scientific community. He had also just received his PhD with the acceptance of his thesis at the University of Zurich, so he could now be called Dr. Einstein. He found that using his title was sometimes advantageous. He commented in a letter that his title considerably smoothed relationships with people.

The first step toward entering the academic world in Germany and Austria at the time was to become what was called a *Privatdozent*, an instructor at a university who received no salary but collected fees from the students. To be hired as a Privatdozent, you had to present an original paper and give a demonstration lecture.

Einstein sent an application to the University of Bern, encouraged by his PhD thesis advisor, Professor Alfred Kleiner. If selected, Einstein would still be able to keep his day job at the patent office.

Einstein waited impatiently for the reply — so impatiently that he couldn't resist writing letters to the dean and to the head of the faculty, promising that if hired, he would develop an exciting course for the students.

Weeks went by with no response. Finally, the letter arrived in the mail. It was a rejection.

Cutting through red tape

Einstein's application was rejected by the University of Bern because he hadn't included the required original scientific paper. This mistake was strange because Einstein had more papers than anyone else applying for this type of position. He also was very interested in entering the academic world, and this position was his ticket. And he was clearly already experienced in preparing complex papers for publication in scientific journals. An application for a position would be comparatively simple. Nevertheless, Einstein messed it up.

Einstein must've been unhappy with the rejection at the time. Years later, however, he referred to it as an amusing example of academic red tape.

When Professor Kleiner heard about the rejection, he convinced Einstein to resubmit. Einstein sent in a more complete application, and the university officials, now worried that they were rejecting a rising star, reconsidered and hired him. Einstein quickly accepted the offer. He was 29.

The first course that Einstein taught at the University of Bern was "The Theory of Radiation," offered during the winter term of 1908–1909. Only four students enrolled, and all were his own friends. The class was held at night, after he left his day job at the patent office. During the second semester, he had only one student.

Einstein wasn't happy with his night job. Teaching so few students wasn't that interesting, and he still had to prepare the lectures as if he were teaching a full class. On top of that, he now had very little time to do research, which is what he really loved to do. But he was determined to become a professor, so he kept going.

Facing politics in Zurich

In 1909, shortly after Einstein started working as a Privatdozent at the University of Bern, Professor Kleiner set out to hire a theoretical physicist at the University of Zurich. He had two good candidates for the position: his former assistant, Frederich Adler, and his former PhD student, Einstein.

During committee deliberations for the position, it became clear that Einstein was going to be the top candidate. In an attempt to cushion the bad news, Kleiner told Adler that he wasn't on the list of finalists. Adler wrote to his father that day, telling him that he wasn't going to get the position but that the man who most likely would get it was his former classmate Einstein. Adler said that, apart from his own disappointment, he would be very pleased if Einstein did get it, because people in Switzerland and even in Germany were feeling that it was a scandal to have a man like that sitting in the patent office.

The final vote of the committee was ten for Einstein and one abstention. The committee forwarded its recommendation to the university administration for final approval.

The other Dr. Einstein

Einstein's sister, Maja, attended the University of Bern at the time that Einstein was a Privatdozent there and would occasionally drop in for one of his classes. She'd attended the University of Berlin for two years but transferred to Bern.

On December 21, 1908, Maja received her PhD magna cum laude in Romance languages from the university, becoming the second Dr. Einstein in the family.

The administration was opposed to Einstein's candidacy on political grounds. For the most part, members of the administration were Social Democrats who favored Adler, a member of the same party. Adler felt uncomfortable with this situation. He didn't want to be appointed for political reasons and knew that the faculty hadn't chosen him. He decided to remove his name from consideration. In his letter to the administration, Adler said that if the university had the opportunity to hire a man like Einstein, it would be absurd to hire him instead. He added that his abilities were in no way a match for Einstein's.

A short time later, Einstein received an offer for a position as a professor at the University of Zurich. He declined because he didn't like the salary, which was about half of what he was making at the patent office. Kleiner went back to the administration, and they agreed to match Einstein's current salary. Einstein accepted the second offer.

Learning to teach

Einstein resigned from the Bern patent office effective October 15, 1909. His appointment at the University of Zurich was as associate professor of theoretical physics with a salary of 4,500 francs, plus certain lecture and examination fees. He started his university position the same day that he left the patent office.

His duties included teaching six to eight hours of classes and seminars per week, as well as advising students. His first graduate student was Hans Tanner. (But Tanner didn't get his PhD with Einstein, because by the time he finished his studies, Einstein had moved on to another university.)

Einstein wasn't a good lecturer during his early years as a professor. He came to class wearing pants that were too short and carried around a piece of paper containing his lecture notes.

With time, his lectures improved, and eventually, his students came to like him. They liked his informal style and his open, easygoing approach. He allowed his students to interrupt the lecture at any time with any questions, and he even went along with the students to the local coffee houses where he sat and explained physics to them.

When Einstein was offered a position at the University of Prague in 1910, the Zurich students sent a petition to the university administration asking them to do whatever they could to keep Einstein there. Right away, the university raised his salary to 5,500 francs and asked the department to look into reducing his teaching load. Einstein turned down the offer from Prague.

Honorary degree

One day, a short time before Einstein started his new position at the University of Zurich, he received a large envelope at the patent office that contained a stylish sheet of paper with ornate Latin printing on it. Einstein thought that it was some sort of advertisement and threw it in the trash without reading it. Later, Einstein learned that the piece of paper was an invitation to receive an honorary doctorate at the University of Geneva.

Because Einstein didn't respond to the invitation, the university officials asked one of his former students, Louis Chavan, to convince him to attend the ceremonies in Geneva. Chavan succeeded in convincing Einstein but didn't tell him what the purpose of the trip was.

When Einstein arrived at the hotel where most of the honorees were staying, he learned that they were all there to receive an honorary degree. Einstein hadn't brought proper attire and ended up marching in the procession and attending the entire ceremony wearing street clothes and a straw hat, while everyone else wore academic robes.

Einstein taught at the University of Zurich from October 1909 to March 1911. In these two years, he published eleven papers on theoretical physics, a remarkable output for a new professor. Most of these papers dealt with the problems of radiation and were connected with his idea of the quantum of light that he had proposed in his first paper of the miracle year.

Even while at the patent office, Einstein had been thinking about extending his special theory of relativity to include nonuniform motion. As he found out a couple years later, this task wasn't going to be easy.

Part III
The Special Theory of Relativity

The 5th Wave   By Rich Tennant

1905 At a lunch counter in Bern, Einstein formulates his Special Theory of Relishivity.

In this part . . .

You're finally here! This part focuses on Einstein's great discovery, the special theory of relativity. First, I show you the original theory of relativity, developed by Galileo Galilei, which makes good common sense. (You're on a train that's going 100 kph, and you walk from the back to the front of the train at 10 kph. Someone by the railroad tracks will clock you moving at 110 kph.)

Then Einstein came along and changed all of this straight-forward stuff. I explain what Einstein meant by relativity and what relativity did to our ideas of time and space. You'll also see what Einstein's famous equation, $E = mc^2$, really means.

Chapter 13

"Black Holes Ain't So Black"

*E*instein's general theory of relativity shows how light can be trapped in a *black hole* — a star with such strong gravity that nothing can escape. Although his own theory of general relativity led to the prediction of the existence of black holes, Einstein never liked the idea. He thought that black holes "smelled wrong" and died before one was actually discovered.

In this chapter, I explain how the idea of black holes emerged, starting two centuries before Einstein's theory. I discuss how our thinking about black holes has evolved since Einstein's time. And what about the possibility that black holes may allow time travel? Stick with me — I get to that topic as well.

Finding the Geometry of Spacetime from Einstein's Field Equation

Einstein completed his general theory of relativity in 1915, after struggling for eight years in search of the right equations. When he was finally finished, he called it a "theory of incomparable beauty" and "the most valuable discovery of my life." Physicists since that time have agreed with him. In a seminar in Trieste, Italy, in 1968, the famous English scientist Paul Dirac said that the general theory of relativity was "probably the greatest scientific discovery ever made."

The general theory of relativity is summarized in an equation, called *Einstein's field equation,* which says that the curvature of spacetime is determined by matter and energy. Einstein's field equation breaks down into a set of ten separate equations that are extremely difficult to solve. Even today, few exact solutions to these equations have been obtained.

Measuring how spacetime warps

According to general relativity and Einstein's field equation, the sun stretches the spacetime around it, warping it in such a way that it changes the motion of anything traveling through that spacetime (see Chapter 12 for details). The sun isn't the only thing that warps spacetime. Everything, even you or me or an apple, warps spacetime. But you can't measure the amount of warping that occurs from ordinary objects. It'd be extremely hard to measure the warping even for the Earth. Only really large objects, like the sun, the stars, and galaxies, can warp spacetime to a measurable extent. The sun, for example, warps spacetime by just two parts in a million.

The warping of spacetime can be measured directly. (As I explain in Chapter 12, Arthur Eddington's expedition to measure the bending of starlight by the sun in 1919 did just that.) But the warping can also be calculated from the theory, with Einstein's field equation. That's how Einstein discovered it and how he predicted what the exact bending of light that Eddington measured was going to be.

Einstein's first book

After the publication of his final paper on general relativity, Einstein thought he needed to write a complete and clear presentation of the theory so that other physicists could study and understand it. The elements of the theory were scattered in many of the papers that he wrote during the eight years he spent developing it. Many of those papers contained mistakes that he corrected later on, or were dead ends that he backed out from. He wanted to put the theory all together in a single and coherent article, but he felt that perhaps someone else ought to spare the time to do it.

Einstein knew that Hendrik Antoon Lorentz was excellent at presenting this kind of work and dropped hints to try to convince him to write it. He told Lorentz that he had "unfortunately been denied by nature the gift of communication, with the result that what I write may be correct but is highly indigestible."

Lorentz didn't bite, and Einstein had to write the article. He finished it in March 1916, and it ended up being 50 pages long. Einstein submitted it to the *Annalen der Physik* with the title "The Foundation of the General Theory of Relativity." The publisher of the journal decided to print it as a separate brochure, which became Einstein's first book.

Einstein's field equation gave physicists a powerful tool to calculate the exact way that stars and galaxies move and interact, and how the entire universe evolves. The field equation of general relativity provides answers to all these questions. Getting the answers, however, isn't easy.

Developing Schwarzschild's geometry

The first attempt at using Einstein's field equation was made by the great astrophysicist Karl Schwarzschild in December of 1915. Schwarzschild read Einstein's final paper on the general theory of relativity in the November 1915 issue of the *Proceedings of the Prussian Academy of Sciences.* Right away, he set out to calculate what the theory would predict about stars.

Schwarzschild divided the problem into two parts:

✔ First, he restricted the problem to the exterior of the star. In a few days, he had the exact solution to the field equations for the curvature of spacetime outside any star. (To be able to perform the calculation, Schwarzschild confined the solution to a star that doesn't spin.)

The first solution was very elegant. Schwarzschild immediately sent it to Einstein, who was pleasantly surprised. Einstein replied right away, telling Schwarzschild that he "had not expected that one could formulate the exact solution to the problem in such a simple way." Einstein presented the paper on Schwarzschild's behalf at the meeting of the Prussian Academy of Sciences on January 13, 1916.

✔ A few days later, Einstein received a second paper from Schwarzschild, this time with the calculations for the geometry of spacetime inside any star. Einstein presented the second Schwarzschild paper at the Academy a few weeks later.

In these two papers, Schwarzschild established the geometry of spacetime around stars. Within a few years, the Schwarzschild geometry became the standard working tool for physicists.

What's remarkable about this work is that Schwarzschild wasn't in his comfortable office at the Potsdam Astrophysical Observatory near Berlin (where he was the director) when he did it. Instead, he was in the Russian front of World War I, having volunteered to serve in the German army. He performed his calculations under the rough conditions of war, in severe weather, and with serious health problems.

Sadly, Schwarzschild wouldn't live to see the remarkable implications of what he had done. He contracted a disease in the Russian front and died at the age of 41, only four months after Einstein presented his second and last paper on general relativity.

Formulating the Black Hole Idea

The idea of a black hole didn't originate with Einstein or with Schwarzschild. It actually dates back to the late 1700s when the British scientist John Michell wrote a paper about what he thought would happen to the light from a star that shrunk below a certain size but kept all its mass.

Trapping light

Michell was thinking about Isaac Newton's idea that light was made up of tiny particles — or *corpuscles,* as Newton called them. These corpuscles should have very small masses, and they should feel the gravitational attraction of the star.

Think of a corpuscle of light as being a tiny ball. If you throw a ball upward from the surface of the Earth, it slows down as it goes up, eventually stops, and falls back down (as shown in Figure 13-1). If you throw it harder, with a greater speed, it goes higher before stopping and returning. If you throw it at 11 kilometers (7 miles) per second, the ball will leave Earth and never return. This speed of 11 kps is called the *escape velocity.*

Figure 13-1:
Gravity
slows the
ball down
until it stops
and falls
back, unless
you achieve
the escape
velocity
(right).

If you could stand on the surface of the sun, you'd need to throw the ball at about 617 kps (385 mps) to have it leave the sun and not fall back. Because the speed of light is much higher than that, Michell thought that the corpuscles of light leaving the sun wouldn't be affected much by the sun's gravity. (The speed of light was known with some accuracy at Michell's time; see Chapter 7 for details.)

But what if a star existed that was much smaller than the sun but had the same mass? In this case, the escape velocity would be larger than the sun's. Michell used Newton's universal law of gravity to calculate the escape velocities of small, massive stars. The smaller the star, the closer its surface is to its center, the stronger gravity is at the surface, and the larger the escape velocity is.

Predicting dark stars

Michell realized that it was possible for a star to exist that was small enough and massive enough that its escape velocity would be the speed of light. A star smaller than that and with the same mass would have a gravitational field so strong that light would not be able to leave it. Light would be trapped inside. The corpuscles of light would rise up at first, then slow down, stop, and fall back to the surface of this star (see Figure 13-2).

Figure 13-2:
Light will be trapped in a star that is small and massive enough.

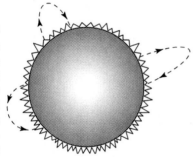

Michell calculated this *critical size* of the star, the size at which the escape velocity is the speed of light. A star with the mass of the sun would have to be just under 6 km (3.7 mi) across in order to be a *dark star* — a star from which light cannot escape. A star with a mass twice as large as the sun would have a critical diameter twice as large, or about 12 km. For a star with a mass equal to three suns, the critical diameter triples (see Figure 13-3).

Michell thought that the universe should contain a large number of stars smaller than the critical size. These dark stars would be invisible to us — they would be black holes.

Michell presented his calculations and ideas at the Royal Society of London in November of 1783. A few years later, the French mathematician and philosopher Pierre Simon de Laplace mentioned the possible existence of these dark stars in his popular book *The System of the World,* without mentioning Michell. (Laplace, a brilliant and accomplished man, was sometimes reluctant to give credit to others.)

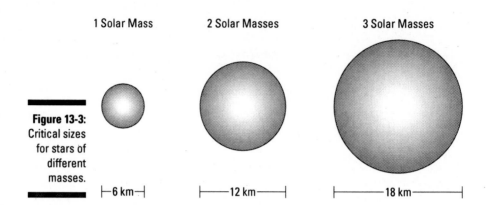

| 1 Solar Mass | 2 Solar Masses | 3 Solar Masses |

Figure 13-3:
Critical sizes
for stars of
different
masses.

├─6 km─┤   ├────12 km────┤   ├──────18 km──────┤

In the early 1800s, the corpuscle view of light was questioned by the experiments of Thomas Young, who showed that light is actually a wave. His wave theory of light, which explained all the observations about the behavior of light, became universally accepted. (In Chapter 7, I describe Young's experiment. As I explain in Chapter 16, Einstein later showed that light is more complicated than what Young proposed.) By the end of the 19th century, scientists believed that because light is a wave and not a particle, it couldn't be affected by gravity. And that was the end of the dark star idea. For a while.

Reintroducing the theory of black holes

The idea of dark stars, or black holes (as we call them today), was still on ice when Schwarzschild solved Einstein's field equations and proposed his geometry. The Schwarzschild geometry revived the idea of black holes, because it predicted that there is a critical size for each star that depends on the star's mass. The critical size that Schwarzschild calculated was the same as what Michell had come up with: 6 km (3.7 mi) in diameter, or 3 km in radius, for a star the same mass as the sun. This critical radius is now called the *Schwarzschild radius*. If a star was smaller than this critical value, light would be trapped. The black hole idea came back.

But here's the problem with the way Michell had been thinking of dark stars: You can't treat light like you do balls that you throw up in the air. The balls slow down because of gravity. But Einstein's special theory of relativity says that light always travels at the same speed; gravity won't slow it down.

How did Schwarzschild's calculation revive Michell's idea, then?

Einstein's relativity opened the door. In Newton's mechanics, space and time are absolute, but the speed of light can change. In Einstein's relativity, space and time are relative, but the speed of light is absolute. (Check out Chapters 9 and 10 to refresh your memory.)

As I explain in Chapter 12, according to the theory of general relativity, the light emitted from a strong gravitational field is Doppler-shifted to stretched waves. The stronger the gravitational field, the greater the shift. Light isn't slowed down as the field increases; it continues to travel at the same speed that special relativity mandates *(c)*. But its wavelength changes.

Look at Figure 13-4, where each star has the same mass but a different radius. The middle star has a smaller radius than the top star and, therefore, a stronger gravitational field. Its light wave is stretched in comparison with the light wave of the top star.

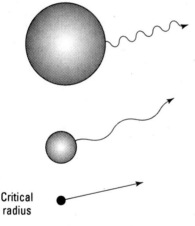

Figure 13-4:
Light emitted from a gravitational field is Doppler-shifted to stretched waves. Time also runs more slowly. Critical radius

If a star has a strong enough gravitational field, the light becomes stretched out so much that it's flat — its wavelength is infinitely long (it can't be measured). The bottom star in Figure 13-4 shows this situation. Because there is no wave, there is no light. The gravitational field that stretches the wavelength to infinity corresponds to that of a star at the Schwarzschild radius.

Another way to consider this situation is to realize that in a gravitational field, time is slowed down (see Chapter 12). The stronger the gravitational field, the slower time flows. (For example, a clock runs ever-so-slightly faster in the attic than in the basement, because gravity is stronger in the basement.) At the Schwarzschild radius, as seen from the outside, time is dilated an infinite amount; time doesn't flow. From our point of view outside the star, light doesn't exist. Because the star is still emitting light, light must be trapped. The star is a black hole.

Facing Einstein's skepticism

Einstein was very pleased with the first exact solution to his field equation that Schwarzschild had obtained. Scientists could now use this solution to calculate the gravitational properties of planets and stars. For example, the orbit of Mercury was quickly calculated as the result of Schwarzschild's work. Einstein had used approximation methods to calculate Mercury's orbit as the first proof of the power of the general theory (see Chapter 12). But he hadn't obtained an exact solution. Thanks to Schwarzschild, the exact solution became possible. When the calculation was done, the result matched what Einstein had previously obtained.

However, Einstein wasn't happy with the idea of black holes. He didn't think that the universe was made that way. He didn't like the fact that his equation broke down at the center of the black hole or at the surface of the Schwarzschild radius. (Before the term *black holes* came into being, these entities were called *Schwarzschild singularities*.)

In 1935, Einstein published a calculation that he interpreted as showing that black holes couldn't exist. Einstein chose a cluster of particles held together by gravity and moving in circular orbits around a center, forming a sphere. He then made the cluster smaller and smaller, with the particles moving faster and faster to maintain equilibrium. When the radius of his sphere reached about 1.5 times the Schwarzschild radius, his calculations showed that the particles would need to move at speeds greater than the speed of light to avoid being pulled in, with the whole thing collapsing into a single point. And nothing could move faster than the speed of light. "The essential result of this investigation," wrote Einstein in his paper, "is a clear understanding as to why the 'Schwarzschild singularities' do not exist."

Einstein's calculation was correct, which obviously created another problem for the black hole theory. But even Einstein made a mistake every once in a while.

Einstein assumed that he needed to keep the whole cluster of orbiting particles from collapsing into itself. At the time, that was the only logical thing to do, based on observations. No one had yet discovered the possibility that a star could collapse. To prevent the cluster from collapsing, the particle's speeds had to increase beyond the speed of light, which would contradict the theory of special relativity. But, by not allowing the cluster to collapse, Einstein missed the whole point. (This wasn't the first time that he didn't let his equations take him to new places. I describe the other time in Chapter 18.)

Studying Collapsing Stars

Despite Einstein's skepticism about the existence of black holes, other scientists continued to use the foundation laid by the general theory and Schwarzschild's calculations to study the behavior of the stars.

For example, a few years after Einstein tried to prove that black holes couldn't exist, J. Robert Oppenheimer and his graduate students at the University of California, Berkeley were trying to find out what would happen to a star after its nuclear fuel was spent. Oppenheimer, who would later lead the team of scientists that invented the nuclear bomb, was at the time one of the top U.S. scientists.

Oppenheimer knew that the Indian physicist Subrahmanyan Chandrasekhar had recently calculated that a star with a mass that was just under 50 percent larger than the sun's would contract into a *white dwarf,* a star with the mass of the sun and the size of the Earth. Because you can fit more than 1 million Earths in the volume of the sun, that's an astonishing contraction. The contraction isn't sudden, however; it takes place over millions of years.

Identifying other extreme stars

Oppenheimer wanted to know what would happen to stars that were even larger. His calculations showed that a larger star would collapse into a *neutron star,* a star composed mostly of neutrons (one of the particles that make up the nucleus of an atom). Neutrons were discovered in 1932, and within a year, two physicists at Caltech — Fritz Zwicky and Walter Baade — proposed that stars made up of only neutrons could be the end result of the collapse of stars larger than the ones Chandrasekhar had studied. They suggested that neutron stars form in *supernova* explosions. Their proposal was generally ignored until Oppenheimer and his graduate student performed their calculations.

J. Robert Oppenheimer

Oppenheimer graduated from Harvard in 1922 with a B.S. in chemistry but switched to physics in graduate school. He decided to attend grad school in Europe, which was the mecca of theoretical physics. He attended the University of Göttingen and obtained his PhD working with Paul Dirac, Max Born, and other luminaries.

After graduating, he found himself in high demand, with offers from Caltech, Berkeley, Harvard, and two European universities. Berkeley intrigued him because, at the time, it didn't have a theoretical physics program, and he saw the opportunity of building it himself. But he feared being isolated. He decided to accept the offers from both Berkeley and Caltech, spending half a year at each. Caltech was the place to go and "be checked if I got too far off base," he said.

Real neutron stars were discovered in the 1960s and have been studied since. They are so dense that if you could bring to Earth a piece of a neutron star the size of sugar cube, it would weigh 100 million tons.

Theorizing the ultimate collapse

Oppenheimer's calculations showed that there was an upper limit to the size of the stars that would collapse to neutron stars. The range of masses was from 1½ to 3 solar masses. (Stars smaller than 1½ solar masses collapse to white dwarfs.) What would happen to stars larger than 3 solar masses?

Oppenheimer gave that problem to Hartland Snyder, another of his graduate students. He calculated that if the original star had a mass larger than 3 solar masses, when its fuel was all spent, the star would start collapsing and continue collapsing without stopping. Snyder and Oppenheimer wrote in a paper that "when all . . . sources of energy are exhausted, a sufficiently heavy star will collapse; [its contraction] will follow indefinitely."

Oppenheimer was puzzled; "the results have been very odd," he said to a friend. And physicists found the results fascinating. The paper written by Snyder and Oppenheimer was published in 1939. However, at the time, political events in Europe were forcing physicists to think about the possibility of nuclear fusion. Neutrons were at the heart of these nuclear processes. No one could take time to think about nuclear processes in stars anymore. Oppenheimer himself was soon called to lead the Manhattan Project.

Reviving Interest in Black Holes

After World War II, very few scientists remembered Oppenheimer's papers about collapsing stars. Oppenheimer himself was involved in other matters.

During the 1950s, interest in general relativity began to grow. In 1955, for the first time, there was an international conference on relativity theory, which was followed by a series of international conferences on relativity and gravitation that continues today.

Calculating spacetime for rotating black holes

In 1963, Roy Kerr, a New Zealander who was then working at the University of Texas, found a new solution to Einstein's field equation, this time describing the spacetime curvature outside a rotating star. Soon, Brandon Carter, Roger Penrose, and other relativists found that this solution described the spacetime geometry not just of a rotating star but of a rotating black hole.

Kerr's black hole was an extension to Schwarzschild's black holes, which didn't rotate. It was a more general solution and had very important new properties. Kerr's work rekindled interest in black hole physics.

Discovering quasars and pulsars

In 1960, U.S. astronomer Allan Sandage used a 200-inch telescope at Mt. Palomar, north of San Diego, California (which was the largest optical telescope in the world at the time), to discover a "star" at the location of a very strong radio source that had been detected a year earlier. A couple of things were odd with this discovery. First, ordinary stars usually are not strong sources of radio emissions. Second, the star's spectrum had several features that astronomers couldn't identify, which is not normally the case.

Soon, other such "stars" were discovered. The most famous one was named 3C 273. Astronomers soon discovered the reason for the strange features in the spectrum of 3C 273 and the other "stars": The spectrum was Doppler-shifted due to the star's extremely large speed moving away from Earth. Calculations showed that 3C 273 was moving at 45,000 kps, which is 15 percent the speed of light. The objects in question weren't stars. They were new strong radio sources. Astronomers named them *quasi-stellar radio sources,* or *quasars.* Soon, astronomers found other quasars that weren't radio emitters. (It turns out that only about 10 percent of quasars are radio emitters.)

Quasars are astonishing objects. Most are very far away, more than 3 billion light-years from Earth. They're extraordinarily bright, which allows them to be seen from Earth at those large distances. They're actually brighter than many galaxies. Our galaxy, the Milky Way, shines with the light of 25 billion suns. 3C 273 is as bright as 35 *trillion* suns.

In 1968, the British astronomer Donald Lynden-Bell, who was working at Caltech at the time, proposed that this incredible energy output was powered by an extremely massive black hole that pulls in surrounding gases. As these gases fall, gravitational energy is released in the form of radiation. That's the consensus today.

At about this time in England, astronomers discovered a new pulsating radio source that they named *pulsar.* (See the sidebar "Little green men.") Eventually, many other such pulsars were found. They turned out to be neutron stars that are spinning very fast.

Little green men

In 1967, Jocelyn Bell was working toward her PhD in astronomy at Cambridge University under Anthony Hewitt. Her thesis was related to the study of radio emissions from several astronomical sources. She had just finished helping to build a large array of radio antennas in a four-acre field in the English countryside and was collecting data when she noticed that one of the antennas was picking up a very regular signal from one particular location in the sky. The signals were all one and one-third seconds apart. She immediately telephoned Hewitt, who rushed over and observed the phenomenon. For some time, half-jokingly, they called the signals *LGM,* for Little Green Men.

Before Christmas, Bell went to Hewitt's home to discuss ways to announce the discovery without setting off a media circus. They couldn't think of any. She went back home that evening feeling upset about trying to finish her PhD dissertation while "some silly lot of little green men had to choose my aerial and my frequency to communicate with us."

After dinner, Bell went back to the lab and found that her telescope had picked up a similar signal from another part of the sky. That ruled out the LGM idea in her mind. But not for the British tabloid press. After Hewitt announced the discovery, reporters swarmed the place, trying to interview the young, attractive female astronomer who'd been talking to extraterrestrials.

Bell's radio sources were named *pulsars,* and many more have been detected since. Astronomers later discovered that pulsars are rapidly rotating neutron stars that emit strong radio sources from their polar regions.

These discoveries fueled the interest of physicists and astrophysicists in black holes. In the past three decades, black hole physics has been an extremely active area of research.

Starting the Hunt

After Oppenheimer's discovery in 1939 that stars with masses larger than 3 solar masses will keep collapsing, a few scientists began to consider the possibility of finding real black holes. But it was tough to figure out how to go about it since you really can't see one.

In 1964, Yakov Zel'dovich in the Soviet Union came up with a way to see a black hole. He knew that a wind of gas blows off the surfaces of many stars. The sun, for example, has its solar wind, made mostly of protons and electrons, which streams off of the sun in all directions at speeds of about 400 kps (about 1 million mph). The solar wind isn't particularly strong when compared with the wind of many other stars.

If a star with a strong solar wind was located near a black hole, the strong gravity of the hole would pull in this gas, heating it up. Zel'dovich calculated that the gas would heat up to several million degrees. Hot objects radiate energy. Normally, this energy is in the infrared part of the spectrum (see Chapter 7) and sometimes in the visible spectrum. When the temperature is in the millions of degrees, the radiated energy is in the form of x-rays. Zel'dovich thought that he'd be able to "see" black holes by detecting these x-ray emissions near a star.

There was a problem, though (there's always a problem). You can't detect x-rays from space down here on the ground. And in 1964, there weren't any space telescopes that could detect them in space.

Several resourceful scientists tried sending x-ray detectors in rockets and were able to detect some x-ray sources. However, the real search for black holes started in 1970 with NASA's launch of the satellite *Uhuru*, dedicated to x-ray astronomy. This satellite discovered 339 x-ray stars. *Uhuru* was followed eight years later by NASA's *Einstein* x-ray telescope.

With *Uhuru* and *Einstein,* scientists discovered several black hole candidates. The most promising was named Cygnus X-1, which scientists call Cyg X-1 (see the sidebar "Betting on black holes").

There are several other candidates today. Scientists are now trying to detect the energy flowing into a black hole. It they succeed, that will be a more direct method of detecting black holes. One day, we'll be as certain that black holes exist as we are that the sun exists.

Understanding How the Universe Makes Black Holes

The constellation of Orion the hunter has three bright stars in the middle that are supposed to represent the belt of the hunter. Three dimmer stars below the belt represent the sword of Orion. A dim, middle star in the belt is not actually a star but a large cloud of gas called the Orion Nebula. This *nebula,* which is located at 1,500 light-years from us and is about 15 light-years across, is a birthplace of stars.

In this nebula, some regions of higher concentration of dust separate them- selves into large spheres. These spheres, or *protostars,* begin to shrink because of gravity, and the temperature rises. At some point, the temperature is high enough for nuclear fusion to start. The star is born.

Giants

That's how our sun started its life some 5 billion years ago. The sun is a middle-aged star and will shine for another 5 billion years before using up all its nuclear fuel. After 10 billion years, with no more fuel to spend, the sun (and any other star with a mass up to about 4 solar masses) will begin to contract. Without fuel, the sun's core won't be able to withstand gravity. This contraction will heat up the core again, which will begin to radiate energy out. The sun's outer layers will then start expanding, eventually forming a *red giant.*

When this second phase is over, gravity will start to compress the core of the sun once more until it becomes a *white dwarf.* In this stage, the sun will get a second lease on life and will radiate for a few million years more. After that, it will be all over. The sun will become a *black dwarf,* a burned-out mass — a dead star.

There are no dead stars of this kind anywhere yet. The universe hasn't lived long enough for a star like the sun to live out its life and die.

Supernovas

Not all stars live out their lives like the sun. Stars that are more massive explode into supernovas. One was discovered in our back yard in 1987. It was seen in the Large Magellanic Cloud, a satellite galaxy to our Milky Way. The core of supernovas like this will collapse into a neutron star.

Betting on black holes

Scientists calculated that Cyg X-1 should have a mass of about 6 solar masses, in the right range for black holes. In 1974, everything pointed toward Cyg X-1 being a black hole. In spite of this, renowned physicist Stephen Hawking of Cambridge University made a bet with the U.S. physicist Kip Thorne of Caltech that Cyg X-1 wasn't a black hole. If Hawking won, Thorne would buy him a one-year subscription to *Private Eye* magazine. If Thorne won, Hawking would buy him a one-year subscription to *Penthouse* magazine.

In his best-seller *A Brief History of Time,* Hawking explains that his bet was an insurance policy for him. He'd spent a lot of time working on black holes, and if black holes didn't exist, he'd at least win his subscription to *Private Eye*. In his well-known book *Black Holes and Time Warps,* Thorne explains that although his wife, mother, and siblings were mortified by the stakes, he didn't think he'd win. He was convinced that Cyg X-1 was a black hole but didn't think he could prove it.

When Hawking and Thorne made their bet, scientists estimated that they were about 80 percent certain that Cyg X-1 was a black hole. In 1988, when *A Brief History of Time* was published, the level of certainty had gone up to 95 percent, but Hawking hadn't accepted defeat.

One night in 1990, while Thorne was in Moscow, Hawking and his friends broke into Thorne's office at Caltech, found the bet, took it out of its frame, and wrote the note of concession on it with Hawking's thumbprint as signature. The certainty that Cyg X-1 was a black hole was still 95 percent.

Most scientists agree that Hawking was right in conceding. Cyg X-1 is very likely a black hole. Today, the evidence is still about the same. The certainty isn't 100 percent because Cyg X-1 is being detected indirectly, and you can always find another less likely but possible explanation for it.

Much more massive stars, with cores of more than 3 solar masses, will also collapse. As Oppenheimer and Snyder discovered theoretically, in this situation, nothing stops the collapse. The star becomes a black hole.

So, What Is a Black Hole Anyway?

Do scientists know what the properties of a black hole are?

During the 1960s and 1970s, the "golden age" of black hole research, many scientists spent a great deal of time performing complicated calculations with the general relativity equations, trying to come up with what they thought black holes should be like. They also did computer simulations and modeling to help guide some of the complicated calculations.

Out of all this activity came several interesting results. The most important one is that a black hole is always perfectly spherical, regardless of the shape of the star that originated it. If the star has a mountain, the black hole ends up round. If the star is deformed in any way — even if it is a square star — the black hole that it forms is still round (see Figure 13-5). What happens to the mountains or the deformations? They are radiated away, in the form of gravitational waves.

Figure 13-5:
Black holes
are round,
no matter
what shape
the stars
were.

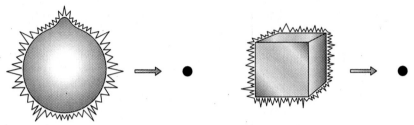

These answers seem simple, but to get to them required years of extremely complicated calculations and discussions among the scientists involved. These scientists also discovered that if the original star had a magnetic field, the resulting black hole sucks this field down behind its *event horizon,* the surface of the sphere at the Schwarzschild radius or the boundary of a black hole. No magnetic field lines remain sticking out of the black hole.

Black holes have no hair

In fact, nothing sticks out of a black hole: no mountains, protrusions, or magnetic fields. This finding prompted the renowned U.S. physicist John Wheeler, who earlier coined the term *black hole,* to declare that a black hole has ho hair. With this apparently crude statement, Wheeler wanted to drive home the concept of how a black hole modified many physical properties to end up in a very simple form.

The phrase caught on fairly quickly at international conferences and meetings. When it came time for scientists to publish research papers on this topic in respected journals, things became a bit more difficult. The editor of the prestigious U.S. journal *Physical Review* told the scientists that his journal would not permit such obscenities. Some European journals and Russian journals, published in languages where the phrase had similar connotations, also refused to use it.

Physicists continued to use the phrase in their conference presentations. Eventually, the phrase lost its lewd interpretation and became synonymous with what Wheeler intended. The journal editors gave in, and now you can find it in countless scholarly papers and books. You'll be hard-pressed to find a popular book dealing with black holes that doesn't use it.

If black holes have no hair, do they have anything?

It turns out that they can't really get rid of everything. (They still have some hair!) Black holes must keep all the things that physics says cannot be destroyed — things that obey what are called *conservation laws*. Physics says that black holes must keep their masses, electric charges, and spin. If they were to get rid of those things, physicists would have to revise all their laws and start over again. (They'd rather stay with the laws that they've discovered and see how far they can go.)

In 1965, the well-known British physicists Stephen Hawking and Roger Penrose showed that spacetime becomes infinite inside a black hole. This means that gravity inside a black hole is infinite. This infinite stretching of spacetime is called a *singularity* (see Figure 13-6).

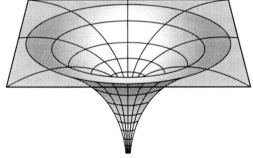

Figure 13-6:
Spacetime is stretched to infinity inside a black hole.

"Black holes ain't so black"

Black holes seem to swallow everything within sight and don't let anything come out. Even light is trapped inside black holes.

In 1971, Yakov Zel'dovich, one of the founders of the Soviet Union's nuclear weapons program, came up with the strange idea that a black hole sends off radiation as well as particles. Didn't everyone know that nothing comes out of a black hole? Why was Zel'dovich claiming that something does come out?

Zel'dovich was attempting to apply some ideas of quantum physics to the study of black holes, which are studied with general relativity. However, Zel'dovich didn't know enough general relativity to perform the actual calculations for black holes, so he made calculations for a rotating metal sphere instead. His analysis showed that the sphere must radiate a tiny amount of energy because of its interaction with the surrounding spacetime.

Zel'dovich published his idea in a prestigious physics journal, but no one paid much attention to it. Most thought that it was crazy.

In 1973, Stephen Hawking visited the Soviet Union to discuss physics with the Russian physicists. When Hawking and Zel'dovich met, they discussed Zel'dovich's idea of radiating black holes. Hawking was interested but didn't like the way Zel'dovich had used quantum physics and general relativity. Hawking decided to do it right. When he was done, he confirmed what Zel'dovich had said, that a spinning black hole emits energy and particles. But he went further. Hawking showed that even after the hole stops spinning, it continues to radiate and emit particles. His discovery was coined *Hawking radiation*.

As Hawking likes to say, "Black holes ain't so black." Initially, Hawking maintained that the radiation that comes out of the black hole is random and carries no information about what went in. Other scientists disagreed. In 1997, Hawking and Kip Thorne bet John Preskill of Caltech that if an encyclopedia is sucked in by a black hole, the information would be lost forever. The Hawking radiation emitting from the black hole would be meaningless; it wouldn't contain any of the information in the encyclopedia.

Recently, Hawking came around and accepted that he'd been wrong. His calculations are showing that Hawking radiation *is* related to the information that goes into the black hole. The contents of the encyclopedia should slowly come out in the radiation. Hawking conceded his bet at the conference where he presented his paper. He gave Preskill a baseball encyclopedia.

Journey into a black hole

If an astronaut were brave enough to travel into a black hole, what would he see?

Imagine an interstellar spaceship arriving to the region near a black hole of 4 solar masses. If the ship commander does it right, he can park his spaceship in an orbit around the black hole. The astronauts on this ship won't feel anything different from what they feel and see when in orbit about the sun, for example.

When an intrepid astronaut leaves the ship on a small runabout and heads toward the black hole, things begin to move away from the ordinary. Suppose the astronaut is reporting back to the station at ten-second intervals. At first, the signals received at the ship come in every ten seconds, as planned. When the astronaut in the runabout gets close to the black hole's event horizon, the intervals received by the spaceship become longer and longer. Instead of one every 10 seconds, they are now coming every 20, 45, 90 seconds. Soon, the ship's astronauts are waiting minutes to get the next signal. Then, the minutes become hours, days, months. Eventually, they find themselves waiting a couple years before the next signal arrives. Finally, years pass without receiving a signal. The astronaut passed the event horizon and went into the black hole.

To the astronaut, however, time is flowing as usual. Every ten seconds, she sends a signal. She crosses the event horizon, and her watch keeps ticking at the normal rate. She dutifully continues sending her signals.

But the signals have been Doppler-shifted because of the enormous gravitational field of the black hole. From the spaceship, the astronaut's time is slowed down. When the astronaut crosses the event horizon, her signal is Doppler-shifted an infinite amount, which is another way of saying that the signal disappears.

Although the astronaut in the runabout sees her watch running as always, things are far from normal for her. The worst problem she has is the enormous tidal forces that are tearing her craft and herself apart. This imaginary trip doesn't have a happy ending. Our astronaut won't survive for long.

Contemplating Time Travel

Could black holes offer the possibility of time travel? As I discuss in Chapter 12, time travel to the future is possible. In fact, we all do it (to a very small degree) all the time. Every time you get on an airplane, a train, or a car, you are moving relative to those who stay behind. According to general relativity, time flows more slowly in the accelerated frame. Since you need to accelerate to reach cruising speed, your time will pass at a slower rate compared to those who stay behind. And while you're traveling at cruising speed relative to us, special relativity says that your time flows more slowly.

At the end of your trip, you'll be younger than those who didn't travel with you. However, the age difference is measured in extremely small fractions of a second. On a flight from Los Angeles to Tokyo at 1,000 kph (625 mph), you travel ten nanoseconds into the future, which is the same as saying that you'll be ten nanoseconds younger. If you get on a spaceship that travels at $0.99995c$ and go for a nice 10-year tour of our neighborhood in the galaxy, you'll travel 1,000 years into the future. When you return to Earth, you won't recognize the place!

Visiting the past

If you travel to the future, can you get back? Or better yet, can you travel to the past from the present?

Special relativity allows you to *see* the past. In fact, this phenomenon happens all the time. When you look at the sun, you're seeing it as it existed 8 minutes ago. That's how long it takes light to travel from the sun to the Earth. The images that we get from a NASA rover on Mars also travel at the speed of light. The scientists at Jet Propulsion Laboratory (JPL) see the rover as it existed 20 minutes earlier. For all they know, the rover malfunctioned 15 minutes ago.

When you see your friend across the table, you're seeing her as she was 3 nanoseconds ago. She doesn't change that much in 3 nanoseconds, so there's no difference in her appearance. But if she travels to another planetary system 20 light-years away, the image that you receive of her will be the one she sent 20 years ago.

What you really want to know is if you can visit the past and come back to the present. We're talking real time travel, like in *Back to the Future* or *Peggy Sue Got Married.*

The short answer is: Perhaps, but not with present-day technology.

Exploring wormholes

In 1988, Kip Thorne and Michael Morris at Caltech and Ulvi Yurtsever at the University of Michigan published the first serious paper on the possibility of building a time machine. It was entitled "Wormholes, Time Machines, and the Weak Energy Condition," and it was published in the prestigious *Physical Review Letters,* a journal with a very strict acceptance policy. In the paper, the three physicists presented their conclusions about their study on the possibilities of time travel.

The idea for the study began with Carl Sagan, who at the time was writing his science fiction novel and movie script *Contact*. Sagan's story deals with time travel, and he wanted to know from Thorne if time travel was scientifically feasible. Sagan was an astronomer and was well acquainted with the theory of relativity and black holes and what the theories say today about time travel. However, he wanted to know from the top scientists working on relativity and black holes whether time travel is possible for a sufficiently advanced civilization.

Einstein had looked at a related problem. In 1935, Einstein and his collaborator, the physicist Nathan Rosen, used general relativity to examine the shape of spacetime near a very massive star. They found that spacetime became warped into a tunnel, a hole in the universe. Einstein examined the equations more carefully and realized that this tunnel would lead to another region of the universe (see Figure 13-7). Einstein was disturbed with this strange solution.

Figure 13-7:
The
Einstein–
Rosen
bridge,
connecting
two parts of
the universe.

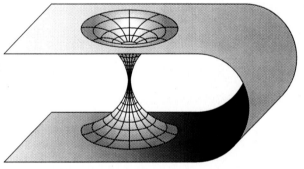

Einstein knew that getting through the tunnel required speeds greater than the speed of light. Because that wasn't allowed by the special theory, he took his conclusions to be a mathematical quirk, with no physical reality. Later, the *Einstein–Rosen bridge,* as it is called, appeared in other solutions to Einstein's field equation. But Einstein wasn't concerned with the reappearance of the bridge, because relativity didn't allow travel through the bridge.

In 1963, when Kerr obtained his solution to Einstein's field equation describing a rotating black hole, the Einstein–Rosen bridge idea was revived. Kerr found that his spinning black hole doesn't collapse to a point, like Schwarzschild's. Instead, it collapses to a ring. If that's the case, then you could in principle travel through the tunnel. You'd have to do it very carefully, moving through the middle of the tunnel, not deviating much from the axis (see Figure 13-8). The Einstein–Rosen bridge is a *wormhole* connecting two regions of the universe.

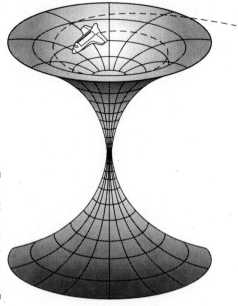

Figure 13-8:
An astronaut
traveling
through an
Einstein–
Rosen
bridge.

Using a time machine

Thorne and his collaborators realized that the Einstein–Rosen bridge could be used as a time machine. If you move one of the openings of the bridge to the neighborhood of a neutron star while the other opening remains here, the much greater gravity of the neutron star would slow down the flow of time.

If the time difference between the two openings of the wormhole is 100 years, an astronaut entering our opening to the wormhole will come out at the other end, 100 years into the future. When the astronaut returns, he will be back in our time.

However, Thorne warns us that for the wormhole to be passable, it must contain some undiscovered exotic matter. Thorne was looking to see if any laws of physics would prohibit the existence of a time machine. The exotic matter that he required for the wormhole doesn't exist today, but the laws of physics don't prevent it from existing. This exotic matter must generate antigravity or gravitational repulsion to allow the astronaut to pass through the wormhole without having it collapse on himself. Gravitational repulsion can be generated with negative energy or negative pressure.

Physicists have discovered negative energy in some quantum systems. Back in 1948, the Dutch physicist Hendrik Casimir had predicted the existence of these systems. The *Casimir effect* was observed for the first time in 1958 (see Chapter 19). Today, scientists are trying to apply this effect to operate micro-machines. Thorne's exotic matter with negative energy that can produce antigravity may someday be discovered.

Prohibiting time loops

Suppose that scientists one day are able to solve all of the engineering problems and construct a time machine using the Einstein–Rosen bridge. Is time travel really possible with all the paradoxes that it creates?

Imagine that you travel back in time and find yourself witnessing a man about to commit a crime. You decide to alert a policeman and the man is killed in a shootout. Later on you discover that the man was your own grandfather and that he hadn't even met your grandmother at the time. Since he is dead, your parents aren't going to be born, and you won't ever exist to travel back in time and alert the policeman.

You could also travel back to January 1905 and meet Albert Einstein at his home in Bern, perhaps the evening after he returned from his long discussion with Michele Besso about the problems with electromagnetism and the principle of relativity (see Chapter 9). You can then tell him that the solution is to keep the principle of relativity and to make the speed of light constant for all nonaccelerated observers. Then you leave his apartment, climb on your time machine, and return to the present. The next day, Einstein tells Besso that he has figured out the problem and proceeds to develop relativity.

Who discovered relativity? You told Einstein how to do it. Einstein listened to you and developed it. Then he published his theory and became famous. You learned about his discovery in this book and then traveled back in time to tell him how to do it.

Equally disconcerting is the time traveler from the future who studies how the time machine he is about to use is made. Then he travels back in time and meets the inventor of the time machine and tells him how to do it.

All these paradoxes prompted Stephen Hawking to propose that there seems to exist a Chronology Protection Agency that protects history and prevents time travelers from changing the past. His chronology protection hypothesis, which comes out of general relativity calculations that he performed, outlaws these time loops.

However, the theory of relativity permits these time loops. Hawking's chronology protection hypothesis would have to be supported by some new physics. Physicists have suggested that perhaps quantum mechanics may support it. Some calculations indicate that if particles travel to their own past, the interaction with the previous form of the particle creates a runaway surge of energy that destroys the wormhole.

Is time travel possible? The present laws of physics don't prohibit it, but they don't support it either. New physics has to be discovered to answer the question.

If time travel is possible, where are the time travelers? As Stephen Hawking says, "the best evidence we have that time travel is not possible, and never will be, is that we have never been invaded by hordes of tourists from the future."

Chapter 14

Was Einstein Right about Relativity?

* *

In This Chapter

▶ Looking at early tests of relativity

▶ Testing general relativity with spacecraft

▶ Understanding the GPS connection to relativity

▶ Using NASA missions to check Einstein's theories

▶ Realizing that theories can never be proved absolutely

* *

Scientists have tested Einstein's predictions from Mars, from the moon, and from orbit. NASA's latest effort, *Gravity Probe B,* was launched in April of 2004 after 35 years of design and testing. The mission will measure, very precisely, how space and time are warped by the presence of the Earth and, more profoundly, how the Earth's rotation drags spacetime around with it. These effects, though small for the Earth, have far-reaching implications for the nature of matter and the structure of the universe.

Gravity Probe B is among the most thoroughly researched programs ever undertaken by NASA, but it certainly isn't the first attempt to test Einstein's theory of relativity. In this chapter, I summarize other tests that have been conducted in the past century. I also show you how thousands of people test the theory of relativity every day by using GPS locating devices. Finally, I show you why we can't be 100 percent certain that Einstein was right.

Conducting Early Tests of Relativity

Einstein's scientific work is at the heart of today's physics. For example,

- His special theory of relativity, which I discuss in Part III of this book, showed that Isaac Newton's laws of motion (see Chapter 4) are only an approximation.

- His general theory of relativity, which I detail in Chapter 12, made radical changes to our notions of gravity and space and also showed that Newton's mechanics is an approximation. According to Newton, gravity is a force that makes objects feel each other's presence. But Einstein said that gravity is geometry, the result of the distortions of spacetime.

- His introduction of the light quantum idea, which I discuss in Part V, led to a whole new area of physics that didn't exist before.

But how do we perceive these theories in the everyday world? Can we *see* what Einstein was talking about?

The discrepancy between special relativity and Newton's mechanics, for example, is imperceptible in the motions that we experience in our everyday lives. Even for astronauts flying on the Space Shuttle, the discrepancy can't be measured. The speed of the Shuttle in orbit is about 28,000 kilometers per hour (kph), which is 17,500 mph or 23 times the speed of sound (Mach 23). While the Shuttle is traveling a whole lot faster than your car can ever go, it's only moving at about three-hundredths of a percent of the speed of light. At such slow speeds, the relativistic effects Einstein described aren't noticed; space and time are not seen as being connected into spacetime. The speed measured on the Shuttle matches the speed that tracking stations measure on the ground. The distances that the Shuttle travels don't change for the astronauts or for the technicians on the ground.

The subtle changes that general relativity brought to Newton's theory of gravity also seem far removed from our everyday lives. The warping of spacetime can't be measured without extremely precise instruments looking at distant galaxies and quasars.

Yet both theories, along with quantum physics, are closer to our lives than you may think. Digital cameras, cellular phones, computers, and GPS units all use one or several of Einstein's theories.

In this sense, Einstein's theories have been tested. The proof is in the pudding. However, scientists continue to perform sophisticated tests of the special and general theories of relativity. Do a Web search for "tests of relativity," and you'll find over 1,000 entries, many of them current research papers explaining delicate tests of the theories.

How do you test a theory? You test its predictions.

The special theory of relativity predicts that

- ✔ Clocks run more slowly in the moving frame.
- ✔ Lengths are shortened in the moving frame.
- ✔ Mass increases in the moving frame.

The general theory of relativity predicts that

- ✔ Gravity slows time. Time runs more slowly in the basement (where the gravitational field is stronger) than it does on the top floor of a structure.
- ✔ Signals are Doppler-shifted in gravitational fields.
- ✔ Spacetime is curved.

Testing special relativity: Life extension

One of the early tests of relativity involved the *muon,* a short-lived elementary particle that has its lifetime extended when traveling close to the speed of light. (I describe the effect in Chapter 10.) The muon travels at $0.998c$ in the atmosphere, and at that speed, its lifetime is extended 16 times. When scientists measure muons' lifetimes in laboratories (where the muons are at rest), the lifetimes are extremely short — much too short for muons to travel from the Earth's upper atmosphere, where they are born, to the ground. Yet they are detected on the ground because their lives are extended when they travel at such high speeds.

In 1976, physicists at the European Particle Physics Laboratory (CERN) in Geneva, Switzerland, accelerated muons that had been generated in the lab to $0.9994c$ in a particle accelerator (see Figure 14-1). The muon lifetimes increased by a factor of 30. At rest in the lab, the particles have a lifetime of 2.2 microseconds. Taking a leisurely trip around a 14-meter (46-foot) diameter track, a typical muon would complete 14 circles before its life was over. But at 99.94 percent of the speed of light, the muon would manage more than 400 turns around the track before it died. These measurements agree with the prediction of special relativity to within 2 parts in 1,000.

Since this experiment was conducted, similar experiments have increased the accuracy even more. Today, measuring the relativistic increase in the lifetime of muons is a lab exercise for graduate students at CERN and at other high energy laboratories around the world.

CERN Photo

Getting younger by flying east: Relativistic time

In 1971, J.C. Hafele of Washington University in St. Louis and Richard Keating of the U.S. Naval Observatory took two atomic clocks on commercial flights around the world to test the time dilation effect predicted by special relativity. One of the flights was eastbound and the other westbound. The clocks were compared with the reference atomic clock at the U.S. Naval Observatory in Washington, D.C.

Hafele and Keating did their experiment on a shoestring budget and bought tickets on commercial flights rather than chartering planes. Their clocks were connected to the airplanes' power and placed against the front walls of the coach class cabins. (As a government employee, Keating wasn't allowed to fly first class!)

According to special relativity, the clock on the eastbound flight should tick more slowly, because it is moving relative to the clock in the Naval Observatory. (As I explain in a moment, the effect on the westbound clock is different, because the plane is moving opposite the Earth's rotation.) But general relativity says that both flying clocks should run faster, because gravity is slightly weaker in the air than on the ground. The two effects tend to offset each other, and the final result depends on how fast the planes fly and on the altitude.

For Hafele and Keating's experiment, special relativity predicted that the flying clock on the eastbound plane should run 184 nanoseconds behind the ground clock. And general relativity predicted that both flying clocks should run 144 nanoseconds faster. The net effect predicted by relativity was that the flying clock on the eastbound plane would lose 40 nanoseconds on the trip around the world. The actual observed loss was 59 nanoseconds.

Relativity gives you a way to stay young: Fly fast and low. But you have to fly eastbound always. If you fly westbound, you'll get older because you'll be flying opposite to the Earth's rotation. Looking from space, a clock on the ground is actually moving faster than your westbound plane (see Figure 14-2). The result is that your clock will run faster when flying westbound than a clock on the ground, and you'll age faster — but only by a few nanoseconds. (You don't have to worry about getting any more gray hairs during your next flight west than you'd get on the ground.)

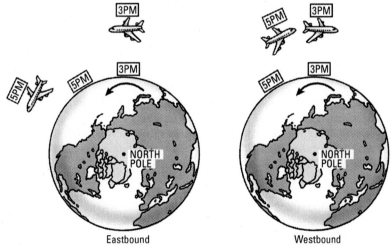

Figure 14-2: When you travel westbound, a clock on the ground moves faster than your plane as seen from space.

Eastbound   Westbound

Hafele and Keating's results with their flying atomic clocks agreed very well with the time predictions of both the special and the general theories of relativity. Other more recent and more sophisticated experiments have also been in agreement with the time-dilation prediction of special relativity and with the time-lengthening prediction of general relativity.

Probing gravity: NASA's first test of relativity

Hafele and Keating's experiment was a nice first attempt at a direct test of relativity. But flying atomic clocks on commercial planes isn't an ideal way to conduct a precision experiment. A better method is to fly the clocks on a satellite.

That's what NASA proposed to do in 1970 with Robert Vessot and Martin Levine of Harvard as principal investigators. The idea was to put an atomic clock in orbit with a Titan rocket. But budget constraints forced NASA to switch to a suborbital flight on a Scout D rocket — the *Gravity Probe A* mission that flew in 1976.

In June of 1976, Vessot went to NASA's Wallops Island rocket launch facility in Virginia to man the rocket clock while Levine traveled to the Kennedy Space Center in Florida to take charge of the ground clock. At 6:41 a.m. on June 18, the *Gravity Probe A* mission was underway. It took an atomic clock to an altitude of 10,000 km (6,200 mi) for a two-hour suborbital flight.

The atomic clocks transmitted their signals continuously. The electronic instrumentation hooked up to the atomic clock aboard the rocket was designed to compensate for the Doppler shifts of the rocket signal during ascent and descent. (This Doppler shift is the stretching of the wavelength of the signal emitted by the rocket as it moves away from the detector on the ground, and the subsequent shortening when the rocket approaches the ground during descent. I explain this effect in Chapter 12.)

With the standard Doppler shift out of the way, things would be simpler; the signal received from the rocket clock should reflect only changes due to relativity. With the rocket in motion, the clock on board should run more slowly than the one on the ground. And as the rocket gained altitude, the weaker gravitational field should speed up the clock on board.

Initially, the high speed of the rocket caused the clock to run slow. The rocket hadn't yet gained too much altitude, so gravity hadn't changed enough to speed up the clock. Therefore, the rocket clock was initially ticking at a slower rate than the one on the ground. Some three minutes later, when the rocket had slowed down some and had also gained elevation, the two clocks were ticking in step. Later, the rocket clock sped up because of the increased altitude (weaker gravity) and slower speed. Figure 14-3 shows the various stages of the rocket's movement; the dots in the figure represent the clocks' ticking rates.

Figure 14-3: When the rocket speed is high, the clock on the rocket slows down. When the altitude is high, the clock speeds up.

The Scout D rocket reached maximum altitude at 7:40 a.m. On the way down, as the speed of the rocket increased and its altitude decreased, the two effects reversed, canceling each other out sometime around 8:31 a.m. After that, the special relativity time dilation took over, and the rocket clock slowed down.

The rocket splashed into the Atlantic Ocean, about 900 miles east of Bermuda. It took the science team two years to analyze all the data. The final result was that the special relativity time-dilation and the general relativity time-contraction effects agreed with the theory to a precision of 70 parts in 1 million.

With this delicate experiment, Vessot and Levine's team showed with great precision that time does slow down in the moving frame and in strong gravitational fields. Time really runs more slowly when you are moving and when you go down to the basement.

Confirming Gravity's Effects on Light

The special theory of relativity is based on the constancy of the speed of light. Many tests have shown that Einstein's assumption is correct: You always measure light traveling at the same speed c regardless of how fast you are moving. Light travels at exactly 299,792 kilometers per second (kps) in a vacuum. In air, light slows down a very tiny amount. When it goes through glass, it slows down just a bit more. When it comes out, it resumes its slightly faster speed. This change in the speed of light doesn't contradict relativity. The speed of light in air is the same, regardless of how fast you're moving through the air when you measure the speed.

It turns out that gravitational fields, in addition to bending light, also appear to slow it down. But you need a very strong gravitational field if you're thinking of measuring this effect, which is the combined result of the strong gravity warping space and the gravitational time delay. Einstein actually came up with a gravitational model with this light time-delay effect built in. However, he didn't pursue the model fully.

Calculating the sun's impact

Light coming to Earth from a distant object travels along the distorted space and appears to slow down due to the curvature of space around the sun. The closer the path is to the sun, the more it appears to slow down. For example, a light signal coming from Mars takes longer when it grazes the sun because of the dip in space (see Figure 14-4). Away from the sun, the curvature is not as pronounced, and the path is more like in the flat Newtonian space.

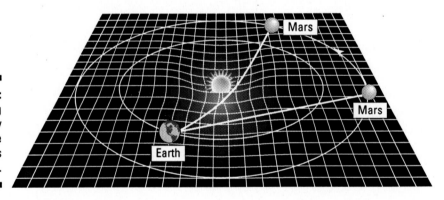

Figure 14-4:
The strong gravity around the sun warps space.

In the 1960s, MIT physicist Irwin Shapiro did some calculations to see how much longer it would take a signal from a distant object to arrive at the Earth if its path grazed the sun. As in Einstein's earlier model, Shapiro's calculations showed that the signal would be delayed due to the sun's gravity. In the case of a radar signal bouncing off Venus, Shapiro calculated that the signal would take an additional 10 microseconds to arrive when Venus was on the other side of the sun.

At about the same time, Duane Muhleman and Paul Reichley at NASA's Jet Propulsion Laboratory (JPL) came up with a similar calculation while studying the effects of general relativity on a radar signal bouncing off Venus. Like Shapiro's calculation, their results showed that the signal would take an additional 10 microseconds to travel from Venus, pass by the sun, and arrive at the detectors on Earth.

Getting radar echoes from the planets wasn't easy in the 1960s. But the Lincoln Laboratories at MIT were up to the task. In 1967, Shapiro and his group verified the time delays for the first time. They measured several hundred radar signals bouncing off Venus and performed the detailed calculations. The results came within 20 percent of the predicted amount that light is delayed due to the general relativity effects.

Testing the time delay from Mars

Also during the 1960s, NASA's JPL was busy exploring Mars. The *Mariner 4* spacecraft arrived at Mars in 1965 and changed our view of the planet. It was the first spacecraft to make it to Mars safely, and it took the first close-up photographs of the surface: 21 astonishing pictures of another planet. In the wake of its success, NASA sent two more spacecraft on a flyby mission to Mars, *Mariner 6* and *Mariner 7*. The two spacecraft sent back 58 close-up photographs of the Martian surface and important data on the composition of the southern polar cap.

After the flybys, the two spacecraft were locked in an orbit around the sun that was similar to the orbit of Mars. Muhleman and Reichley at JPL knew that the Mariners would be close to Mars later on when the planet was going to be located on the other side of the sun from Earth. Although their missions would be over by then, the two scientists asked NASA Headquarters to extend the missions long enough to time the signals and do the general relativity test. NASA approved. The results confirmed the predictions to within 5 percent.

NASA planned a large mission to Mars for the following decade. The *Viking* landers would be the first robotic craft to land on the surface of another planet. Their mission was to look for life or signs of it. Testing relativity wasn't in the plans, but Muhleman and Reichley, teaming up with Shapiro, convinced NASA Headquarters to approve relativity measurements.

The twin *Viking* missions of 1976 and 1977 were extremely successful, electrifying not just the scientists but the general public with beautifully detailed color photographs of the surface and atmosphere of Mars. The missions were also a success for Einstein's general theory of relativity. Although Einstein himself never proposed this particular test of the apparent time delay of light by gravity, it proved to be the most accurate test of relativity ever. According to the *Viking* landers' measurements, general relativity's time-delay effect is correct to within 1 part in 1,000.

Making GPS Accurate

A test of the time-delay effects of both special relativity and general relativity is done daily by millions of people around the world — the users of Global Positioning Satellite (GPS) receivers.

The GPS system, which started in 1978 with the launch of the U.S. Department of Defense *Navstar* satellite, is an array of 24 satellites that orbit the Earth at 14,000 kph (8,600 mph) at an altitude of 20,000 km (12,000 mi). Each satellite carries an atomic clock so accurate that it will lose or gain only 1 second in 3 million years.

The receiver has a less accurate quartz clock, like the one in your digital watch. Without a correction, receivers will get out of sync with the satellites. To synchronize the clocks, at least four satellites are always in line of sight of any receiver on the ground. The signals from three satellites provide enough information to triangulate the position, while the fourth satellite measurement provides a correction factor.

With a moderately priced GPS receiver that you can buy at the mall, you can locate your position to within a couple of meters and get the local time to 50 billionths of a second. The GPS receiver in a car can give you position, speed, and direction in a few seconds.

To get this kind of precision, the receivers must keep pace with the satellite clocks to within 20 to 30 nanoseconds. But even with the correction factor of the fourth satellite, the clocks will get out of sync and lose this accuracy because of relativistic effects:

- ✔ At 14,000 kph, the satellite clocks circle the Earth twice a day; obviously, they move much faster than the clocks on the ground. According to Einstein's special theory of relativity, a clock on a satellite moving relative to one on the ground will run more slowly, by 7 microseconds every day (see the Speed Clock in Figure 14-5).

- ✔ But at the 20,000 km altitude, the gravitational field is weaker than it is on the ground. Therefore, the general theory of relativity says that the satellite clock should tick faster than the clock on the ground by about 45 microseconds per day (see the Gravity Clock in Figure 14-5).

If you combine the effects, the net result is that clocks in the receivers will run 38 microseconds slow in just one day, as shown on the clock on the right side of Figure 14-5. At this rate, the clocks will lose the required 30-nanosecond accuracy (which ensures navigational accuracy to within 10 meters) in just two minutes!

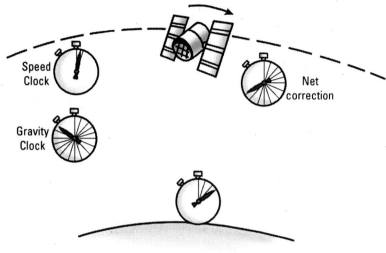

Figure 14-5:
The atomic
clock in the
GPS satellite
and the
one in the
receiver on
the ground
will get out
of sync in
two minutes
because of
relativistic
effects.

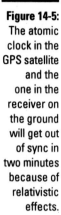

To prevent that problem, the GPS system was designed with a relativistic correction built in. The ticking of the satellite clocks was slowed down before launch to compensate for the gravitational stretching of time once in orbit. And the receiver computers have software that incorporates relativistic formulas. Relativistic errors cancel out in newer GPS receivers, which use the wide-area augmentation system. (See the sidebar "Enhanced GPS systems.")

These relativistic corrections came out of Einstein's theories. The 30 million GPS users getting their accurate locations are constantly testing the accuracy of Einstein's predictions. The GPS system works.

Enhanced GPS systems

The wide-area augmentation system (WAAS), designed by the U.S. Federal Aviation Administration, has improved the accuracy of GPS signals to 1 to 2 meters horizontally and 2 to 3 meters vertically throughout most of the United States. The system uses a network of 25 ground stations that checks GPS readings with map coordinates and issues corrections. These corrections are uplinked to geostationary relay satellites, which broadcast to WAAS receivers. With this method, relativistic errors cancel out.

Measuring the Curvature of Spacetime

In 1959, Leonard Schiff, the chairman of the physics department at Stanford University, was at his regular lunch hour break, swimming 400 yards at the Stanford pool, when two colleagues joined him to talk about gyroscopes. (Gyroscopes are based on a principle of physics that says that an object rotating freely keeps its orientation for as long as it's free of external influences.)

Schiff was a nuclear physicist and had done work in quantum mechanics but had recently become interested in relativity. He'd been thinking about using very precise gyroscopes to test the theory. One of his colleagues, William Fairbank, was a low-temperature expert and had also been thinking about gyroscopes, but he wanted to do experiments with them at low temperatures. The third professor, Robert Cannon, was an expert on gyroscopes and had worked with them in guidance systems for submarines, planes, and missiles before joining the Stanford faculty.

After their swim, Schiff told his two colleagues about an idea he'd had about using gyroscopes to observe the curvature of spacetime and the way the Earth drags spacetime with it as it rotates. According to Einstein, the gyroscope remains fixed in spacetime. If spacetime is curved by the Earth, the gyroscope should "see" that. If spacetime is dragged by the Earth, the gyroscope should be dragged along.

Spacetime drag: The universe in a bucket

Schiff's idea was new, but the effects had been known for a long time. Just two years after Einstein developed his general theory of relativity, two German physicists, Josef Lense and Hans Thirring, used Einstein's theory to show that a large spinning object would not only curve spacetime but also drag spacetime along with it. Physicists call this effect *frame dragging*.

One way to visualize frame dragging is to take a bucket of white paint and pour a small amount of a dark-colored paint in it without mixing it. Spin a small paint brush in the paint, and notice how the paint tends to turn behind it, creating a whirlpool (see Figure 14-6). The spinning brush swirls the paint around it.

The frame dragging effect explains why rotation is relative. Consider another bucket, this time filled with water and hanging by a rope. If you start spinning the bucket, what do you see? Initially, the water slowly begins to spin, trying to catch up to the bucket. Soon, when the water is spinning along with the bucket, the surface of the water becomes curved, concave (see Figure 14-7). That's because the water molecules, once set in motion, want to keep that motion. That's what Newton told us with his first law of motion (see Chapter 4). Some of the molecules end up bunching up against the sides of the bucket. Because there isn't room for every molecule at the sides of the bucket, some bunch up right behind, and the rest are farther back, giving the surface of the water that concave look. The effect seems pretty straightforward nowadays.

Figure 14-6:
The spinning brush drags the paint along with it.

Figure 14-7:
The surface of the water in the spinning bucket takes a concave shape.

Back in 1689, Newton didn't think it was straightforward. Newton wanted to get to the bottom of this phenomenon. With respect to what was the water spinning? Not the bucket, because the bucket is spinning along with the water. The rest of the universe? If that is the case, then imagine that you do the experiment in a completely empty universe: a universe that consists of only a bucket with water. What happens now? Does the water take the same concave shape or stay flat? With respect to what is the water spinning? In an empty universe, there's nothing to refer the motion to.

Newton believed that even in an empty universe, you still have space as a reference. The water spins relative to space.

Newton proposed a variation of his thought experiment. Suppose that you go back to the initial experiment with the bucket hanging from the rope. Now, instead of spinning the bucket, you, the room you're in, the entire building, and everything else in the universe rotates around the bucket. All the solar systems, galaxies, clusters . . . the entire universe spins around the bucket. What happens to the surface of the water then? Does it take a concave shape, or does it stay flat?

Newton couldn't answer this question.

What did Einstein say about these two thought experiments? In relativity, there is no absolute space. That idea is at the core of special relativity (see Chapter 10). Newton's view that in an empty universe the water spins relative to absolute space is wrong. But spacetime is not relative. For Einstein, space is relative and time is relative, but spacetime is absolute. According to Einstein,

> *The water in the bucket in an otherwise empty universe spins relative to spacetime.*

What about the second thought experiment, the one Newton didn't have an answer to? Did Einstein have an answer? In principle, he did. According to general relativity, it shouldn't matter whether you say that the bucket spins and the universe doesn't or that the universe spins and the bucket doesn't. The water takes a concave shape in either case. *Rotation is relative.*

Imagine that you place your bucket inside a large and massive empty shell. Suppose that the shell is actually the size of the Earth and contains all of its mass. Inside this shell, there is no gravity. The shell attracts the bucket from all directions, and all these attractions cancel out. This is true even when you place the bucket away from the center of the shell (see Figure 14-8). The chunk of shell closest to the bucket would attract it with a greater force than the chunk on the other side, except that the bucket "sees" more of the shell that's farther away. This effect is true in Newtonian mechanics and in general relativity.

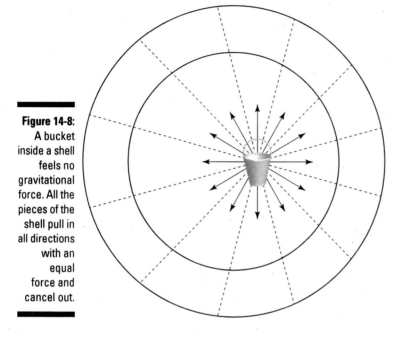

Figure 14-8:
A bucket
inside a shell
feels no
gravitational
force. All the
pieces of the
shell pull in
all directions
with an
equal
force and
cancel out.

Now, imagine starting this hollowed Earth spinning. According to Newton, nothing should happen to the water because the shell doesn't exert a force on the bucket. According to Einstein, the rotating shell drags spacetime along with it. The frame dragging forces cause the water to slightly move over to the sides and take a curved shape. If you enlarge the shell more and more while at the same time increasing its mass, the spacetime effect should increase. If the shell becomes the size of the universe and contains all the mass of the universe, the frame dragging increases in such a way that the curvature of the water matches the shape of the water when the bucket itself rotates.

Proving this idea mathematically wasn't easy. In 1912, even before completing his general theory, Einstein started some calculations of this frame dragging effect in a shell. In 1965, two theoretical physicists were able to partially solve the problem. Finally, in 1985, Herbert Pfister and K. Braun in Germany were able to complete the calculation, showing that, in fact, Einstein was right in his initial insight. Space inside a spinning shell is dragged along.

Can this effect be checked experimentally? That's what Schiff and his swimming buddies wanted to know.

Embarking on the mission

Schiff and his two colleagues pitched to NASA the idea of using a gyroscope to measure the curvature of spacetime and to detect frame dragging. As it turned out, NASA had started plans for an orbiting observatory and was interested in the research. Four decades of planning, development, and deployment started right then.

NASA called the mission *Gravity Probe B*. The *Gravity Probe A* mission in 1976 had flown an atomic clock in a rocket to measure the relativity of time predicted by Einstein. The new mission was going to measure two other predictions of Einstein: the curvature of spacetime and the frame dragging effect.

Gravity Probe B was launched atop a Delta 2 rocket on April 20, 2004, from Vandenberg Air Force Base in California. The satellite was placed into orbit 640 km (400 mi) above the Earth carrying some of the most advanced technology ever built. Unfortunately, Leonard Schiff wasn't around to see the realization of his dream. He passed away in 1971 at the age of 55. The mission is now led by Francis Everitt of Stanford University.

The centerpieces of the mission are the four gyroscopes, each a 4-cm diameter sphere of fused quartz spinning at 10,000 rpm. They are the most perfectly spherical objects ever made, polished to within a few atomic layers (see Figure 14-9). The fused quartz used to make the spheres was refined into some of the purest materials in the world.

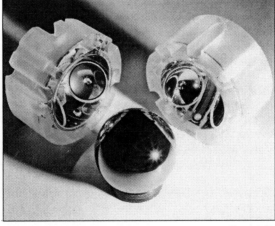

Figure 14-9:
Fused quartz gyroscopes will measure the general relativity predictions.

Courtesy NASA

The gyroscopes needed to be this perfect because the mission will measure the two relativistic effects to an incredible accuracy. If the spheres were not almost perfectly round, the Earth would pull on each of them with a slightly different force, causing the gyroscope to spin and ruining the precision of the measurement. Each sphere also needed to be made up of exactly the same stuff throughout, so that the Earth pulls on all its parts with equal force.

Schiff had calculated that at a 640-km altitude, the curvature of spacetime would turn the gyroscope 6.6 seconds of arc per year and frame dragging would turn it 42 milliseconds of arc per year. A second of arc is a very small angle. If you look at a round clock, each minute mark is 6 degrees apart. One degree has 60 minutes, 3,600 seconds, or 3,600,000 milliseconds of arc. So the minute mark on your clock is separated by 216 million milliseconds of arc (see Figure 14-10). *Gravity Probe B* has to measure the 42 milliseconds of arc with half a millisecond of arc precision. That's like looking at the edge of a sheet of paper from 100 miles away! You can appreciate the reason for the ultra precision in the manufacturing of the gyroscopes.

→ 216,000,000 milliseconds of arc

Figure 14-10: There are 216 million milliseconds of arc in the minute mark of a round clock.

If the gyroscopes are almost perfect spheres, how do you know which way they are moving? The whole purpose of the mission is to measure tiny deviations in the orientation of the spinning balls. To be able to do this, the spheres were coated with a layer of *niobium,* an element that becomes a superconductor when cooled to very low temperatures, close to absolute zero. In a superconductor, there is no resistance to the flow of current. As a result, it generates a magnetic field with the north and south poles lined up with the axis of rotation of the ball. Measuring the magnetic fields gives the scientists the direction in which the balls are spinning.

Because the niobium needed to become a superconductor by lowering the temperature, 650 gallons of superfluid helium went on the mission. That amount will keep the gyroscopes cooled for the 16-month estimated duration of the mission.

Many other technological hurdles had to be overcome to get to this point. About 100 doctoral dissertations were written on the new technologies during the nearly 40 years that it took to develop the mission. If the experiment is successful, it will be the most precise test of general relativity ever conducted.

So, Was He Right?

A scientific theory can never be proven correct. It can, however, be disproved. "There could be no fairer destiny for any . . . theory," wrote Einstein, "than that it should point the way to a more comprehensive theory in which it lives on, as a limiting case."

If scientific theories can't be proven correct, how do scientists know if they are on the right track? The technique is simple and powerful. They use the theory to make predictions of the outcome of experiments. If the predictions turn out to be correct, the theory gains strength. The more confirmed predictions, the stronger the theory.

You can see why theories can never be proven correct. There is always the possibility that someone will make that one experiment or observation that will disprove one or more of the predictions of the theory. If *Gravity Probe B* determines that there is no frame drag, that space isn't dragged along as the Earth rotates, then that particular prediction of general relativity is wrong. But it won't be just that prediction. The entire theory will be shown to be incorrect. Or, most likely, incomplete.

On the other hand, if *Gravity Probe B* measures a frame drag with the values predicted by general relativity, all you can say is that the theory is very strong, that it has passed all the tests that have been designed for almost a century. But you can't say that all future tests will be equally successful.

Part IV
The General Theory of Relativity

The 5th Wave   By Rich Tennant

"Along with 'Antimatter' and 'Dark Matter', we've recently discovered the existence of 'Doesn't Matter', which seems to have no effect on the universe whatsoever."

In this part . . .

The general theory of relativity is Einstein's crowning achievement. It was the successful result of his incredible four-year effort to extend his special theory of relativity. In this part, I tell you what this theory means and what it does to our conception of the universe.

The general theory shows that light can be trapped in a black hole. I describe what these strange objects are and what a trip into one of them might be like.

Speaking of strange objects, I discuss the possibility of tunnels or wormholes into another universe. Can these wormholes be used for time travel? I tell you what Einstein's theories have to say about that.

But, have all these strange ideas been checked? Was Einstein right? You'll see the many efforts to check on Einstein that scientists at universities around the world and at NASA have undertaken, as well as what the results say.

Chapter 15

Atoms Before Einstein

* *

In This Chapter

▷ Considering Einstein's PhD thesis

▷ Exploring the nature of the atom

▷ Refining our understanding of the atom and its components

▷ Explaining light quanta

▷ Introducing Bohr's atom

* *

As I explain in Chapter 4, the idea of the atom didn't originate in the modern world. The Greek philosopher Democritus, who lived in the fifth century B.C., first penned the idea that all things are made up of small, indivisible particles called atoms, meaning "indivisible."

But the human race got a little distracted and forgot all about the atom for about two millennia. In the 19th century, English chemist John Dalton reintroduced the idea and backed it up with some experiments.

In his PhD thesis, Einstein showed the world how to determine the real dimensions of atoms. But he didn't develop his ideas in isolation; as always, he used the existing knowledge of atoms at the time as a springboard. In this chapter, I show you what that existing knowledge was. I give you a quick tour of what Einstein knew about the atom as he was working on his PhD, and I explain some important discoveries during Einstein's lifetime that changed the way we think about matter.

Greek atomic physics

In the fifth century BC, Democritus thought that everything was made up of indivisible atoms that came in different sizes, masses, and colors. He explained that the different substances we see are combinations of these atoms.

But the ancient Greeks didn't really do much science in the way we understand it today. Except for Archimedes (whose work I describe in Chapter 4), the Greek thinkers were thinking, not experimenting. Their ideas were much further ahead than their technology. You need delicate instruments to show that atoms exist, and the Greeks didn't have them.

It's no wonder that the idea of atoms didn't catch on. Aristotle came along with the much simpler idea that everything is made up of only four elements — earth, water, air, and fire. He explained that these four elements have their own natural place, and that motion is an attempt to reach these natural places. His idea, which was easier to digest, caught on.

Proving the Reality of Atoms

Einstein's PhD thesis was entitled "A new determination of molecular dimensions." He wrote it during the incredible output of creativity of his miracle year (see Chapter 3). This thesis was part of his second attempt at getting a PhD. He'd tried before, back in 1901, a year and a half after graduating from the Polytechnic. (At that time, he'd submitted a thesis on molecular forces, but it was rejected. See the sidebar "Einstein's rejected thesis.")

In his PhD dissertation, Einstein described a new method to calculate the diameters of individual molecules, as well as a new way to calculate Avogadro's number. This number had been discovered in 1811 by the Italian physicist Amadeo Avogadro in connection with his suggestion that the same volumes of any gas kept at the same temperature and pressure contain the same number of molecules; the chemical or physical properties of the gas don't affect the number of molecules. Avogadro's theory inspired experiments that eventually determined that a specific volume of any gas (22.4 liters, or the volume of a box that holds a basketball) contains what we now call *Avogadro's number* of molecules. Avogadro's number is 600 sextillion (6 followed by 23 zeros) molecules — a mind-boggling number.

With Einstein's dissertation paper, as well as with a follow-up paper he wrote that explained *Brownian motion* (the constant motion of tiny particles that had been observed by Scottish botanist Robert Brown), Einstein was concerned with "discovering facts which would guarantee as far as possible the existence of atoms of definite, finite size."

Today, we can see atoms. Modern scanning tunneling microscopes can map surfaces with atomic resolution. Figure 15-1 shows a scanning tunneling microscope image of graphite atoms. Graphite is a form of carbon, and each hill is a carbon atom. The distance between adjacent carbon atoms is 25 billionths of a centimeter.

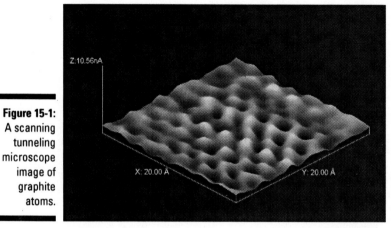

Figure 15-1:
A scanning
tunneling
microscope
image of
graphite
atoms.

Image by the author

Even back in the 1950s, field ion microscopes allowed scientists to obtain direct images of atoms. Not so at the beginning of the 20th century. Although most physicists and chemists accepted the reality of atoms, there were still some doubters. So Einstein set out to offer irrefutable proof of atoms' existence.

Einstein's rejected thesis

Einstein's first attempt at getting a PhD was unsuccessful because of a combination of politics and a bit of immaturity on Einstein's part. After graduating from the Polytechnic, he'd been accepted as a doctoral student by Dr. Alfred Kleiner at the University of Zurich and was working on a thesis on molecular forces.

He became interested in physicist Paul Drude's work on the theory of metals, which indicated that electrons behave as a gas within a metal. Einstein was impressed with this work but found a couple of flaws with Drude's theory. It appears that Einstein didn't agree with Drude's assumption that there were both positive and negative charges within the metal. Einstein's second objection was related to Drude's use of Ludwig Boltzmann's statistical theory on molecular motion, in which he had also found a gap.

Einstein wrote to Drude expressing his concerns. Drude replied to Einstein, dismissing his disagreement and stating that an eminent colleague had agreed with his theory. Einstein became angry. In a letter to his fiancée, Mileva Maric, Einstein promised to attack Drude in the *Annalen der Physik* (which was going to be a bit difficult because Drude was the editor).

Einstein included his criticisms of Drude's theories in his thesis, even though they weren't directly related to his subject matter. Kleiner was not about to approve a thesis that criticized Drude or questioned Boltzmann's well-established theory. He rejected it.

Understanding Atoms with a Grain of Salt

Atoms are complicated little things. Take your salt shaker and sprinkle a few grains on the table. Each one of those tiny grains has one *quintillion* (1 followed by 18 zeros) atoms of sodium and the same number of atoms of chlorine. How did we ever discover what these incredibly small things are made of? It wasn't easy.

Figuring out why balloons pop

The first step on the long road was taken in 1738, when the Swiss mathematician Daniel Bernoulli used the idea that gases are made up of small particles to explain how these gases exert pressure on a container. He explained that the pressure is due to the collisions of these particles with the walls of the container.

According to Bernoulli, if you have a gas in a container, the pressure of the gas comes from the speed of the molecules hitting the walls of the container and how often they hit it. The speed of the molecules is related to temperature. If you keep the same volume, pressure, and temperature, then you always have the same number of molecules.

Eighty years before Bernoulli, Newton's contemporary Robert Boyle had performed experiments with gases and discovered what we know today as *Boyle's law,* which explains how the pressure of a gas increases when its volume decreases (as long as we keep the gas at the same temperature). For example, if you squeeze a balloon, the pressure increases. If you keep squeezing harder and harder, the pressure becomes so large that the balloon pops.

Bernoulli analyzed the increase in particle collisions when the volume of a container (such as a balloon) shrinks. In doing so, he was able to arrive at the same mathematical conclusion stated in Boyle law. Bernoulli's analysis marks the first time that anyone used the idea of atoms as the building blocks of matter to successfully calculate a property of something.

Explaining elements

The next important step toward the understanding of the atom was the discovery that certain substances can't be reduced any further by chemical means. These basic substances, or *elements,* combine in very specific and predictable ways to form all the substances that we know.

In 1808, the great chemist John Dalton showed that you can explain these chemical rules of how the elements combine with each other by assuming three things:

✔ Each element is made of a specific atom.

✔ All the atoms of the same element are identical and different from the atoms of other elements.

✔ These atoms combine in very specific ways to form all the substances we see in the universe.

Another line of work, initially unrelated to the search for the atom, was taking place in the 19th century. Michael Faraday, the self-taught English scientist who invented the idea of fields (see Chapter 6), was studying how electrical currents break up water and other chemical compounds. He proposed that electricity wasn't a fluid but existed as small particles that carry the electric charge, as Ben Franklin had suggested. Some time later, scientists began to call these particles *electrons*.

Discovering electrons

In the late 19th century, scientists studying electricity began to use an apparatus made of a sealed glass tube with no air in it that had two small metal discs at each end (see Figure 15-2). The metal discs were connected to a battery, and the idea was to see what would happen with electricity in the vacuum of the tube.

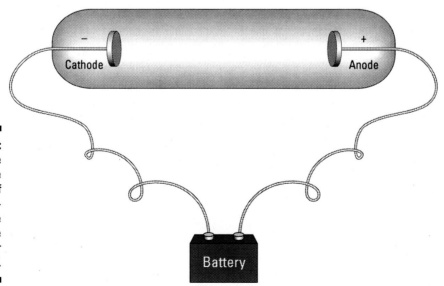

Figure 15-2:
A cathode ray tube, the precursor of the television tube and the computer CRT.

What happened was that the tube glowed with a strange green light. At the time, this phenomenon had no explanation. Physicists called the metal disk that emitted the glow the *cathode* and the opposite disk the *anode*. The cathode was connected to the negative end of the battery and the anode to the positive. The rays were named *cathode rays,* and the whole device was a *cathode ray tube,* or CRT. (You probably use CRTs all the time. Television tubes are CRTs, and older computer models use them as well.)

In 1897, at the Cavendish laboratory in Cambridge, England, the physicist J.J. Thomson, the director of the lab, designed experiments in an effort to understand the nature of the mysterious green glow in CRTs. Thomson and his 20 researchers were able to deflect the green light beam and discovered that it had a negative charge. Thomson concluded that the green glow was made by individual particles passing through the vacuum of the tube, and he was able to measure their charge. These negatively charged particles were later called *electrons.*

Thomson was also able to measure the ratio of the electron's mass to its charge. That measurement told him that these electrons are about 2,000 times smaller than the smallest atom, hydrogen.

Envisioning plum pudding

Atoms, then, aren't the smallest bits of matter, like Dalton had said. These electrons are much smaller still. Are atoms made up of electrons? That possibility sounded interesting to Thomson. However, matter is neutral, and these electrons are negatively charged.

Thomson needed some positive body in the atom that would counterbalance the negative electrons and form a neutral atom. He proposed a plum pudding type of arrangement. The electrons would be the raisins, and the pudding was the positive body in the atom (see Figure 15-3).

As soon as Thomson proposed his model, two major discoveries made it obsolete. In Germany, Wilhelm Roentgen discovered a powerful radiation that he called *x-rays.* In Paris, Henri Becquerel and Marie and Pierre Curie, experimenting with uranium crystals, discovered that certain atoms emit radiation of a type that they hadn't seen before. The new phenomenon was called *radioactivity.*

What was causing these new rays? Thomson's atom, with electrons in a positive "pudding," wouldn't account for these rays coming out of certain atoms. Clearly, there were other things inside the atom.

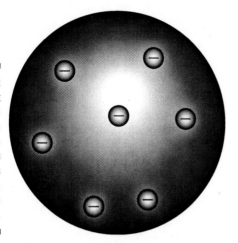

Figure 15-3:
The first model of the atom, with the negative electrons like raisins inside a positive pudding.

One of J.J. Thomson's former students, a New Zealander by the name of Ernest Rutherford, saw that the radioactivity that the French scientists had discovered was of two different kinds. He placed sheets of aluminum foil in front of the device that was detecting the radiation and noticed that he could easily stop one kind of radiation, which he called *alpha rays,* while the other, the *beta rays,* required more sheets of aluminum to stop. (Later, physicists discovered yet another type, *gamma rays.*) As I explain in the next section, Rutherford later showed that the alpha rays have positive charge. And the Paris group showed that the beta rays are negative.

Probing the Atom

What scientists needed was a way to look inside the atom. Physicists knew that atoms were too small to be seen even with the most powerful microscopes available.

Rutherford and his assistant, Hans Geiger, discovered that when an alpha particle hit a screen painted with a specific type of coating, the coating would flash. The coating gave Rutherford the tool he needed. He couldn't see the atom, but he might be able to see what the atom does to the alpha particles if he could throw the particles at the atom. Because he now had a way to detect the alpha particles, he could see where they hit and how the atoms changed or didn't change their path.

Think of Rutherford's experiment this way: If you are in a pitch-dark room and have a ball painted with a fluorescent paint, you can throw the ball around and see how it bounces off any columns or walls (see Figure 15-4). You can't see the walls, but you can deduce their presence by looking at how the ball bounces off them.

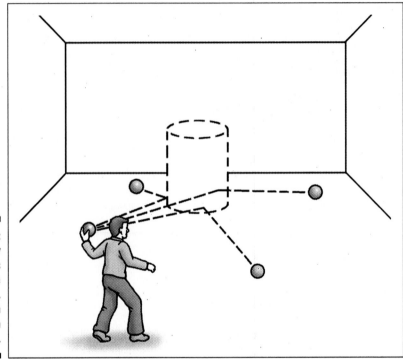

Figure 15-4:
If you throw projectiles at invisible obstacles, you can make them visible.

That's what Rutherford did: He threw alpha particles at gold atoms to see how the particles would bounce off the invisible atoms. With Geiger's help, he used the radioactive element radium as his source of alpha particle projectiles, and he aimed the projectiles at the gold atoms in a thin sheet of gold foil. Behind the foil, he placed a screen painted with his new coating (see Figure 15-5). Rutherford asked Geiger to take data and to change the location of the screen around, to see how the alphas were being deflected.

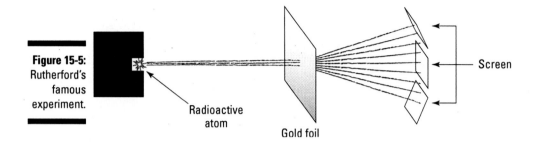

Figure 15-5:
Rutherford's
famous
experiment.

Radioactive
atom

Gold foil

Screen

Recall that J.J. Thomson had found that atoms contain negative electrons. But Thomson and other scientists knew that something positive must be in the atom as well, to balance the negative electrons, because atoms are electrically neutral. *What* was that positive something, and *where* was it? That's what Rutherford wanted to know.

The flashes on Rutherford's screen provided the answer. Geiger was back in the lab taking data. He saw most of the flashes when the screen was placed right on the other side of the gold foil or within a couple of degrees. Rutherford was expecting that. A fast alpha particle would pass through the crowd of electrons in the gold atom and, in general, continue on its path. Every once in a while, one alpha might go closer to an electron or two so that their electrical repulsion would push it away a bit. But the repulsion wouldn't push it much, because the alphas were coming through fast.

Rutherford wanted to see what would happen if they moved the screen farther out still. He asked a bright undergraduate by the name of Ernest Marsden to move the screen up to about 45 degrees and to take the data. Marsden did and got a few flashes. Encouraged by this result, Marsden decided to move the screen out farther. Fifty degrees, sixty. He got some flashes. Seventy? Still some. He was getting counts with the screen at 75 and 80 degrees. Surely, if you placed the screen at right angles with the incoming alphas, you wouldn't get anything. He did, and he saw some flashes.

What if he went to the other side? Still a few counts. All the way to the back? A few counts even there. He reported his results to Rutherford. Rutherford, who understood fully what he was doing, was astonished. It was like firing a 15-inch shell at tissue paper and expecting to see the bullet bounce back at you, he said later.

Creating a new model

These fast alphas were encountering something very strong inside the nucleus that made them bounce back. Rutherford made some calculations and decided that for that phenomenon to happen, the atom had to have a very small core of positive charge in the middle — a positively charged nucleus. And the nucleus would contain most of the mass of the atom (see Figure 15-6).

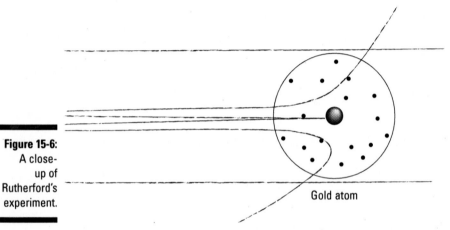

Figure 15-6:
A close-up of Rutherford's experiment.

Gold atom

Rutherford published his results in 1911. In his paper, he proposed a new model of the atom, with a tiny, positively charged nucleus containing 99.9 percent of the mass of the entire atom. In this model, the negatively charged electrons are distributed throughout the volume of the atom, like a planetary system (see Figure 15-7). The total charge of the electrons is equal and opposite to the charge of the nucleus.

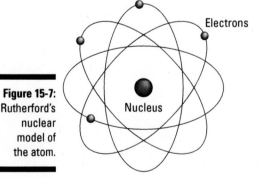

Electrons

Figure 15-7:
Rutherford's nuclear model of the atom.

Nucleus

And, Rutherford said, the atom is very small. If you line up ten trillion atoms next to each other, they measure one centimeter (about half an inch). Also, the atom is almost empty. If the atom was the size of a concert hall, the nucleus would look like a pea at the center with the electrons like bees flying around.

Things were looking bright now. There was even a candidate for the positive particle that lived in the atomic nucleus: the proton. In Germany in 1886, Eugen Goldstein had observed positively charged particles that were 1,836 times more massive than the electron. Although they were more massive, the amount of electric charge these particles carried was the same as that of the electron.

Predicting an unrealized collapse

Soon, physicists calculated that the nucleus of hydrogen is a single proton. Hydrogen is simple: a proton at the center forming the nucleus, and a single electron moving around it.

Other atoms are more complex and were more challenging. Measurements and calculations were not working out for these atoms. The main problem was with the electrons moving around the nucleus. James Clerk Maxwell's electromagnetism said that such an electric charge that moved around in a curved path would radiate energy. That meant the electrons should lose energy as they moved around in the atom, spiraling down and collapsing into the nucleus. Physicists calculated that it would take about a microsecond for this collapse to happen. But the collapse doesn't happen; atoms are stable.

The solution came from two scientists who weren't even working on the physics of the atom at the time, Max Planck and Einstein.

Discovering Quanta

At about the time that J.J. Thomson was doing his experiments with cathode ray tubes, Max Planck in Germany was trying to resolve another big unexplained problem in physics. This problem had to do with the way hot objects radiate energy. His explanation eventually helped scientists explain why the electron in an atom doesn't collapse into the nucleus. But before it did that, Planck's solution needed Einstein's interpretation.

To understand the problem physicists were grappling with, consider an example close to home. When you turn on an electric stove, you can feel the element getting hot before there's any appreciable change in color. Within a couple minutes, the element begins to glow red, and eventually, when it's hot, it has an orange glow.

This thermal radiation is an electromagnetic wave. Sometimes you can't see it, if the radiation is in the infrared range, for example. But sometimes the wavelength is in the visible range of the spectrum. And other times, the radiation is in the short wavelengths of the ultraviolet region.

Max Planck

Planck was born in Kiel, Germany, in 1858, the sixth son of a professor of Law at the University of Kiel. Planck came from a long line of academics; his grandfather and great-grandfather had also been professors.

When Planck was 9, his father accepted a position at the University of Munich. The high school that Planck attended in Munich had a great math and physics teacher, and Planck became very interested in these two subjects. He was always a top student.

Planck entered the University of Munich to study physics but didn't get along with his professor, Philipp von Jolly. Von Jolly told Planck that there wasn't anything new to be discovered in physics. Unhappy with the university, Planck decided to move to the University of Berlin, where the famous physicists Hermann von Helmholtz and Gustav Kirchhoff taught.

Like Einstein would do some years later, Planck became interested in areas that weren't taught in courses, and he studied Rudolf Clausius's work in thermodynamics from original journal papers. After getting his undergraduate degree, Planck wrote a thesis on the second law of thermodynamics and submitted it as a PhD dissertation to the University of Munich. The dissertation was approved, and Planck obtained his PhD in physics when he was only 21 years old.

Like most PhD physicists at the time, Planck was interested in an academic career. At the time in Germany, if you wanted to be a professor, you started as an instructor, or *Privatdozent*— an unpaid position with teaching duties. Privatdozents collected small fees from the students for administering exams. But you needed another job to survive. Planck was a Privatdozent in Munich from 1880 to 1885. In 1885, he was promoted to associate professor, which meant he finally got a regular salary for teaching.

With a steady income, he married his childhood girlfriend, Marie Merck. In 1889, Planck moved to the University of Berlin as a full professor, replacing Kirchhoff, who was retiring.

Planck was also a gifted pianist and seriously considered a career in music before deciding on physics. He became one of the most important scientists of all time, earning the Nobel Prize in physics in 1918 for his discovery of the quantum of energy.

Pitting theory against the real world

What is the source of this thermal radiation? When Planck began to study the problem, the prevalent model assumed that the thermal energy emitted by an object was formed by the continuous changes in energy of charged particles oscillating within the matter (see Figure 15-8). In this model, the distribution of energies at shorter and shorter wavelengths grew larger and larger, eventually tending toward infinity. This prediction was not only impossible; it was completely opposite to what Planck and other scientists were observing.

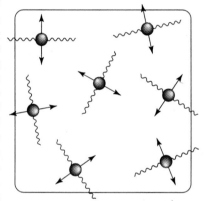

Figure 15-8:
The heat radiated by an object comes from the energy changes of charged particles oscillating inside the body.

What physicists were observing was that at short wavelengths, the energy distributions actually grew smaller and smaller, moving toward zero at the very short wavelengths. These very short wavelengths are in the ultraviolet part of the spectrum, and physicists refer to this problem as the *ultraviolet catastrophe.*

The model predicted that bodies should radiate more energy at short wavelengths. The observations showed that bodies emit less energy at these wavelengths. The problem was serious, because the solutions that physicists were proposing were based on a very solid theoretical framework, but the real world data wasn't matching. Physicists were worried because their failure to explain these new observations meant that *thermodynamics,* the study of heat and thermal effects (see Chapter 5), was flawed.

In 1900, when Planck was a professor of physics at the University of Munich, he decided to tackle the radiation problem. He used Maxwell's electromagnetism to develop a theory that connected the heat or thermal energy of the radiating body and the charged oscillating particles. To do that, he had to use the statistical methods that Ludwig Boltzmann had invented for the distribution of energies in molecular collisions.

Splitting energy bundles

To derive his formula using Boltzmann's statistical methods, Planck first had to split the total energy being radiated from an object into a number of bundles or packets all with the same energy. He then counted the possible ways of distributing these bundles among all the oscillating particles. Planck published his results in a series of papers between 1897 and 1900.

Planck's formula, known today as *Planck's law,* agreed perfectly with the observations. Planck, however, didn't like the method he'd used to derive his equation. He wasn't happy about using statistical methods in physics. But his equation worked.

At first, scientists didn't appreciate the importance of Planck's discovery. Planck himself didn't fully understand what he'd done. His idea of splitting the total energy of the oscillators into bundles, or *quanta* (as they are called today), marked a turning point in the history of physics and made possible the development of the physics of the atom by Einstein and others.

Exploring the Bohr Atom

Planck's law with the total energy radiated by a hot object split into bundles or quanta of energy was later generalized by Einstein into a revolutionary idea that started quantum theory. I discuss that development in Chapter 16. Here, I return to the problem of the collapse of the electron in orbit about the nucleus in Rutherford's model.

In James Clerk Maxwell's theory of electromagnetism, the charged electron moving around the nucleus gives off energy. (In the same way, Planck's oscillating charges give off the energy of radiation in a hot object.) As these charges give off energy, they should fall into the nucleus in about a microsecond. But they don't. Atoms are stable.

Rutherford proposed his model in 1911. Planck had published his solution to the ultraviolet catastrophe and the explanation of the energy distribution of objects in 1900. During his year of miracles, in 1905, Einstein generalized Planck's idea of the energy quanta into a property of light and radiation.

All the elements were there to solve the riddle of the collapsing atom. But no one did. At least not right away.

Kicking marbles on a staircase

In 1913, the Danish physicist Niels Bohr came up with a new model of the atom that avoided the collapse of the electron. His model was similar to Rutherford's planetary model but had an important difference. In Bohr's model, the electrons orbit the nucleus in very specific orbits that he called *stationary orbits*. In these orbits, the electrons are safe. They don't radiate any energy.

In Bohr's theory, the electrons are allowed to move between orbits. When they jump to a lower orbit, they give off energy. After they arrive there, they are safe again, in another stationary orbit. If they gain energy, they jump to a higher orbit.

The electrons in Bohr's atom are like marbles on a staircase (see Figure 15-9). If you carefully place a marble at the edge of one of the steps, it stays there safe. You can give the marble some energy by kicking it up. If you do that, the marble will land one, two, or any other number of steps higher and stay there. When the marble loses energy, it falls down, landing one, two, or several steps down. You can't kick a marble so that it moves two and a half steps up. A marble that rolls off a given step won't move down and stop in the middle of two steps, floating there. The *allowed orbits* for the marble are the steps.

Bohr said the same is true with electrons. Electrons can stay only in the *allowed orbits*. The places in between aren't allowed.

Figure 15-9:
Electrons in
the Bohr
atom are like
marbles on
a staircase.
They are
allowed only
on certain
specific
orbits.

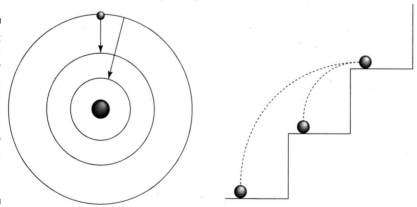

The energies that the electrons give off or gain when they jump around in their orbits are Planck's bundles or quanta. Electrons are allowed to give off or gain energy only in the form of these quanta.

Bohr used Planck's theory to calculate the energies of the allowed stationary orbits for the atom. When he compared his calculations with experimental data, his theory agreed exactly.

Needing a new physics

Bohr's theory provided a great advance toward the understanding of the atom. But it wasn't the final word. When Bohr tried to apply his theory to other more complicated atoms, things didn't work out as nicely. The energies of his allowed orbits didn't quite match the energies measured for those atoms.

Soon, physicists realized that they needed something else. The physics of Newton and Maxwell, patched up with Planck's and Bohr's discoveries, wasn't cutting it. A few physicists knew that a new physics was needed. The 26-year-old Einstein would give them the key to this new physics. Take a look at Chapter 16 for the details.

Chapter 16

Quantum Leap: God Plays Dice

*R*elativity was not Einstein's only revolutionary theory. He also made possible quantum theory.

Quantum theory was born in March of 1905, with Einstein's first paper of his year of miracles (see Chapter 3). The title of the paper was "On a heuristic point of view concerning the production and transformation of light." If you look up *heuristic* in a dictionary, you'll find that it means "serving to guide, discover, or reveal; valuable for empirical research, but unproved or incapable of proof." That definition summarizes Einstein's feelings about quantum theory.

After helping create quantum theory, Einstein had second thoughts about its implications. He could never accept that "God would play dice with the universe," as he put it. Throughout his life, Einstein thought that quantum theory was not the final word and that one day it would be replaced by the true theory of the atom.

However, as I show you in this chapter, scientists think that quantum theory is here to stay.

Discovering the Quantum

In 1900, Max Planck applied Ludwig Boltzmann's ideas on statistical mechanics to the data that physicists were getting for the radiation of hot objects. The problem that physicists hadn't been able to solve was in the high-energy region, where their equations were giving them nonsense answers.

Planck came up with a solution, but in doing so, he had to split the total energy being absorbed by an object into bundles of energy, each containing the same amount. In Chapter 15, I explain that Planck wasn't too happy about using statistics in physics, and he didn't fully understand the implications of what he'd done. But until 1905, when Einstein published his "heuristic" paper, Planck's paper remained a successful method to reproduce the data.

Revealing Einstein's "revolutionary idea"

In his March 1905 paper, Einstein started by showing why existing equations couldn't really be applied to the problem of the radiation of objects. The old equations worked fine in the low energy region, but they failed in the high energy region. Einstein explained why, in the high energy region, the equation solutions indicated there was an infinite amount of energy.

Einstein then set out to study the problem in a way "which is not based on a picture of the generation and propagation of radiation." In other words, he wasn't using Planck's method. He decided to start from basic physics principles. When he was done, he'd shown that the radiation of hot objects behaves as if it were made up of separate *quanta* (bundles or packets) of energy. Einstein assumed that the energy of each quantum is related to the wavelength of the radiation emitted: The shorter the wavelength, the larger the value of the energy.

Up to this point, there was no revolution. Like Planck and everyone else had assumed, these light quanta could be interpreted as a curious property of the radiation from hot objects. But Einstein took a bold step (which eventually gained him the Nobel Prize in 1922). He declared that matter and radiation can interact only by exchanging these energy quanta.

Here is what Einstein said:

> ✔ Light (and all electromagnetic radiation) is made up of quanta of energy, bundles or packets with energies that are related to the wavelength of the light.

✔ The shorter the wavelength, the larger the amount of energy of a light quantum, or *photon*.

✔ These photons cannot be split.

Light isn't just a wave, as Thomas Young's experiments had shown (see Chapter 7). Instead, Einstein said, light is made up of quanta of energy, and these quanta (or photons) are like particles. They're not exactly like little dust particles, but light has particle properties. A photon has a fixed amount of energy, and it exerts pressure on objects. It interacts with other particles in a particle-like way, not in a wavelike way. Light is lumpy.

In Chapter 7, I explain that Young's experiment showed once and for all that light is a wave, and his famous interference experiment is repeated today in schools all over the world to show students the wave nature of light. Waves aren't particles. Waves and particles have very different properties. These two ideas are mutually contradictory. It's like day and night, on and off. If you have one, you can't have the other. What gives? Is light a wave, or is it a particle?

It's both. Before Einstein came along, this statement would have been non-sense. But in the quantum physics that Einstein started, it makes sense. However, it would take 20 years for scientists to resolve the seemingly inherent contradiction.

Identifying quanta of various energies

With Einstein's new view of the nature of light, Planck's radiation law became the accepted explanation for the radiation of hot objects. This law indicates that the thermal energy emitted by an object comes from charged particles oscillating inside the object and that these oscillations have only some specific energies. Einstein hadn't been satisfied with Planck's radiation law before, because it hadn't made sense. With his new insight, it made sense, and he was ready to embrace it. "Planck's theory makes implicit use of the . . . light-quantum hypothesis," he said.

Einstein's light-quantum idea explained the strange results that physicists were seeing in their study of the radiation from hot objects. They'd been measuring the energy radiated at different lengths and were seeing that at long and inter-mediate wavelengths, things made sense. But at very short wavelengths, their measurements were showing very little radiation. They couldn't understand that result. Their equations predicted that as they looked at shorter and shorter wavelengths, the energies should be larger and larger. As Figure 16-1 shows, the results of their equations differed greatly from the results of their experiments.

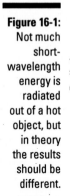

Figure 16-1:
Not much
short-
wavelength
energy is
radiated
out of a hot
object, but
in theory
the results
should be
different.

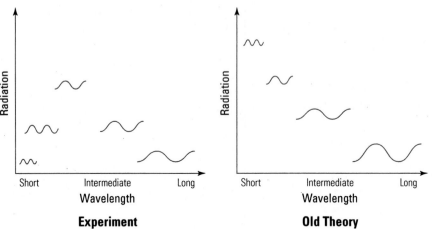

Experiment

Old Theory

The light quantum idea made the experiment results clear. Planck had proposed that the thermal energy emitted by an object comes from charged particles oscillating inside the object (see Chapter 15). The energy of each photon depends on the wavelength of the oscillating particle (see Figure 16-2). At short wavelengths, the radiation from a hot object is made up of high-energy photons. (Short wavelength photons have larger energies.) Very few oscillators have photons with these energies, so only a few of these high-energy photons are emitted. That's why the scientists were detecting very little radiation at these short wavelengths.

Figure 16-2:
Low-energy
photons
have long
wave-
lengths,
while high-
energy
photons
have short
wave-
lengths.

Low energy photon
(long wavelength)

High energy photon
(short wavelength)

At long wavelengths, the photons have low energies, and many more oscillators have these energies. Many more of these low-energy photons can be emitted, but because each one has little energy, the total amount of energy from all of them is not too large. At the middle wavelengths, you have quite a few oscillators that emit photons of moderate size. As a result, the largest emission of energy occurs at the middle wavelengths, as the experiments were showing.

Planck's great insight, validated by Einstein's generalization, was to realize that the energies are related to the different wavelengths of the light emitted by the oscillators, instead of assuming that the energies are all equally distributed, like previous theories had done. Einstein's great insight was to make this idea a fundamental property of nature. Light and all electromagnetic radiation are made up of quanta; light is "quantized."

The step size of these quanta is determined by a constant now called *Planck's constant*. As Figure 16-3 shows, radiations of shorter wavelengths carry more energy (larger steps) and are identical to each other. But those radiations are different from the ones that consist of larger wavelengths. Just as you can't split the steps of a staircase, you can't split photons.

According to Einstein and Planck, then,

> *The energy of a light quantum or photon is related to the wavelength of the light; this energy is "quantized" with the step size determined by Planck's constant.*

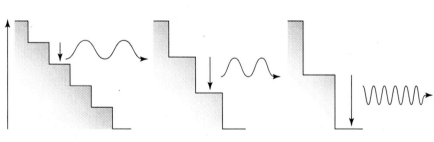

Figure 16-3:
Light and all electromagnetic radiation is quantized. All the photons radiated at one wavelength have the same energy and are identical.

Solving the photoelectric effect

Another nagging problem in physics, called the *photoelectric effect,* had also resisted all attempts at explanation. Heinrich Hertz had seen this effect in 1887, and physicists were puzzled by it.

What is the photoelectric effect? If you shine a beam of light on a certain material, you can detect electrons that are ejected from the metal. (That's what happens in the solar cells that power our modern devices, from calculators and swimming pool heaters to the Martian rovers.) The electrons that are ejected form the electric current that runs the device. If you increase the brightness of the light, you get more electricity out of the cell (see the top of Figure 16-4). However,

- ✔ The speeds of the electrons emitted don't change when you increase the brightness.

- ✔ What's worse, if you increase the wavelength beyond a certain value, you won't get anything out of the cell, regardless of how bright the light is (see the bottom of Figure 16-4).

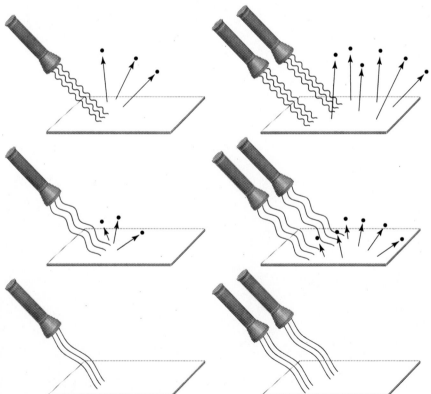

Figure 16-4:
Puzzling
experiments
when
shining a
light on
certain
materials.

The solution again came from Einstein's light-quantum idea. How does the light quantum solve the first problem? When you shine a light at the material, you are sending photons of a certain energy. Suppose that the light is *mono-chromatic* (of a single color). In this case, the wavelength of light is fixed, and all the photons that strike the surface have the same energy. When one of the photons strikes the material, all of its energy is transmitted to an electron in the material. The electron then takes in one of these photons and uses its energy to get out of the material. When you increase the brightness, you aren't increasing the energy of each photon, you are simply sending in more photons all of the same energy. The chances of one electron taking in more than one photon are very small, so increasing the brightness releases more electrons. However, it doesn't affect their speeds.

The solution to the second problem is simpler. It takes energy for the electron to negotiate its way out of the material. The energy that it receives from the light comes in these photons of fixed energy. Each single photon has to provide one electron with enough energy to leave the material. If you shine a light of low-energy photons, ones from a light with long wavelength, these photons may not have the minimum energy needed. Increasing the brightness of the light only increases the number of these low-energy photons, not their energy.

Imagining Waves of Matter

How did physicists react to having these two nagging and long-standing problems solved? Not surprisingly, with skepticism. In 1905, Einstein was an unknown. However, after the barrage of amazing papers he published that year, it was difficult *not* to know about him. Planck was one of the first physicists to acknowledge his brilliance and one of the early proponents of the theory of relativity.

The light-quantum idea was another matter. Not even Planck accepted it, even though it helped explain his own discovery. As late as 1913, when Einstein was recognized as one of the top European physicists (and at that time, physics was done mostly in Europe), there was strong opposition to his quantum idea. When Einstein was proposed for membership in the Prussian Academy of Sciences in 1913, Planck and other illustrious physicists wrote in their official recommendation as follows:

> *One can only say that there is hardly one among the great problems in which modern physics is so rich to which Einstein has not made a remarkable contribution. That he may sometimes have missed the target in his specula-tions, as, for example, in his hypothesis of light-quanta, cannot be held too much against him.*

For 15 years, Einstein stood alone in his belief of the light-quantum idea. In 1918, Einstein said that he no longer doubted the reality of quanta, "even though I am still alone in this conviction." After that, things began to change very rapidly.

Finding a new way to count

In June of 1924, Einstein received a letter from a young, unknown Indian physicist by the name of Saryendra Bose, who was a professor at the University of Dacca. With the letter came a paper in which Bose derived Planck's radiation formula by imagining a gas of photons, applying the statistical methods used with regular gases to count the photons in a new way, and assuming that you couldn't distinguish the photons. Einstein was immediately interested in Bose's derivation and translated the paper into German for publication in a journal. Einstein then extended this new counting method and applied it to atoms and molecules. The method is known today as *Bose–Einstein statistics.*

Again, Einstein made a leap. From these studies, he concluded not only that light has the dual character of being a wave and a particle, but also that matter shows the same duality. Matter should also have wavelike behavior.

Measuring electron waves

That same year, a graduate student at the University of Paris, Louis de Broglie, finished his PhD dissertation in which he proposed to extend Einstein's dual character of light to particles of matter. Matter, de Broglie said in his thesis, should also have wave properties. "After long reflection," wrote de Broglie, "I had the idea, during 1923, that the discovery made by Einstein in 1905 should be generalized by extending it to all material particles and especially to electrons." In his thesis, de Broglie calculated what the wavelength of an electron should be.

Professor Paul Langevin was a good friend of Einstein's. When his PhD student, de Broglie, gave him the thesis requesting his approval, he wasn't sure about granting a PhD for research based on an idea that could turn out to be incorrect. He asked his student to make a third copy of the dissertation, and he sent it to Einstein for his comments. "A very notable publication," Einstein wrote back. De Broglie defended his thesis on November 25, 1924. He received the Nobel Prize in physics in 1929 for his discovery.

De Broglie suggested ways to test his idea of matter waves by trying to observe interference patterns with electrons. Three years later, two U.S. physicists saw an interference pattern with electron beams. Interference patterns are the trademark of waves; only waves can interact in such ways. De Broglie's matter waves are the basis for the electron microscopes in use today.

Superatoms

The 2001 Nobel Prize in physics was given to three physicists for their experimental creation of the first Bose–Einstein *condensate,* a new state of matter predicted by Bose and Einstein when they first proposed their theory. The three scientists are Carl E. Wieman of the University of Colorado in Boulder, Eric A. Cornell of the National Institute of Standards and Technology, and Wolfgang Ketterle of MIT.

In a Bose–Einstein condensate, a gas is cooled to temperatures so low that the atoms all share the same quantum energy level. The billion or so atoms in the gas become a single "superatom." To create this superatom, the three scientists had to bring the gas to temperatures less than a few billionths of a degree above absolute zero,

all the while preventing the gas from liquefying or even solidifying. The feat was accomplished by trapping the atoms with lasers.

This new state of matter will give scientists a new window to the quantum world, allowing them to probe further the nature of matter. The condensate also has possible practical applications. In 1997, Ketterle's group at MIT was able to extract parts of the condensate like drops from a faucet. They hope to be able to create an atom laser that could be used to build better gyroscopes and more accurate atomic clocks. Other scientists have been able to manipulate condensates on microchips, which eventually will allow the creation of new small instruments and electronic gadgets.

Discovering the New Mechanics of the Atom

During the summer of 1922, Niels Bohr gave a series of lectures at the University of Göttingen in Germany about the new advances in physics. A 22-year-old graduate student by the name of Werner Heisenberg from the University of Munich was in the audience. At one of the lectures, the young Heisenberg made a critical remark. Bohr was intrigued by this student and invited him to go hiking in the Hain Mountain to discuss his questions. Bohr was impressed with Heisenberg and invited him to join his institute in Copenhagen after graduation. "My scientific career only began that afternoon," wrote Heisenberg years later.

In 1924, after getting his PhD, Werner Heisenberg took Bohr up on his offer and joined the Niels Bohr Institute. He was 23 years old. There, he joined a group of young and bright physicists from Europe, the United States, and Russia who were studying the problems of the atom. After about a year, he was invited to return to Göttingen as an assistant to Max Born, the director of the physics institute.

Studying the spectra of atoms

At Göttingen, Heisenberg began to look at the spectra of atoms that scientists were obtaining at the different labs around the world. Scientists had been studying the spectra of atoms for many years.

To observe a particular spectrum, you can place a gas of a particular element (helium, for example) in a glass container and pass a high-intensity light through it (see Figure 16-5). If you then look at this light through a prism, you'll see the *spectrum,* the rainbow of colors. If you place the prism right in front of the incoming light, you notice that the rainbow has some gaps, some small dark areas where the light is missing. If you move the prism to the side and look at the light scattered by the gas, you notice that instead of the dark areas, you see bright areas on top of the rainbow.

Each element has its own very specific set of lines. Hydrogen, for example, has a characteristic set of bright red, blue, and purple lines, while helium is easily identified by its two bright yellow lines very close to each other. The sets of lines are the fingerprints of atoms.

Heisenberg was interested in finding a mathematical expression for the lines of the hydrogen spectrum. He couldn't come up with an equation for them, but in the process he solved another problem.

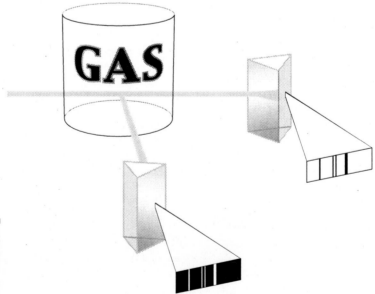

Figure 16-5:
Taking the spectrum of a gas.

In Bohr's model of the atom (which I explain in Chapter 15), the electrons orbit the atom with very specific energies. These energies are quantized, with the electrons jumping from one of these orbits to another as they absorb or eject a photon with the right energy. But what are the actual orbits of the electrons in the atom? Are they circular or near circular, like those of the planets? Heisenberg discovered that there is no need to answer this question. The only thing that matters is what can be measured, like the wavelengths and brightness of the spectral lines of the atom.

In the spring of 1925, Heisenberg had a bout of spring fever and asked Born for a few days off. He went to Helgoland, a small island in the North Sea. Away from the pollen, Heisenberg could think clearly. He realized that he needed to simplify the problem if he wanted to get anywhere. He started from scratch, modeling the atomic vibrations after the simple back-and-forth motion of a pendulum. In a few days, he had some promising calculations. When he got back to Göttingen, he had discovered the new mechanics of the atom.

By July, he'd finished writing his first paper on the theory of this new mechanics. In it, he described the changes in the energy of the atom using an array of numbers that followed some simple rules. He asked Born to check his paper. Born immediately recognized the arrays as being *matrices* — devices that mathematicians had invented some time before. (See the sidebar "The matrix" in this chapter.) The rules that Heisenberg had discovered were the rules of matrix algebra. Born sent the paper for publication and, with his student Pascual Jordan, helped Heisenberg to develop the theory further.

Realizing the world is grainy

The important discovery that Heisenberg made is that quantities that can be measured, like position or speed, can't be represented by plain numbers, like you are used to. They must be represented by these arrays, these matrices, and must follow their special rules.

The matrix

A matrix is a mathematical entity with specific rules on how you must work with it. When Heisenberg discovered that matrices are the correct tools to describe atomic processes, physicists began to take an interest in them. Until then, very few scientists knew that they even existed. Now, the standard college training for scientists in the physical sciences includes a thorough review of matrices. Matrix algebra isn't difficult and can even be fun. The movie is better, though.

For example, with regular numbers, if you multiply 2 times 3 you get 6. You also get 6 if you flip the order of the multiplication: 3 times 2 is the same as 2 times 3. Not so with matrices. Matrices are finicky about the way you manipulate them. For example, the way you rotate an object in space is described with matrices. Take a look at Scenarios A and B and Figure 16-6 to get an idea of how this works.

Scenario A

Suppose that you start with a book sitting flat on your desk, with the cover facing up so that you can read it (see Figure 16-6). Now make these two rotations:

1. **Flip the book toward you holding the far edge, so that the book rests on its bottom edge.** The cover should be face up in front of you now.

2. **Rotate the book counterclockwise from its present position.** You end up with the spine of the book in front of you.

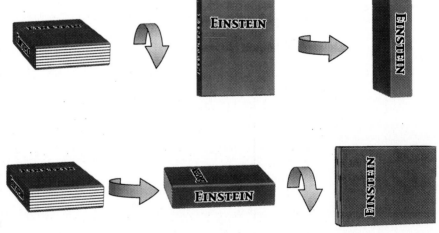

Figure 16-6:
The order in which you rotate a book matters. Atoms have similar properties.

Scenario B

Now, return to the original configuration of the book sitting on the table, and reverse the order of the two rotations:

1. **Rotate the book counterclockwise from its initial position.** The book sits flat on the table with the spine facing you.

2. **Flip the far edge toward you.** The book is now resting on the spine.

The order in which you perform the two rotations matters. There is a difference in the final position of the book. Heisenberg, Born, and Jordan found out that when you do the same sort of thing to atoms, when you flip the order of the operations that you perform, the final configuration changes. And the difference is related to Planck's constant.

Planck's constant measures the "step size" of quanta. If Planck's constant was zero, it wouldn't matter which way the operations with atomic quantities are done. But Planck's constant isn't zero. Therefore, the world is grainy, quantized — changing by steps, not continuously. The steps are extremely small (Planck's constant is very small), and in the normal world of our experiences, you don't see them, not even with precision instruments. (Think of a digital photograph; unless the photo is enlarged substantially, you don't realize the photograph consists of individual pixels.) The world seems smooth and continuous. The size of the graininess is determined by Planck's constant.

That Heisenberg discovered all this in a few days, along the way reinventing some of the mathematical tools he needed, can only be explained as the result of a privileged mind.

Contemplating Wave Mechanics

Erwin Schrödinger, a physics professor at the University of Zurich, wrote to Einstein on November 3, 1925: "A few days ago I read with the greatest interest the ingenious thesis of Louis de Broglie, which I finally got a hold of; with it . . . your second paper . . . has now become clear to me for the first time."

In his thesis, de Broglie stated that a wave must be associated with an electron (see Figure 16-7). The associated wave of an electron orbiting an atom should close in on itself when the electron is in one of the allowed orbits, one of the steps in Bohr's atomic model. If you were to try to calculate the electron wave for a nonallowed orbit, the wave wouldn't close in.

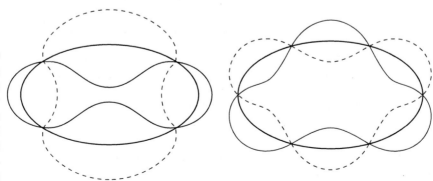

Figure 16-7:
De Broglie's waves for electrons in orbit around the nucleus of an atom.

Doing the math

Schrödinger was intrigued with this idea and decided to apply the mathematics of regular waves (waves on a string or sound waves, for example) to calculate the allowed atomic levels. However, the results that he got didn't agree with the spectral data. Schrödinger decided that this avenue wasn't worth pursuing, and he set the calculations aside for several months.

Luckily, Schrödinger was asked to give a seminar on de Broglie's work at the university. The discussion during the seminar motivated him to return to his work. In a couple of months, he came up with a wave equation that described the wavelike behavior of the electron in space and time and that established the connection between the wave and the particle. With his new equation, Schrödinger calculated the correct light spectrum of hydrogen, matching the experimental data very well.

Schrödinger published a paper on his wave equation in January of 1926, about six months after Heisenberg's publication of his own theory. The world had not just one atomic theory but two: matrix mechanics and wave mechanics. Some time later, the English physicist Paul Dirac showed that these two versions are equivalent. Both versions survived, and we use them today. Schrödinger's wave mechanics is the version that physics students learn first, because it's easier to grasp if you're familiar with regular waves. In graduate school, students move on to the more abstract and somewhat more powerful matrix mechanics. (There is even a third version, invented by Dirac himself, that's a bit more sophisticated and powerful. Grad students sometimes use it in their theses.)

Accepting the uncertainty principle

What are the waves in Schrödinger's wave mechanics? Are the particles themselves moving up and down like a wave? Max Born provided the answer. The waves are waves of probability: the probability of finding the electron at a particular location in space and time.

Are electrons particles or waves? Like light and electromagnetic radiation, electrons are *both* particles and waves. How can this be? You know the drill already. It's a quantum physics thing. In Thomas Young's experiment (see Chapter 7), you pass two coherent light beams (light beams that oscillate in step) through two narrow slits. The two beams overlap, producing bright areas where the waves reinforce each other and dark areas where they cancel each other out. The bright and dark areas form the interference pattern that's the signature of the wave (see Figure 16-8).

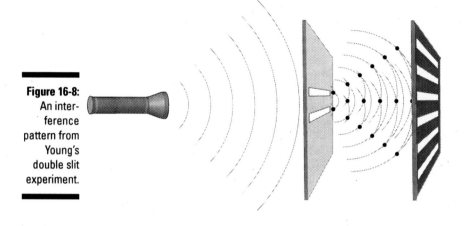

Figure 16-8:
An inter-
ference
pattern from
Young's
double slit
experiment.

Einstein showed that light also has particle properties, the photons. But can you think of light as being made up of these particle-like photons and still have an interference pattern? You might argue that photons, traveling at the speed of light, are really not quite the same as "real" particles, like electrons. But you'll see that electrons are also very alien to the ideas we have in our minds about nature and reality. Let's experiment with an electron and see what happens.

We'll use the same setup from Young's experiment: two narrow slits and a screen. The source of electrons is an electron gun from an old television set. The electrons that come out of the gun form the image on the TV screen when each one of them strikes the phosphor of the screen and lights it up. When you leave both holes open and turn the electron gun on, you see an interference pattern on the screen. Fine. The electrons are behaving like waves, and waves interfere like that (see Figure 16-9).

Figure 16-9:
Electrons
demonstrate
an inter-
ference
pattern,   Electron
which is   gun
characteris-
tic of waves.

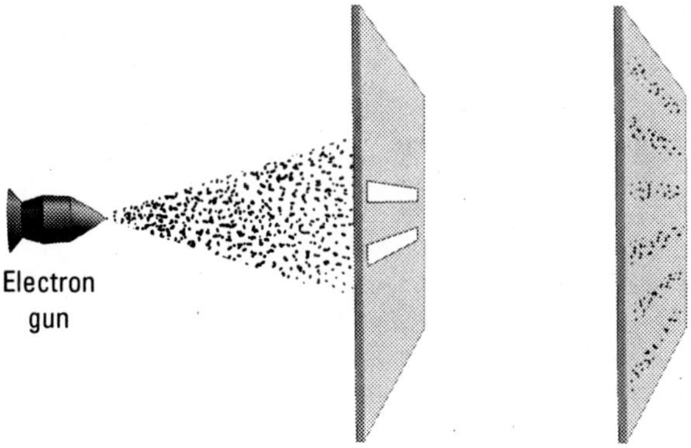

Now, cover one slit and turn the gun on (see Figure 16-10). No interference this time — just a bright area on the screen, the result of the many electrons that went straight through the hole and the ones that might've grazed the edges and got deflected a bit, you think. You get the same result with either hole.

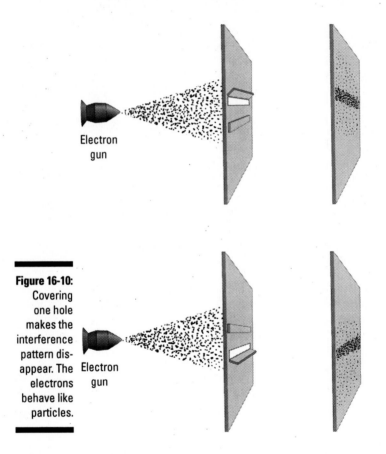

Electron gun

Figure 16-10:
Covering one hole makes the interference pattern disappear. The electrons behave like particles.

Electron gun

The electrons are now behaving like particles. How do they know that you covered one hole?

Open both holes again and try to watch the electrons as they go through. To do that, you install small detectors by each hole and observe. (The detectors may shine some light on the electrons and detect the reflected light.) What you see is that single electrons pass through one hole or the other and hit the screen. Nothing strange — this is what you expect particles to do. But now the interference pattern isn't there. The electrons are acting as particles (see Figure 16-11).

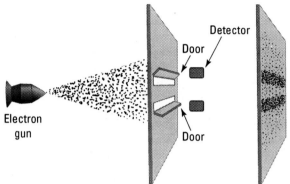

Figure 16-11:
When you watch every single electron that goes by, the interference pattern disappears.

Could it be that the detector is disturbing the electrons when you try to observe them? You can reduce the brightness of the detector light. But light is made up of photons. Reducing the brightness is the same as sending fewer photons to interact with the electrons. You can reduce the brightness until you send just one photon for every electron that passes by. (That's okay, because your detector is very sensitive and can detect single photons.) When you do the experiment, watching every single electron with one single photon, you don't get any interference patterns. The electrons behave like particles.

Reduce the brightness some more. Now you have fewer photons and some electrons go by undetected. When you observe the screen, you see the bright spots in front of the holes that particles form, but you also see a faint interference pattern overlaid on the bright spots. Reduce the brightness some more, and the interference pattern becomes stronger at the same time that the bright spots in front of the holes get fainter (see Figure 16-12).

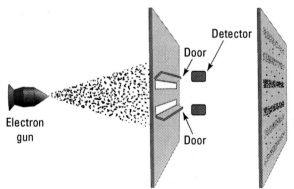

Figure 16-12:
When you don't watch every electron that goes by, the interference pattern begins to reappear.

You can't win. The electrons outsmart any attempt at watching them without disturbing them. The electron is a particle when you try to detect it as a particle, and it's a wave when you try to observe it as a wave. Heisenberg discovered this phenomenon early on, calling it the *uncertainty principle*. The problem is not that you aren't being clever enough or that you lack better instruments. This is just the way the universe is.

Young's experiment is an experiment to detect waves. When you don't attempt to watch the electron, it behaves as a wave and forms an interference pattern. When you try to watch it, you are looking for it as a particle, and that's what you see. Trying to observe the electron changes its behavior.

Succumbing to the New Physics

What is the true nature of the electron? After many years of deep thought and numerous discussions with Einstein, Niels Bohr came to the conclusion that the question doesn't have any meaning. According to Bohr, it's meaningless to ask what an electron really is. Physics isn't about what *is*; it's about telling us something about the world.

Heisenberg's uncertainty principle says that you can't determine with complete accuracy the position of an electron and at the same time measure where and how fast it's going. An electron occupies a place in space only when you measure it at that location. If you measure its location again and find it some place else, that's all you can say. How it got from here to there is a question that has no meaning in physics.

The uncertainty principle doesn't apply just to electrons and atoms. It applies to everything. However, because it involves Planck's constant, which is very small, you don't notice its effects when you are watching baseballs, cars, or planets move.

Einstein didn't buy it

Einstein, the scientist who started quantum physics, didn't buy Bohr's interpretation. He didn't think that the universe was built on the type of uncertainty that quantum physics brings. "God doesn't play dice with the universe," he said once. He couldn't accept that the universe is made with uncertainties and unpredictabilities.

Einstein believed instead that the uncertainties exist only because we don't know enough. There are hidden variables that we aren't seeing yet, but one day we will discover them. In other words, quantum physics isn't complete.

In 1935, Einstein proposed a very clever experiment to show that the uncertainty principle and the unpredictable nature of quantum physics weren't correct. He published a paper with his collaborators Boris Podolsky and Nathan Rosen.

In his *EPR experiment* (as it is called, after the authors' names), Einstein imagined that a particle at rest in a laboratory splits into two equal pieces that fly away from each other (see Figure 16-13). Einstein proposed letting the fragments fly away for a long distance. Suppose that the original particle was in a laboratory on the ground on Earth. Also suppose that the arrival of the two particles is monitored by two detectors: one on the International Space Station, and a second in the Space Shuttle (see Figure 16-14). An astronaut in the Space Station measures the speed of one fragment when it gets there. That's also the same speed of the other fragment moving in the opposite direction toward the Shuttle.

Figure 16-13:
EPR thought experiment. A particle initially at rest splits into two pieces that fly away from each other.

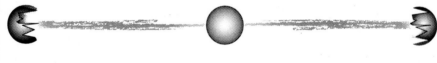

Figure 16-14:
Astronauts in the International Space Station and in the Shuttle perform measurements on the fragments.

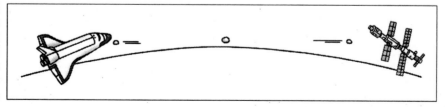

The astronaut in the Space Shuttle measures the position of the fragment arriving there. At that point, she knows the position, the speed, and the direction of her particle, even though she measured only one quantity. And she knows them accurately. No uncertainties here. Heisenberg's uncertainty principle says that you can't know the speed and the location of one of these fragments with complete accuracy. If you know one, you can't know the other. Here was Einstein proposing a clever experiment to do just that.

Bohr sticks to his interpretation

Was it that easy to dethrone quantum physics? This simple thought experiment was saying that Heisenberg's uncertainty principle wasn't right. And the uncertainty principle is at the heart of quantum physics. If the principle doesn't hold, the whole building comes crashing down.

Bohr's response to Einstein's EPR argument was unexpected. He said that because the two fragments were once in contact with each other, they remain linked forever, regardless of how far apart they are. After they break apart, they continue to form the system that you measure.

When the astronaut in the Space Station measures the speed of the fragment arriving there, the position of the fragment arriving at the Shuttle changes in such a way as to make it impossible for the other astronaut to measure it with any accuracy.

Einstein never accepted that idea. He called it "spooky action at a distance." How can one particle at one location be affected by the measurements that you make to another particle very far away? For that to happen, an instantaneous signal must travel from one particle to the other, and according to relativity, no signal can travel faster than light.

It would've been easier to figure out what really happens by performing a real experiment. But an experiment this sophisticated was beyond the technological capabilities when Einstein and Bohr were alive.

The argument was not settled during their lifetimes. Most physicists sided with Bohr. His *Copenhagen interpretation* of quantum physics, as it is called, was what most scientists followed.

In 1965, ten years after Einstein died, the Scottish physicist John Bell, working at the European particle accelerator in Geneva, began to study the EPR experiment and came up with a powerful mathematical theorem that we know today as *Bell's inequality*. This theorem made possible real EPR experiments.

The theorem is statistical in nature, and the reason it's needed is that Heisenberg's uncertainty principle applies only to many measurements. It doesn't apply to a single measurement but to the measurement of many electrons. It's a statement about a statistical average over many measurements.

Einstein was wrong

In 1982, French physicist Alain Aspect performed the first real EPR experiment with photons. Instead of position and speed, he measured another property called the polarization. *Polarization* is the orientation of a photon's electromagnetic field. His results were clear. The world behaves like Bohr said it did. There are no hidden variables to be discovered; there is no theory to be proposed that would change quantum physics at its roots.

Einstein was wrong this time. The electron isn't a particle or a wave. While you aren't observing it, it doesn't occupy a location in space. If you observe the electron, it is where you find it. If you measure it again at another location, that's where it is. But the electron doesn't travel from one location to the other. Physicists say that it "tunnels" through space between the two locations. Although not entirely accurate, the term helps scientists to at least talk about the phenomenon. It's easier than saying that the electron was measured here, then it spread out throughout all space and reappeared at the second location when they made another measurement. This last statement is actually more accurate, but you can see how cumbersome it can become. Physicists working with quantum physics deal with this situation on a daily basis and usually leave it in the mathematical world, where the equations describe it correctly.

Does all of this sound very strange? That's the way the universe is. What's interesting is that scientists have come up with real applications that take advantage of this weird behavior. The first one is the *Josephson junction,* a type of electronic component that uses the "tunneling" of electrons between superconducting materials in actual devices with a variety of applications.

According to quantum physics, electrons, protons, atoms, and all the other particles that have been discovered are the representation in the physicists' minds of what are really mathematical relationships connecting their observations.

Scientists arrived at this discovery slowly. Initially, they thought that they were dealing with tiny objects, very small particles that were much smaller versions of the tiny dust or smoke particles they had studied. When they finally discovered quantum physics and what it says about the world, the names had stuck.

Teleportation

"Beam me up, Scotty." The famous command from the *Star Trek* television series was invented because of budget limitations. During the production of the original series, there wasn't a good way to land the ship in every episode, so the producer came up with the idea of teleporting people and things. Today, scientists at IBM and at the University of Michigan are getting us a little closer to achieving teleportation.

The first attempt ever at teleportation took place in 1997, when two research teams used a method proposed by Charles Bennett of the IBM Watson Research Center in Yorktown Heights, New York, which was based in the original EPR thought experiment. The first team, in Austria, reported results of the teleportation of a photon. A similar experiment was also done in Italy. In these experiments, two correlated or *entangled* photons were emitted from the same atom with the same polarization. When the polarization of one photon was changed, the entangled partner immediately polarized itself in the opposite direction. Bennett had proposed going one step further, using the information sent to the entangled partner to reproduce the state of the first particle, which has changed because of the measurements. Because all photons are identical, reproducing the state of the original photon on the second one amounts to transmitting the particle.

Since then, several other groups have attempted similar experiments. In 2004, Boris Blinov and his collaborators at the University of Michigan were able to entangle a photon and an *ion* (an electrically charged atom). The next step for his team is to entangle two widely separated ions by first entangling each ion and its photon and then entangling the two photons.

The conclusion you can take with you after all of this is that on the very small scale of the atom, the world doesn't look like the world we see every day. This world is impossible to visualize, and only through the mathematics of quantum physics can scientists make sense of it and use it for practical applications. Electrons exist. And they can be manipulated. Watch television tonight and see how amazingly accurate these electrons that you can't visualize are aimed at all the different places on the screen to form the ever-changing images that give us the illusion of motion.

Chapter 17

Einstein and the Bomb

*O*f the many applications of the $E = mc^2$ equation, perhaps the most dramatic is the atomic bomb. Quantum physics and the equation made it possible.

How did physicists get from $E = mc^2$ to chain reactions and the bomb? It wasn't easy, and it wasn't planned. The physicists weren't interested in making a bomb or any other kind of weapon. They were trying to discover the structure of matter, the composition of the atom, the way the universe works. In doing so, they stumbled upon the enormous energies stored in the atomic nucleus and discovered, slowly but steadily, how to unleash them. Political events changed what was an intellectual pursuit into a war effort. And the rest is history.

In this chapter, I explain where the bomb came from and its connection with Einstein's theory. I discuss Einstein's letter to President Franklin Delano Roosevelt and his subsequent efforts to discourage war. I retrace the main steps of the scientific history that led from $E = mc^2$ to the bomb. (Yes, the subject matter is nuclear physics, but you'll be surprised at how understandable it is.) By the end of the chapter, you'll know how the nuclear bomb works. (But, thank heavens, you still won't be able to build one!)

Warning the President: Einstein's Letter

"Sir: Some recent work by E. Fermi and L. Szilard, which has been communicated to me in manuscript, leads me to expect that the element uranium may be turned into a new and important source of energy in the immediate future." With these now famous words began the letter that Einstein sent to President Roosevelt in 1939.

Einstein didn't send the letter to brag about his fellow scientists' work. He wrote to warn the president of the possibility that Nazi Germany was developing a nuclear bomb and to urge him to start a serious effort to see that the United States developed it first.

As I explain later in the chapter, in the section "Remaining a Pacifist," the author of the letter was actually the physicist Leo Szilard. However, Einstein wrote an early draft, and he signed the final letter as if the words were his own. Einstein was the greatest scientist in the world, and Szilard — a nuclear physicist working in chain reaction and uranium research — thought that the only way the president would pay attention was if Einstein authored the letter. Reluctantly, Einstein signed it ("Yours very truly, A. Einstein"). And in doing so, he made what he called "the greatest mistake" of his life.

The letter doesn't mention $E = mc^2$, relativity, or any of Einstein's work. The bomb would be a direct application of the equation, and at the time, the physicists involved in developing the bomb knew it. However, Einstein wasn't involved in this research. Nuclear physics was perhaps the only field in physics that he didn't know. It had been developed while he was busy trying to unify gravity with the rest of physics (see Chapter 19).

Szilard wasn't trying to lure Einstein to join the research effort. Instead, he had a sense of urgency in reaching the president. Germany had invaded and conquered Poland and was close to overrunning Belgium. What the scientists were hearing from Germany regarding the development of the bomb wasn't good, and the president needed to be notified without making too much noise. Szilard wasn't important enough to be heard. Einstein was.

In the final section of this chapter, I explain how Einstein came to sign the letter and what happened after the president received it. Before I get there, we need to travel the road that led to the development of the nuclear bomb.

Nuclear Physics in a Nutshell

The energy of a nuclear bomb comes from inside the nucleus of the atom. Mass is converted into energy according to $E = mc^2$. This energy is the binding energy of the nucleus, the glue that keeps the nucleus of the atom together. (Take a look at Chapter 11 for details about this binding energy.)

Radiating particles

In some cases, the nuclear force is not able to keep a nucleus all together, and the nucleus loses some of its particles. French physicist Henri Becquerel accidentally discovered this effect in 1896. He'd been intrigued by the experiments with x-rays that Wilhelm Roentgen had been doing in Germany (see Chapter 15). Becquerel obtained a uranium salt to see if he could observe these x-rays.

In his laboratory at the Museum of Natural History in Paris (where his father and grandfather had also been physics professors), Becquerel started his experiments by exposing to the sun a photographic plate with the uranium salt sprinkled on it, thinking that sunlight would activate the x-rays. One cloudy day when he couldn't perform one of his experiments, he placed the photographic plate with the uranium salt in a drawer. A few days later, he went ahead and developed the plate anyway, thinking that he was going to get a faint image. But the image was very sharp, with high contrast. He soon realized that he'd discovered a new type of energetic radiation.

When Pierre and Marie Curie heard of Becquerel's experiment, they began to search for other elements that could emit similar rays. They found that thorium and uranium emit the same radiation. And in 1898, they discovered two new elements: polonium (named after Marie's native Poland) and radium. The Curies named the effect *radioactivity.*

In England, Ernest Rutherford designed experiments to investigate this new radioactivity phenomenon and was able to show that these rays come in two varieties, one more penetrating than the other. The less penetrating one, which he called *alpha,* has positive electric charge. The Curies in Paris discovered that the other one, called *beta,* is negatively charged.

Realizing limitations of the nuclear force

Why are these nuclei giving off particles? The nuclear force is supposed to be extremely strong (see Chapter 11). Why isn't it able to keep all these particles inside the nucleus?

The answer is that the nuclear force has a very short range of action. It's able to tie in particles that are close to each other. If the particles are too far apart, the force stops working. If the particles happen to be protons, which have positive charges, the electric force acting alone will push them apart (see Figure 17-1).

Figure 17-1:
Nuclear particles feel the nuclear force only when they are very close together.

Electrical
Nuclear

When the nuclear particles are bundled up in a nucleus of an atom, each particle interacts only with its nearest neighbors. In a nucleus with more than 30 particles, a particle in the middle of the nucleus won't feel the nuclear force of a particle at the edges. For example, in the left image in Figure 17-2, each of the nuclear particles in the cluster feels the nuclear attraction of the other particles in the cluster (its immediate neighbors). However, these particles don't feel the force of the particle near the edge.

Think of it this way: Imagine that you and a group of several friends are trying to stay together while swimming in rough waters. If you all decide to hold hands, each one of you will be holding on to the two nearest neighbors. The grip of a swimmer at one end of the large chain, no matter how strong it seems to his immediate neighbor, has no influence on a swimmer at the other end. If the water gets too rough, the whole group may break apart, creating small groups of two, three, or maybe four, as shown in the right image of Figure 17-2.

Like the rough waters that break apart your group, the electrical repulsion of the protons tries to break apart a large nucleus. However, in the nucleus, certain helpers try to keep the whole thing together: the neutrons. Neutrons don't have an electric charge, and the only force they feel is the nuclear attraction. They are the skilled swimmers who won't be pushed away by the rough waters. If you have enough of them in your group, it will stay together.

Figure 17-2:
Nuclear
particles in
a cluster are
attracted to
the other
clustered
particles,
just as
swimmers
are attached
to their
neighbors.

Studying alpha decay

Like the swimming group with the skilled swimmers, a nucleus with a balanced number of protons and neutrons is stable and stays together. But if a nucleus has too many protons, the total electric repulsion can overwhelm the attraction of the nuclear force, and a piece of the nucleus can fly apart (see Figure 17-3).

Figure 17-3:
A nucleus
with too
many pro-
tons can
jettison
an alpha
particle.

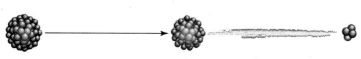

The piece that leaves the nucleus is usually in the form of an *alpha particle,* a cluster of two protons and two neutrons. (This particle is also the nucleus of the helium atom.) It turns out that these four particles are held together very tightly by the nuclear force, so this cluster is a very stable configuration of nuclear particles. These are the particles that Rutherford identified as alpha radiation. Physicists call the effect of the alpha particles leaving the nucleus *alpha decay.*

Detecting beta decay

It seems as if having a lot of neutrons is good for a nucleus because neutrons don't feel the electrical repulsion but do feel the nuclear attraction. They are the skilled swimmers in rough waters. However, these skilled swimmers don't have a lot of stamina. A neutron on its own, away from the nucleus, lasts for only about 15 minutes. After these 15 minutes, it changes into a proton, an electron, and another small particle called the *neutrino*. This effect is called *beta decay*.

Inside the nucleus, surrounded by the other particles, neutrons last much longer. When there are enough protons around, a quantum physics effect prevents neutrons from creating more protons. Quantum physics describes it by giving each proton in the nucleus its own space or slot. When there are enough protons, all the slots are taken and no additional protons are allowed (see Figure 17-4).

Figure 17-4: When all the proton slots are taken, no additional protons are allowed in the nucleus.

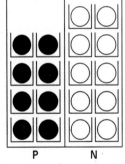

P   N

In a nucleus with too many neutrons, a neutron at the outer edges of the nucleus can decay into a proton because there will be empty slots for this new proton to stay in. Therefore,

> *A nucleus with too many neutrons is unstable and decays into a proton, an electron, and a neutrino.*

The protons created by this decay stay in the nucleus. The electrons don't belong in the nucleus; there are no slots for them there. The same goes for the neutrinos. Therefore, the electrons and neutrinos are both ejected (see Figure 17-5). Neutrinos are extremely difficult to detect. They can go through the entire Earth and come out at the other end without a single collision. But electrons are easy to detect. These breakaway electrons create the *beta rays* that the Curies and Rutherford saw.

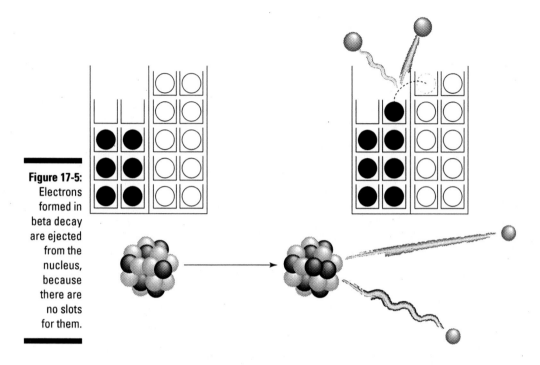

Figure 17-5:
Electrons
formed in
beta decay
are ejected
from the
nucleus,
because
there are
no slots
for them.

In both cases, the alpha and beta decays, the radioactive nucleus changes into the nucleus of another element when it gives off the alpha or the beta particle.

A third type of radioactive decay exists in which the unstable nucleus gives off only very energetic radiation, but no particles are ejected. The radiation is electromagnetic and is called *gamma rays*. In this case, the nucleus simply gives back some energy that it gained previously, but it doesn't lose its identity (see Figure 17-6).

Figure 17-6:
A nucleus
can also emit
high-energy
electro-
magnetic
radiation in
the gamma
region of the
spectrum.

Gamma ray

Discovering Nuclear Fission

In the 1930s, when physicists were applying the rules of quantum physics to the nuclei of atoms and were able to explain the effects I describe in the previous section, they began to look at other possible ways that a heavy nucleus could decay and give off energy. Keep in mind that their goal was to understand the nature of the atom; no one had weapons in mind (yet).

Misreading results

In 1934, in his laboratory in Rome, Italian physicist Enrico Fermi was using neutrons from a radioactive nucleus as projectiles to bombard uranium nuclei. He thought that he was producing new heavier elements — *transuranic elements,* as he called them. He published a paper in the journal *Nature* describing his experiments. Scientists around the world became very excited about Fermi's new elements.

A chemist named Ida Noddack wrote a paper arguing that Fermi hadn't really proved that he was producing these transuranic nuclei. She thought instead that the experiments were showing that Fermi had actually split the uranium nucleus into two smaller nuclei. She published her paper in the *Journal of Applied Chemistry* in Germany, a journal that physicists didn't normally read.

A few physicists did read the article, but it didn't make sense to them. They all thought that the new element formed in Fermi's experiments had to be close in mass to the bombarded element. Fermi also read it and, after performing some calculations, decided that Noddack was wrong; the possibility of generating much lighter elements, as she suggested, was very low.

As it turned out, Noddack was ahead of her time. The physicists simply didn't know enough about the properties of nuclei to realize that what she was proposing was actually happening in Fermi's experiments.

Realizing that uranium is being split

The final answer to this problem came a few years later, in the middle of World War II. Austrian physicist Lise Meitner and her research group conducted a four-year investigation in her laboratory that not only explained what Fermi had done but, in the process, discovered *nuclear fission,* the mechanism for the bomb.

Like Noddack and most scientists working in nuclear physics at the time, Meitner was interested in Fermi's experiments. But unlike Noddack, Meitner and her collaborators initially concluded that Fermi was making new transuranic elements.

In Germany, Meitner began to work on a model that would explain Fermi's experiment, but things were not falling into place. She couldn't see how bombarding uranium with one slow neutron, as Fermi was doing, could produce four or five beta decays. In a paper she wrote in 1937, she said that the results were "difficult to reconcile with current concepts of nuclear structure."

The Curies in Paris also looked at Fermi's experiment results. From his data, they identified new evidence that he was creating another element, but they couldn't figure out what it was.

As I explain in the sidebar on Lise Meitner, she was forced to flee Nazi Germany in 1938, and she went to Stockholm to continue her work.

Back in Germany, Meitner's longtime collaborator Otto Hahn and his assistant identified the element that Fermi was creating as *radium,* the radioactive element that the Curies had discovered several years earlier. Mail between Stockholm and Berlin was delivered overnight, and Meitner received Hahn's interpretation right away. She didn't think Hahn was right. For radium to be produced, two alpha particles needed to be emitted. She didn't think that the slow neutron in Fermi's experiment would have enough energy to knock out even a single alpha.

Lise Meitner

Lise Meitner was born in Vienna of Jewish descent but was baptized and raised as a Protestant. She became interested in physics when she read about Marie and Pierre Curie's work. She studied at the University of Vienna, where Ludwig Boltzmann was a professor, and obtained her PhD in physics in 1906.

The next year, she joined the University of Berlin, where she began a collaboration with Otto Hahn, a chemist who was the same age. The two young scientists worked in radioactivity and were very successful; in 1918, they announced the discovery of a new radioactive element. By then, they both had moved to the Kaiser Wilhelm Institute, where she directed the physics lab and he directed the radiochemistry lab.

By 1938, Meitner was considered one of the top nuclear physicists in the world. Einstein called her "our Madam Curie." An organic chemist at the institute named Kurt Hess, an unknown and envious researcher who became the institute's first active Nazi, began a campaign to get rid of Meitner. When she mentioned this fact to Hahn, her collaborator and lifelong friend, Hahn went straight to the top administrator at the institute. He was told to fire Meitner.

Hahn fired her. They'd been working together for more than 20 years and knew and respected each other well. "Hahn says I should not come to the Institute anymore. He has ... thrown me out," she wrote in her diary.

Hahn might've been afraid both for the future of the institute and for his own future. But without Meitner in the picture, he would be the sole recipient of the glory that their success would bring. He would benefit from Meitner's absence.

In August of 1938, Meitner fled Nazi Germany for Stockholm, Sweden.

Meitner suggested a new experiment for Hahn's group to try. "Fortunately, her opinion and judgment carried so much weight with us that we immediately began the . . . experiments," wrote Hahn's assistant. The experiment proved that the element being produced wasn't radium — it was *barium*, an element much lighter than uranium.

Meitner and Hahn had just discovered nuclear fission. Noddack had been right. Fermi wasn't producing transuranic elements; he was splitting atoms.

Hahn published the results of the experiments, suggesting that the uranium nucleus had been split in two fragments. Meitner was extremely disappointed that she couldn't be part of that "beautiful discovery." But she knew that a "non-Aryan" couldn't be included in the publication.

Imagining liquid drops

In December of 1938, Meitner traveled to Copenhagen to visit her nephew, Otto Frisch, who was a physicist in Niels Bohr's institute. Aunt and nephew went out for a walk in the snow one cold winter morning. They began to discuss the results from her former group in Berlin. She'd suggested that the uranium nucleus had split into two similar fragments, one of them a barium nucleus. But how could a slow neutron pack enough energy to accomplish that division?

Frisch's boss, Niels Bohr, had been advancing the idea that a large liquid drop would be a good model for a heavy nucleus. A large liquid drop is fragile and can be easily split into smaller droplets. If there is enough energy, the drop begins to take on larger and larger elongated shapes, vibrating back and forth until it splits (see Figure 17-7). The new smaller droplets are more difficult to split and are much more stable. The *surface tension* — the forces keeping the water molecules bound to each other on the surface — is much larger for these smaller drops. (Large soap bubbles are more fragile than small ones for the same reason.)

Figure 17-7:
If you add enough energy, you can split a large liquid drop into smaller droplets.

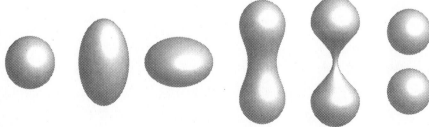

If a heavy nucleus is somehow disturbed, Bohr said, it would behave like this oscillating drop, vibrating until it breaks into two pieces. Although the nuclear force is very strong, it has a short range. Frisch knew that for a nucleus as large as uranium, the surface tension isn't very large. Meitner did the $E = mc^2$ calculation in her head and came up with the value for the huge amount of energy that is released when the uranium nucleus is split. Things were making sense now. Frisch suggested the name *fission* for the effect.

In Fermi's experiments, the neutron provides the energy needed to start the vibrations of the uranium nucleus. When the vibrations become large enough, the nucleus breaks up into the two fission fragments (see Figure 17-8).

Figure 17-8:
Nuclear fission as explained in the liquid drop model. When the nucleus breaks apart, it releases new neutron projectiles that can cause more fissions.

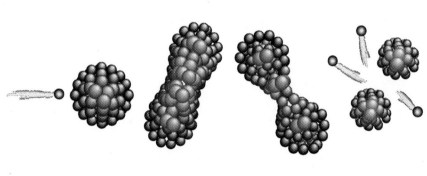

The new smaller fragments, like the smaller liquid drops, are more difficult to break apart. Their surface tensions are much larger. The nuclear particles — the protons and neutrons — in their nuclei are much more tightly attached to each other. In these smaller nuclei, each particle senses the nuclear force of most of the other particles, because none are too far away (see Figure 17-9). Being more tightly bound, the new nuclei (the fission fragments) have less mass than the larger uranium nucleus, with its more loosely bound particles (see Figure 17-10). The difference in masses is the energy, the $E = mc^2$, that keeps them together in the larger nucleus. This energy is released when they break apart.

During that morning walk in the snow, Lise Meitner and her nephew, Otto Frisch, figured out the physics of nuclear fission. They came up with the correct explanation of the experiments that Fermi was doing in Rome and for the experiments that her former research group in Berlin, with Otto Hahn, had done at her suggestion. Hahn's paper came out in January of 1939 without Meitner's name. Meitner and Frisch published their interpretation of the phenomenon in *Nature* a couple weeks later.

Figure 17-9:
The smaller
fission
fragments
are much
more stable.

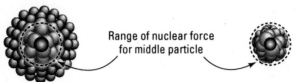

Range of nuclear force
for middle particle

Figure 17-10:
The fission
fragments
have a
smaller
mass than
the original
uranium
nucleus.

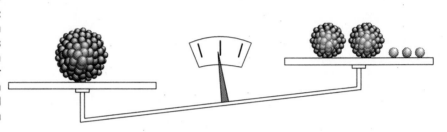

Otto Hahn won the Nobel Prize in chemistry in 1944 for the discovery. Alone.

The Nobel committee thus made one of its greatest mistakes. Hahn had contributed substantially to the discovery, but Meitner had guided the research from the beginning through completion. The prize should've gone to both. The committee didn't do in-depth research and failed to see the political reasons behind the omission of Meitner's name from several key papers.

Making the Bomb

Meitner and her team discovered a way to unleash the enormous energies stored in the nucleus. But they still weren't thinking about building bombs.

The energies in the nucleus are huge only by comparison. The energy released in the splitting of a single uranium nucleus is only about a trillionth of the energy used in lifting a baseball from the ground to your chest. Even when you consider the enormous number of atoms in a sample of uranium, how can you bombard all of them at once so that you get a large enough amount of energy to be useful? Because if you don't, the nuclei will give off their tiny amounts of energy at different times — not enough to do anything with.

Creating chain reactions

One scientist *was* thinking about bombs at the time, but no one was listening. Back in 1932, Leo Szilard came up with the idea that neutrons would make better probes for the nucleus than the alpha particles that Rutherford and the other scientists were using.

Szilard also came up with a way to release the energy all at once. He thought that if you used neutrons, you could perhaps find an element that could release two or more neutrons when bombarded with one neutron. Then, you could use those two neutrons as probes that would generate four more neutrons with which you could bombard four nuclei, and so on. Szilard called the phenomenon a *chain reaction* (see Figure 17-11).

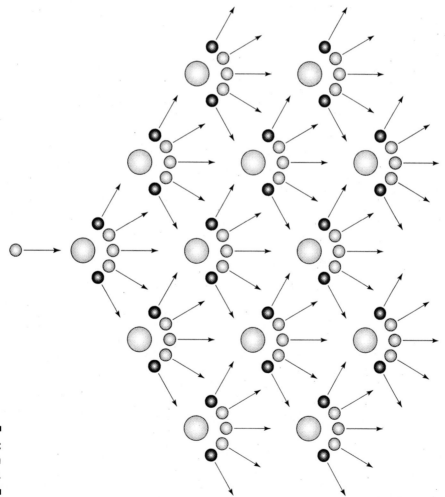

Figure 17-11:
A chain
reaction.

In a chain reaction, when an element that's bombarded with a neutron releases neutrons, these new particles can be used as projectiles to bombard other nuclei. The result is an uncontrolled reaction that may release a great deal of energy.

When scientists were asked to develop a nuclear bomb to help the war effort, Szilard's idea of a chain reaction took center stage. When he first proposed it, nuclear fission hadn't been discovered, and no one knew that large nuclei could be split into two by a relatively slow neutron. Szilard had proposed to bombard every element with neutrons until one that would give off additional neutrons was found. That wasn't going to be practical.

When nuclear fission became understood, the path was clear. Splitting uranium into two fission fragments with one neutron generated three new neutrons that could serve as projectiles for three new possible fissions. These three fissions would generate nine new neutron bullets, which would turn into 27 new neutrons, and so on. Szilard had his chain reaction.

In 1942, Enrico Fermi achieved the first chain reaction in the nuclear physics laboratory that he'd set up at the University of Chicago. (Fermi had moved to the United States from his native Italy to escape Mussolini's Fascist regime.)

In Fermi's chain reaction, the mass of the uranium nucleus plus that of the neutron that splits it is much larger than the total mass of the fission fragments produced. Einstein's $E = mc^2$ tells us that the energy of the uranium nucleus and the energy of the neutron together are greater than the energy of all the fission fragments. This energy is released when the uranium nucleus is split.

Sensing the force

The very limited range of the nuclear force is the reason the nuclear particles in the uranium nucleus are not as tightly bound together as they are in the fission fragments. A particle in a nucleus with a large number of nuclear particles, such as uranium, won't feel the nuclear force of particles located at the other side of the nucleus. They are beyond the reach of the nuclear force (see the right side of Figure 17-12).

On the other hand, a nuclear particle in a nucleus with very few particles, like helium (which has only four particles) feels the nuclear force of each of the others (see the left side of Figure 17-12). But the total force that it senses is not as large. A nuclear particle sensing the force of all 16 particles in oxygen, for example, is much larger.

Figure 17-12:
A particle
in a small
nucleus
senses all
the others. A
particle near
the edge
of a large
nucleus
doesn't
sense
particles in
the middle.

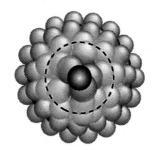

Identifying the most stable nucleus

There is an maximum size for a nucleus in which all particles sense the presence of all the others. In a nucleus this size, adding one additional particle won't increase the total force on each one of the other particles. Particles in a smaller nucleus will sense a smaller total force.

When you consider the electric repulsion of the protons, the range of the nuclear force is just enough to keep the 56 nuclear particles of the nucleus of iron all bound to each other. *Iron-56,* as it's called, is the most tightly bound, the most stable nucleus there is. A heavy nucleus like uranium-235 (with 235 nuclear particles) has too many particles not bound to too many other particles. When this nucleus is disturbed by an incoming neutron, for example, it easily splits into two much more stable clusters, releasing energy.

Imagining magnets

You can see the reason for the energy release if you imagine, for example, four horseshoe magnets tangled together (see the left side of Figure 17-13). In this configuration, the magnets aren't paired up, and their mutual attractions are weakened. You could easily separate them.

If you shake the tangle of magnets enough, they'll pair up in two groups of two magnets, attached to each other with their opposite poles facing (see the right side of Figure 17-13). It will be harder to separate the pairs than it was to separate the tangled magnets.

Figure 17-13:
It takes
more energy
to separate
magnets
when they're
paired up
than when
they're in a
tangle.

Imagine that when the magnets are in a tangle, you hold on to only one of them. When you shake it, you'll feel it pulling on you when it finds its partner. If you imagine doing this experiment with a gigantic magnet, you could get hurt with the energy released by the magnet as it pairs up with its partner.

Splitting a nucleus of uranium-235 releases energy for the same basic reason. The energy released by the gigantic magnets comes from their masses; the conversion of mass into energy according to $E = mc^2$. If you had a super-precise balance, you'd find that the magnets weigh slightly less after they pair up than they did when they were in a tangle. The energy released from your magnets is tiny compared with the energy released from a chunk of uranium-235. The nuclear force is just much stronger.

Moving on to nuclear bombs

Fermi's first chain reaction in 1942 wasn't allowed to go uncontrolled. In his nuclear reactor at the University of Chicago, he used a neutron absorber to control the rate of the reaction. In a nuclear bomb, the chain reaction is allowed to take place without control.

For a nuclear explosion to happen, you need to have enough uranium to sustain the chain reaction. But just having the right amount is not enough. Generating an uncontrolled chain reaction also depends on the design of the bomb. If you have a good design, 1 kilogram of uranium-235 is enough. That amount is called the *critical mass.*

If you have the critical mass of uranium-235, it will explode on its own; any stray neutron can start the chain reaction. In a nuclear bomb, then, the critical mass is assembled only at the time of the explosion.

Note that *nuclear* bomb is a more accurate term than the old name *atomic* bomb, because the energy comes only from the nucleus of the atom.

In *Little Boy,* the bomb dropped on Hiroshima, Japan on August 6, 1945, the uranium was kept in two halves at the two ends of a cigar-shaped design (see Figure 17-14). At the time of detonation, an explosive propelled the two pieces together, forming critical mass.

When critical mass is achieved, the uranium explodes in about one microsecond. However, 99.9 percent of the energy in a nuclear bomb is released during the last tenth of a microsecond of the explosion. The sudden release of energy in such a short time is what makes the bomb so powerful.

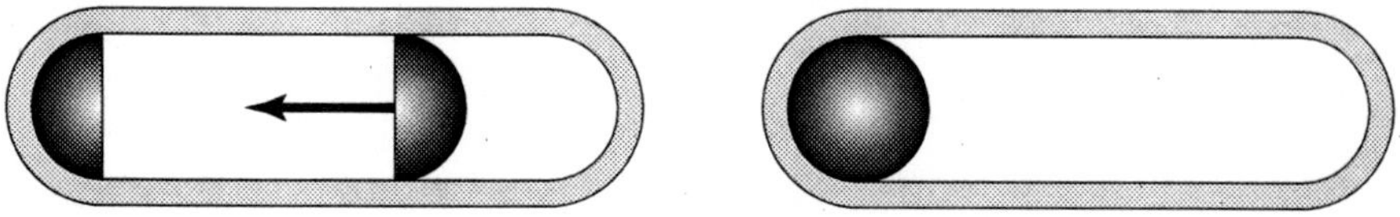

Figure 17-14:
The design for *Little Boy,* the nuclear bomb dropped on Hiroshima in 1945.

Creating the H bomb

Another, more powerful bomb was invented in the United States several years after the nuclear fission bomb I've described so far. This one is called the *hydrogen bomb,* or *H bomb.* Another name for it is *thermonuclear bomb.* Its source of energy is the same as the source of energy that powers the sun, nuclear fusion. And Einstein's $E = mc^2$ equation made it possible as well.

Nuclear fusion is the combination of two light nuclei into a more massive nucleus. Einstein's $E = mc^2$ says that things that are sticking together have less mass than when they are apart. Before they're combined, the masses of the two nuclei add up to a larger value than the mass of the final nucleus they create. When the two light nuclei are combined to form a new nucleus, energy is released.

A typical thermonuclear bomb fuses together the nuclei of two varieties of hydrogen, *tritium* (one proton and two neutrons) and *deuterium* (one proton and one neutron) to form *helium* (two protons and two neutrons). The fusion releases one neutron and energy (see Figure 17-15).

The great technological difficulty that needed to be solved in the development of this weapon, the "secret" of the hydrogen bomb, was how to bring these nuclei close enough together that the nuclear force would overcome the extremely large electrical repulsion of the protons in each of the original nuclei. The solution was to surround the hydrogen bomb with a fission bomb and to invent a technique that made possible the use of the gamma rays from the fission bomb to force the nuclei together.

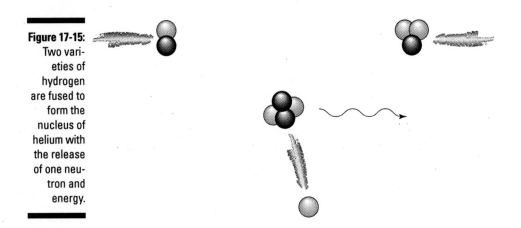

Figure 17-15:
Two varieties of hydrogen are fused to form the nucleus of helium with the release of one neutron and energy.

Remaining a Pacifist

Einstein didn't have anything to do with the development of either nuclear bomb invented in the United States during World War II and the Cold War. As I explain in the following sections, his involvement stopped soon after he signed his famous letter to President Roosevelt.

Fearing a Nazi bomb

After Fermi's experiments showed the feasibility of a chain reaction, Leo Szilard, who'd been proposing the idea for a long time, went to Princeton, New Jersey, and consulted with the renowned physicist Eugene Wigner. (Like Szilard, Wigner was a refugee from Hungary.) They knew that Belgium controlled large quantities of uranium in the Congo, and Nazi Germany was knocking on Belgium's door. Both men worried about the possibility that the Germans would get their hands on enough uranium to create a nuclear bomb.

Writing to the president

Szilard knew that Einstein was a good friend of the queen of Belgium and thought that Einstein should write her a letter explaining the urgency of the situation. Wigner and Szilard went to visit Einstein at his house near the Institute of Advanced Studies. They didn't even get past the porch of Einstein's house before he agreed to write the letter. But he wanted to send it to the Belgian government instead of to the queen.

Einstein wrote a draft and gave it to Szilard and Wigner. Szilard then spoke with one of his colleagues, who put him in contact with Alexander Sachs, a banker and adviser to President Roosevelt. Sachs recommended taking the letter to the president instead.

With guidance from Sachs, Szilard wrote a draft of the letter that was to be given to Roosevelt. He sent it to Einstein, explaining what had happened. Einstein wanted a second meeting. Wigner was traveling on the west coast, so Szilard came with Edward Teller, a noted physicist who was also from Hungary. At this meeting, Einstein dictated another draft to Teller. A few days later, Szilard sent Einstein two versions of the letter that he'd written based on Einstein's new draft. Einstein signed both letters and returned them to Szilard.

Sachs personally carried the longer version of the letter to the president on October 11, 1939. Roosevelt understood right away the importance of the letter. "Alex," he said, "What you are after is to see that the Nazis don't blow us up." The president then called his secretary and told him, "This requires action."

The action that resulted wasn't what Szilard wanted. The president formed a committee with Fermi, Szilard, Teller, and Wigner. Einstein wasn't a member. After the committee's recommendations were sent to the president, the government authorized all of $6,000 for one year's worth of research on uranium fission and chain reactions.

Szilard went back to Einstein requesting a second letter, which Einstein wrote. After receiving the second letter, the president decided to increase the size of the committee to include Einstein. Einstein declined.

Regretting his support

Einstein's letters didn't really inspire the United States to work on building a bomb. The inspiration, instead, was a two-part report written by Otto Frisch, who had fled to England, and the British physicist Rudolf Peierls. The two parts were titled "On the construction of a 'super-bomb'; based on a nuclear chain reaction in uranium," and "Memorandum on the properties of a radioactive 'super-bomb.'" The report was sent to Washington through official channels.

On December 6, 1941, the day before the Japanese attack on Pearl Harbor, President Roosevelt set up the secret Manhattan Engineering District project — the *Manhattan Project,* as it came to be known. Three days later, Germany declared war on the United States.

The bomb was never used against the Nazis. Nazi Germany collapsed in May of 1945, before the bomb was ready. Instead, bombs were dropped on Hiroshima and Nagasaki and ended the war with Japan.

After the war, Einstein's letter to the president became well-known. His $E = mc^2$ equation, an essential tool in the development of the bomb, was also well known. Some people began to call Einstein the "superfather" of the bomb (J. Robert Oppenheimer, who led the Manhattan Project, was called the father.) Einstein disliked this label very much. "If I had known that the Germans would not succeed in building the atomic bomb, I never would have supported it," he said.

Striving for peace

"I would unconditionally refuse to do war service, directly or indirectly, and would try to persuade my friends to take the same stand, regardless of the cause of the war." These were Einstein's words during an interview in 1921. The fact that he went against this stance by writing a letter to the president in 1939 only shows the magnitude of the threat that Hitler presented to the world. After World War II ended, Einstein returned to his strong pacifist stance.

Einstein had been a pacifist since his youth. He said that his pacifism was an instinctive feeling, "the feeling that possesses me because the murder of men is disgusting." His pacifism didn't come from intellectual theories, "but from my deepest antipathy to every kind of cruelty and hatred . . . my pacifism is absolute."

In 1930, during a visit to the United States, Einstein made a controversial speech in which he said that "if only 2 percent of those called up declared that they would not serve, and simultaneously demanded that all international conflicts be settled in a peaceful manner, governments would be helpless." The 2 percent included so many people, he thought, that there wouldn't be enough jails to put them in. The speech appeared in *The New York Times* the next day and made many people uneasy.

The threat of Hitler forced Einstein to become what he called "a militant pacifist." During the war, Einstein agreed to serve as a consultant to the Navy. His job was to point out flaws in the designs of new weapons and to present ideas for improvement. This job was easy for Einstein and was somewhat similar to his old job at the Bern patent office.

After the war, and until he died in 1955, Einstein opposed the proliferation of nuclear weapons and campaigned constantly for their abolition. With Szilard, he founded the Emergency Committee of Atomic Scientists in 1946 and served as its president and chairman of trustees. The organization's goal was to educate the public about the nature of atomic weapons. Besides Einstein and Szilard, the committee included Linus Pauling, Harold Urey, and the famous physicists Hans Bethe and Victor Weisskopf. However, the organization didn't make the impact that its founders were looking for. The committee was active until 1950.

A similar organization, the *Bulletin of the Atomic Scientists,* was founded in 1945 by scientists who worked on the Manhattan Project at the University of Chicago. Einstein was one of its first sponsors. The Bulletin continues its mission of education today.

Chapter 18

Einstein's Greatest Blunder

*A*fter Einstein completed "his most beautiful discovery," the field equation of the general theory of relativity (see Chapter 12), he began to use it as a tool to discover nature's secrets — to find out how the world works. The first secret he tackled was the most basic one of all: the nature of the universe. He wanted to know how the universe was made and how it works. When he was done, he'd created a new area in physics. He'd also made a big mistake.

In this chapter, I introduce Einstein's equations for the universe and the early models that were developed with them. Uncharacteristically, Einstein was afraid of his own equations and introduced what he called his greatest blunder.

Looking for the Edge of the Universe

In February of 1917, Einstein submitted a paper to the Prussian Academy of Sciences presenting his model of the universe. His model was in sharp contrast to the previous attempts based on Isaac Newton's physics.

Deconstructing Newton

Einstein began his paper by listing all the things that weren't right about Newton's universe. Newton constructed an unchanging universe that extended to infinity and was filled with stars that felt each other's gravity according to his universal law of gravitation (see Chapter 4).

Einstein and others pointed out that gravity wouldn't allow Newton's universe to remain unchanged. Also, the idea of an infinite universe was problematic, and eventually, scientists were able to show that it couldn't exist. An infinite universe would collapse.

But a finite universe is also problematic. If the universe doesn't extend forever, if space has an end, then the next question is: What's on the other side? What lies beyond the edge of the universe? Answering with "another universe" doesn't cut it. You can simply keep asking the same questions. Is the other universe infinite, or does it have an end? And so on.

If a universe has an edge, you could travel to the edge of the universe and stick your hand out. Do you extend the universe by doing that? Are you creating more universe?

These questions about a universe based on Newton's physics have never been answered. Newton's mechanics showed us how the solar system works, how stars move and live within galaxies, and how galaxies interact with each other. Scientists use his mechanics even today with great success to calculate satellite and space station orbits, and to send spaceships to Mars. But you can't use it to figure out how the entire universe works or whether it extends forever or has an end.

Reconciling "finite" with "unbounded"

Einstein's model, as outlined in his paper to the Academy ("Cosmological observations on the general theory of relativity"), presented an unchanging universe that has no boundaries but is finite in size. Einstein built his universe with the following properties:

- ✔ Except for local differences, everything in the universe is made of the same stuff.
- ✔ The universe looks the same in all directions and from every place (in a large scale, with local differences).
- ✔ The universe is unbounded and finite.
- ✔ The universe is static, which means that it has existed forever and will continue to exist forever in the same general form. There was no beginning and there will be no end, but there are local changes.

Einstein found out very quickly that this last assumption was incorrect. Except for that, Einstein's model is, in very general terms, close to what we use today.

The first property of Einstein's model of the universe makes life easier. If you assume that the universe changes from place to place, your model becomes extremely complicated. Although scientists are now talking about strange forms of matter that they've discovered, according to observations over the last 100 years, at the large scale, the universe appears to be made of the same stuff. Take a look at Chapter 19 for more information.

The second property has been corroborated recently (see Chapter 14). Matter in the universe, in the form of galaxies and clusters of galaxies, seems to be distributed the same way in all directions.

At first glance, the third property seems like a contradiction. Einstein says that the universe doesn't extend forever, but that it doesn't have an edge. Einstein didn't just come up with this property out of the blue. His field equation required it. He told his friend Michele Besso that "in gravitation I am now looking for the limiting conditions in the infinite. Surely it is interesting to reflect to what extent there exists a finite world, i.e. a world of naturally measured finite extension, in which all inertia is really relative."

The universe that Einstein's field equations gave him has a finite extension in space. The three dimensions of space are closed, similarly to the way the two dimensions of the surface of a sphere are closed. Imagine a two-dimensional universe where two-dimensional beings live (see Figure 18-1). There are stars and planets in this universe. The stars are discs made out of hot gases that emit light and heat. The planets are much smaller dark discs, and they orbit some of these stars. Everything takes place on the surface of the sphere. There is no "up" or "down" in this universe.

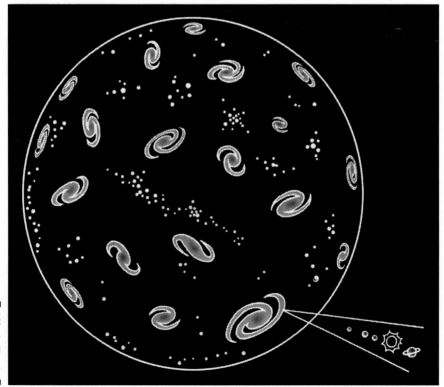

Figure 18-1:
A two-dimensional universe.

The surface of this two-dimensional universe is finite and unbounded. A two-dimensional being traveling in this universe will move along the surface of the sphere, never encountering an edge. Eventually, the traveler will end up at the starting position. Because there are no edges to this universe, the traveler can't stick her flat, two-dimensional hand out. (She can't stick it up, because there is no up.) She is forever stuck on the surface.

Einstein's model of the universe is the three-dimensional version of this spherical universe. Our space is unbounded but has a finite size. Einstein's universe doesn't have the problems that Newton's universe had. It doesn't extend forever, but you can't travel to the edge and stick your hand out. There is no edge. There is no other side.

Calculating the Curvature of the Universe

How would you go about discovering the shape of the universe? It's easier to think about in a fictional two-dimensional universe.

A two-dimensional example

Imagine that Roundworld is one of the inhabited planets in orbit around a yellow star in this two-dimensional universe. Roundworld is a very flat world, and its inhabitants had always thought that their entire universe was flat, like a disc. Scientists had made very precise measurements of different geometrical shapes, and everything worked out according to the theorems of plane geometry, which everyone learned in school. For example, the sum of the angles of a triangle was always 180 degrees.

Over the years, scientists argued whether their flat universe extended forever, with infinite stars and planets, or whether it was finite, with an edge. But if it was finite, what was beyond the edge?

About 90 years ago, a famous scientist discovered that their universe is not flat but curved. Roundworld is still flat, but the entire universe is actually spherical. If one of the Roundworlders could travel for millions of years along a straight line, he would eventually come back around, having traveled all the way around the universe. He would end up at the starting point.

The scientist proposed making a huge triangle with laser beams sent out from spacecraft that had been launched for such a mission several years in advance. When the angles of the triangle formed with the laser beams were measured, the sum of these angles came out to be larger than 180 degrees (see Figure 18-2). The universe is curved, the scientist concluded. It's a sphere.

Everyone was astonished but happy that they had discovered the shape of the universe. But they couldn't visualize it. They knew about curved lines, like circles, but didn't have the concept of a curved surface. Curved in what direction? They didn't have up or down. But their physicists could see it in their equations.

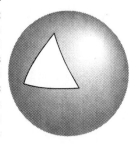

Figure 18-2:
The Roundworld scientists measured the angles of a large triangle in space.

A four-dimensional cylinder

Einstein didn't propose sending out spacecraft with laser beams to measure the curvature of the universe. He performed a thought experiment.

Imagine a spinning disc or wheel. You know from the geometry we all learned in school that if you measure the circumference of the disc and divide it by its diameter, you get the value π. According to special relativity, however, you'd measure a smaller value for the circumference when the wheel is spinning, because the length along the direction of motion is contracted (see Chapter 9). The wheel is in motion relative to you, and you measure a smaller length in the moving frame (see Figure 18-3). The diameter doesn't change because it's at right angles to the direction of spin, and only lengths *along* the direction of motion are shortened.

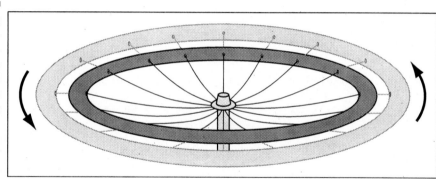

Figure 18-3:
If you measure the circumference of a wheel that is spinning at relativistic speeds, you get a smaller value.

The shortening of the circumference relative to the wheel's diameter is due to the curvature of space. To see why, draw a wheel on a flat sheet of paper. Cut out a wedge of the circle (to get the smaller circumference that you measured above), and then rejoin the paper. The paper will curve (see Figure 18-4). I walk you through the same process to illustrate the orbit of Mercury in the curved spacetime of the sun (see Chapter 12). In that case, the space is locally curved by the sun. In the present case, all of spacetime is curved. The shortening of the spinning disc is a property of spacetime and doesn't depend on being close to the sun or to any other mass.

Figure 18-4:
Cut a wedge out of the wheel. If you rejoin the edges, you get a curved surface.

You can also do what the Roundworld scientists did and try to add the angles of a large triangle in space. You'll discover that they add up to more than 180 degrees. Our spacetime is curved.

Actually, the three dimensions of space are curved. The time dimension isn't. Spacetime is a four-dimensional cylinder, with space curved and the time dimension flat (see Figure 18-5). In what direction does space curve? Just like the Roundworlders who couldn't visualize their curved surface, we can't visualize our curved space. But our physicists can see it in their equations.

Figure 18-5:
Einstein's spacetime is curved like a cylinder.

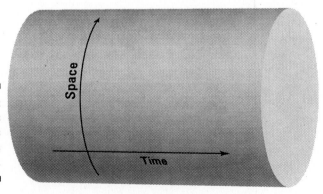

Sphereland

In 1960, the Dutch mathematician Dionys Burger wrote a story about a two-dimensional world, *Sphereland*, describing the trials and tribulations of A Hexagon, one of the two-dimensional Spherelanders. The book was a sequel to the classic *Flatland*, a science fiction story published in 1880 by the Shakespearean scholar Edwin Abbot.

Einstein's Model of the Universe

Einstein's fourth assumption was that the universe is static, existing forever in the same overall form and remaining like this forever. This assumption was very uncharacteristic of Einstein. When he first made the calculations, his field equation gave him a dynamic universe, a universe that was either expanding or collapsing.

Einstein didn't like what his model was giving him. An expanding or collapsing universe was a strange notion. Not that it couldn't happen. The physics of either option was fairly straightforward. A collapse would be caused by gravity pulling in all the stars from their current positions. An expansion required some sort of large explosion in the distant past that pushed all the stars away. His model could represent either possibility. But the observations of the day weren't showing either one. The universe that the astronomers were seeing was static.

Changing his equation to fit reality

Einstein decided to modify his model so that it would represent reality. He saw that by adding a term to his equations that represented the force of repulsion and that exactly counterbalanced the pull of gravity, his universe would become static. It was a frail equilibrium, but it did the trick. He called the term the *cosmological constant* because, in his model, it determined the size of the universe.

It must've been a hard decision for Einstein to make. In his paper to the Academy he wrote: "I shall conduct the reader over the road that I have myself traveled, rather a rough and winding road . . . The field equations of gravitation . . . still need a slight modification."

A model for an empty universe

Shortly after Einstein proposed his model of the universe, the Dutch astronomer Willem de Sitter also used Einstein's field equation to construct a model of the universe. Like Einstein's model, de Sitter's universe was static, but unlike Einstein's, it was empty. Although that may sound strange, taken as a whole, the universe is almost empty; the stars and galaxies are spread out over extremely large distances, making the density of the universe almost zero.

A few years later, scientists realized that de Sitter's model wasn't really static, as he'd thought. You may think that de Sitter was sloppy in developing his model or that the physicists that read the papers weren't paying enough attention. This wasn't the case. The problem was that Einstein's field equation isn't easily solved, and using it to build a model is extremely complicated. Today, physicists have developed sophisticated mathematical tools that help them use general relativity without running into these problems. In de Sitter's model, the universe is empty and there is nothing to expand. But Arthur Eddington — the English astronomer who organized the eclipse expedition to test general relativity (see Chapter 12) — introduced particles of matter into de Sitter's model and discovered that they moved apart.

In Einstein's model, space is curved but time isn't. In de Sitter's model, both space and time are curved. If you imagine space represented by one dimension instead of three, Einstein's model is represented by a cylinder, with time flat along the axis, while de Sitter's universe is more like a sphere, with time also curved.

Einstein wasn't happy with the appearance of de Sitter's model. He'd assumed that general relativity would allow only one unique solution, which was clearly not the case. When the model was first proposed, astronomers and physicists took a great deal of interest in it. Today, we know that the mass density of the universe, although still small, isn't small enough to model an empty universe.

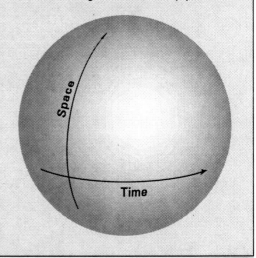

Rejecting a Russian model

A few years after Einstein introduced his static model of the universe, the Russian scientist Alexander Friedmann decided to remove Einstein's cosmological constant from his model. Friedmann wanted to restore the original form of the equations and see what the consequences were. What he found was that the model predicted an expanding universe, as Einstein had first discovered. But Einstein had rejected it from the beginning and hadn't looked into the details of the model before modifying it with the cosmological constant.

Friedmann did study it, and he found that there were two possible outcomes of this expansion, depending on the total mass density of the universe:

- If the universe has a very high mass density, it will first expand, but (because in this case the gravitational field is so strong) the expansion will stop and turn into a contraction. This type of universe is called a *closed universe*. This universe has spherical curvature, like Einstein's model.

- If the mass density of the universe is very low, gravity is not strong enough to halt the expansion, which will continue forever at the same rate. This is an *open universe*. This universe is also curved, but the curvature is not closed, like the spherical curvature of the first type. It's an open curvature that in some way curves away from itself, like the surface of a saddle (see Figure 18-6).

Figure 18-6:
The three types of Friedmann universes.

There is a third case that Friedmann didn't consider at the time. If the mass density of the universe falls right in the middle, at a *critical* value, the universe is a *flat universe* which also expands forever, but the expansion gradually slows down. However, gravity is not strong enough to slow it down completely.

Friedmann published his calculations in two papers in 1924. At first, Einstein didn't think that the model was correct. When he looked closely, he realized that Friedmann's papers were correct, but he didn't think that they represented the real universe. He still believed that the universe was static, not expanding. Friedmann's model was actually his own initial model, before he introduced his correction with the cosmological constant.

If only he hadn't. If only he'd been brave and stuck with what his equation was telling him. If only he'd been more like the rebellious Einstein who stuck with his equations even when they were telling him crazy things that hadn't been observed — that mass warps space, that light is bent by gravity, that time is dilated. He'd been right then. This time he wasn't.

Watching the Universe Expand

At about the time that Einstein was working on his model of the universe, a U.S. astronomer by the name of Vesto Slipher was beginning to see evidence that distant clusters of stars were moving away from us. However, because of World War I, Einstein hadn't found out about Slipher's research.

Slipher had been making his observations of distant stars for several years. By 1914, he'd collected data showing that the light from many of these stars was Doppler-shifted toward the red end of the spectrum (the wavelengths were stretched), meaning that they were moving away from us (see Chapter 12). Slipher was actually looking at galaxies, although at the time, astronomers didn't know that these white smudges in the sky contained billions of stars.

Here's a brief introduction to the structure of the universe: A typical galaxy, like our own Milky Way, contains 100 billion stars that are kept together by gravity. Galaxies are grouped in clusters (see Figure 18-7). Our cluster, the Local Group, contains some 30 galaxies. Clusters also exist in super clusters. The Local Group is part of the Virgo Super Cluster.

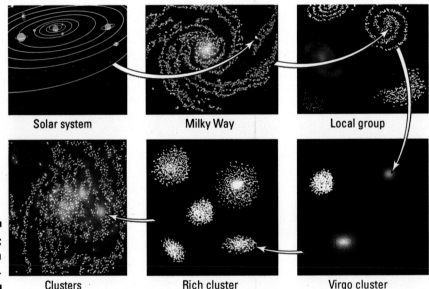

Figure 18-7:
Structure in
the universe.

Solar system   Milky Way   Local group

Clusters   Rich cluster   Virgo cluster

None of this was known when Einstein and Friedmann were working on their models. At the time, astronomers thought that the universe contained stars and *nebulas* (fuzzy bright patches in the sky). Some astronomers had said that these nebulas were perhaps *island universes* — large collections of stars. But because the nebulas were so far away, existing telescopes weren't strong enough for astronomers to determine if they consisted of stars.

Exploring island universes

In 1924, the U.S. astronomer Edwin Hubble showed that nebulas *are* island universes, external to our Milky Way. With a 100-inch telescope that had been recently installed at the Mount Wilson Observatory in California, he was able to make out individual stars in the nebulas. The announcement caused a sensation among the world's astronomers and the scientific community. Hubble had discovered *galaxies,* entire universes of innumerable stars very far away.

Hubble's discovery of galaxies was one of the most important discoveries in the history of astronomy. But it wasn't the most important discovery that Hubble would make. In 1929, he showed that the universe is expanding.

Using a yardstick for the stars

After his discovery of galaxies, Hubble began to measure their properties. The first thing he wanted to know was their distances. Astronomers had developed several methods to measure distances to stars. The simplest was the *parallax method* (see Chapter 4), using simple geometry to figure out the apparent shift in the position of the star as the Earth moved in its orbit around the sun. But that method was good only for nearby stars. If the star was far away, the shift was undetectable.

Eventually, astronomers discovered that some properties of stars could be used to compare their relative distances. They could calibrate a new method by comparing it to the simple parallax method.

In 1912, Henrietta Leavitt at the Harvard College Observatory discovered one such method. She was a research assistant at the observatory and was observing and studying a type of stars known as *variable stars,* which change brightness periodically. She was concentrating on one specific group of these stars in the Small Magellanic Cloud, a cloud of stars visible from the southern hemisphere.

Leavitt measured the times it takes these stars to go from dim to maximum brightness and found that it varies from one day to several months. These stars had been seen before in other places and were known as *Cepheid stars,* because the first one to be discovered was in the constellation Cepheus. Cepheids are very bright giant stars that can be seen at great distances.

After many measurements over four years, Leavitt realized that there is a direct relationship between a Cepheid's brightness and the time it takes the star to go from dim to bright. If a star that is 1,000 times brighter than the sun goes from dim to bright in 3 days, a star that is 10,000 times as bright as the sun does it in 30 days. If you measure these times, you know the brightness of the star. And this is the *actual* brightness of the star, not the apparent brightness that we see from Earth, because these particular Cepheids are all in the Small Magellanic Cloud, meaning that they are all roughly at the same distance from Earth.

Leavitt figured out that she could use the *period-luminosity* relationship, as her method was called, to measure the distances to the stars. But first she needed to calibrate her method. To calibrate, all she had to do was to find a Cepheid close enough to the Earth, so she could apply one of the other distance methods to find the distance. When she knew the distance based on the other method, she reversed the method and used her relationship to find the distance to other Cepheids in other locations.

This is how Leavitt's method works. Suppose you are observing a distant galaxy and you want to know its distance from Earth. You look for Cepheids and measure how long one of them takes to change from dim to bright. The time you measure tells you the actual brightness of the star. When you know the brightness, you can figure out how far it is, in the same way that if you know a light bulb you see shining at a distance is a 100-watt bulb, you can figure out how far it is.

Henrietta Leivitt had discovered the first yardstick to measure the distances to distant galaxies. Her method was perfected over the years and is one of the main distance measurement tools in use today.

Discovering that galaxies are moving away

With the telescopes at Mount Wilson and Henrietta Leavitt's method, Hubble began to measure the distances to his new galaxies. By 1929, he had measured the distances of about two dozen galaxies. He then compared the distances that he was measuring with the spectra that Vesto Slipher had been taking. What he obtained was astonishing. He found that all the galaxies in the universe are rushing away from each other, and the farther they are, the faster they move. The universe is expanding.

Edwin Hubble

Edwin Hubble became one of the towering figures in astronomy. He was also a bit of a ham. He spoke with an English accent, which he acquired when he went to England as a Rhodes scholar. He smoked a pipe and enjoyed blowing smoke rings across the table. He was a showman. But he didn't need to be. Knowing how to strike a pose is the ritual of lesser men. His discoveries and papers were of great historical importance and needed no help.

He had started out his professional life as a lawyer. After studying physics at the University of Chicago, he attended Oxford on his Rhodes Scholarship and studied law there, passing the bar exam when he returned to the United States in 1913. After practicing for a year, he decided to go back to the University of Chicago to study astronomy, obtaining his PhD in 1917.

Soon after graduation, Hubble received an invitation to join the staff at the Mount Wilson Observatory, at the time the best in the world. Hubble sent a telegram to the director of the observatory: "Regret cannot accept your invitation. Am off to war."

After his return from World War I, Hubble did go to Mount Wilson to start his long and successful career there.

Hubble had made the most important discovery in the study of the nature of the universe. Expansion means some sort of explosion. The universe was born out of an explosion, and we are living in it.

Hubble published his results later that year. In his paper, he mentioned that the models of the universe based on Einstein's general relativity had predicted this expansion. But not Einstein's own model. Einstein introduced the cosmological constant to keep his universe from expanding. If he had listened to his equations, he would've predicted Hubble's discovery.

In the face of Hubble's finding, Einstein realized that his static model was wrong and gave in. He hadn't accepted Friedmann's model of the universe, which was essentially his own without the cosmological constant. He now recognized that he'd been wrong. In his book *The Meaning of Relativity*, Einstein later wrote that "Friedmann found a way out of his possible dilemma. He showed that it is possible, according to the field equations, to have a finite [universe] without enlarging these field equations." And without a need to add his cosmological constant.

He told the physicist and cosmologist George Gamow that the cosmological constant idea was the biggest blunder he had made in his entire life.

Was it really? In Chapter 19, I show you why there may be doubts about that claim.

Chapter 19

Not a Blunder After All

As I explain in Chapter 18, Einstein developed a theory of the universe using the field equation of his general theory of relativity. His initial calculations indicated that the universe is either expanding or collapsing, which Einstein considered a mistake. His model was of a static, finite universe — after all, no one had observed the universe expanding.

To make his calculations fit the observations of the time, Einstein introduced a correction factor called the *cosmological constant.* Unfortunately for Einstein, in 1929, astronomer Edwin Hubble showed that the universe *is* expanding. Einstein should've trusted his field equation.

How is it possible that the greatest mind of the 20th century could make what he later called his "greatest blunder"? In this chapter, I show you why Einstein's blunder turned out to be not such a blunder after all. I also explain how Einstein's work led physics and astronomy throughout the 20th century and is still guiding these fields today.

Reevaluating Einstein's Universe

In recent years, Einstein's cosmological constant has been resurrected by scientists to help them understand new, puzzling findings about the behavior of the universe. It turns out that Einstein may have been right all along. To see why, in this section I take a closer look at how Einstein introduced his cosmological constant into his equations for the universe.

Energy creates gravity

In the universe according to Isaac Newton, planets, stars, galaxies, apples, and baseballs feel a force, gravity, whose strength depends on their masses and their separation from each other (see Chapter 4). In Einstein's universe, the strength of the gravitational field isn't just due to mass and distance, but also to energy and pressure.

Einstein realized that energy contributes to gravity. Why? Because $E = mc^2$ says so (see Chapter 11). A bird in flight has slightly more mass than when it is perched on a tree limb. The tiny amount of mass increase comes from the energy of the bird's motion. Any form of energy contributes to the total mass. If the bird basks in the sun, its mass will also increase. The Earth and the warm, flying bird will attract each other with a slightly larger force than when the bird is on a shaded branch. (Not that you could measure the additional force — the increase would be about a one-hundredth of a trillionth of a pound!)

Negative pressure creates antigravity

According to the theory of general relativity, pressure also creates gravity, although the contribution of pressure is usually very small. How small? Consider this: The mass of the air in a room — and its contribution to gravity — is comparatively very small. And the pressure of the air contributes less than a hundred billionth of the small amount that the mass contributes.

Normally, pressure pushes outward, like the air pressure in your car's tires. What would happen if pressure were negative? In general relativity, negative pressure creates repulsive gravity — antigravity!

In Einstein's universe, planets, stars, and galaxies attract each other with attractive gravity. Like in Newton's universe, this attractive gravity comes from the masses of the planets, stars, and galaxies. But in Einstein's universe, the planets, stars, and galaxies attract each other with *additional* gravity from all the forms of energy that they have and from the positive pressures that they exert.

What about the negative gravity? In 1917, when Einstein was developing his model, no one knew about negative pressure. His equations told him that negative pressure was a possibility. Without negative pressure, which produces repulsive gravity, Einstein's universe — like Newton's — could collapse.

Einstein developed his model of the universe 12 years before Hubble's discovery of the expansion of the universe (see Chapter 18). The observed universe wasn't expanding and certainly wasn't collapsing. It was static. Einstein saw that his equations allowed for repulsive gravity. If the universe had the right amount of this antigravity, it would counterbalance the pull of gravity, preventing the universe's collapse and maintaining its perfect, static equilibrium.

That's what the cosmological constant accomplished. By adding this term, Einstein's universe became filled with this exotic form of energy that created antigravity and maintained the universe in balance. For Einstein,

> *The cosmological constant exerts a repulsive gravitational force; it creates antigravity.*

If Einstein hadn't included the term in his equations, he would've realized that to prevent the gravitational collapse, the stars in the universe had to be moving away from each other. He would've predicted the expansion of the universe 12 years before Hubble discovered it.

As I explain in Chapter 18, Hubble showed that it isn't the stars that are moving away from each other, but the galaxies — the island universes that he had discovered. The stars themselves stay more or less at the same distances from each other inside their galaxies.

Exploring the Runaway Universe

With the discovery of the expansion of the universe in 1929, there was no need for the cosmological constant, and Einstein finally gave it up. As Einstein wrote on a postcard that he sent to the German mathematician Hermann Weyl, "If there is no quasi-static world, then away with the cosmological term."

Attention shifted to a new question: Is the universe going to expand forever, or is it going to slow down, stop, reverse course, and collapse? According to the theory of general relativity, the answer depends on the density of matter and energy in the universe — on how much matter is out there.

Discovering dark matter

Just two years after Hubble's discovery of the expansion of the universe, astronomer Fritz Zwicky of Caltech was observing a cluster of thousands of galaxies about 370 million light-years away. He discovered that the outer galaxies in the cluster were moving too quickly for his taste. His calculations showed him that at the speeds he was measuring, these outer galaxies should be thrown away from the cluster; yet, they remained together. To keep them together required gravitational attraction from about 100 times more galaxies than he was seeing. And these extra galaxies weren't there. Zwicky concluded that additional mass may exist that doesn't give off light.

In the 1970s, Vera Rubin and Kent Ford at the Carnegie Institution in Washington, D.C., observed the motions of the stars in many galaxies. They concluded that these motions could be explained only if was a huge halo of invisible *dark matter* surrounding these galaxies.

Now, more than three decades later, astronomers think that the universe is filled with dark matter, an invisible form of matter that can be "seen" only through its gravitational pull on the visible matter that makes up the stars and galaxies.

What is dark matter? No one knows. What scientists do know, however, is that it isn't your ordinary, run-of-the-mill type of matter. Dark matter isn't made of protons, neutrons, electrons, or any of the known building blocks of ordinary matter.

Although they don't know what dark matter is, astronomers have been able to figure out with a great deal of precision that there is as much as five times more dark matter than ordinary matter in the universe. What we see with our eyes and telescopes isn't everything that's out there.

Speeding away: Accelerating expansion

For astronomers and physicists, 1998 was a great year. Two independent groups of researchers, the Supernova Cosmology Project and the High-z Supernova Search Team, came out with the same result: The expansion of the universe is speeding up.

Saul Perlmutter of Lawrence Berkeley National Laboratory and Brian Schmidt of the Australian National University headed the two research teams. They and their researchers were actually trying to measure the *deceleration* of the universe, not its acceleration. They were doing so using what are known as *supernovas,* tremendous explosions of stars that are usually much more massive than our sun (see Chapter 13).

The supernova standard candle

Supernovas are classified into types according to their spectral features. One particular type of supernova, called Type la supernova, comes out of the explosion of a star the size of the sun that's part of a *binary system:* a situation where two nearby stars orbit around each other. When this star uses up its nuclear fuel, it begins to pull matter from its companion, growing in size until it reaches about 1½ solar masses. (In other words, it has one and a half times the mass of our sun.) At this point, called the *Chandrasekhar limit,* the pressure and temperature inside the star are so large that they trigger a nuclear explosion.

Because these explosions always occur exactly when the star reaches the Chandrasekhar limit, these supernovas shine with the same brightness. And they are *bright.* From Earth, you can see them halfway across the visible universe. The Hubble Space Telescope can see them when they are much farther away.

Why is this so important? Because it provides astronomers with what they call a *standard candle,* a way to measure the distances to galaxies. A standard candle is a star that always burns with the same brightness. It's like having known light sources spread throughout the universe. If you know, for example, that all cars have 100-watt headlight bulbs, you can figure out how far the cars are from you by measuring how dim their headlights look from your location.

A long acceleration

Using this wonderful yardstick, Perlmutter and Schmidt's teams discovered that, for the past 5 billion years, the expansion of the universe has been speeding up.

In 2002, NASA outfitted its Hubble Space Telescope with a new instrument, the Advanced Camera for Surveys. This camera turned the Hubble into a supernova-hunting machine. With this new capability, Adam Riess of NASA's Space Telescope Science Institute confirmed that, early in the history of the universe, its expansion was slowing down. But about 5 billion years ago, the slowdown stopped for some time, after which the universe's expansion started its current acceleration.

How can this happen? The accepted model of the universe, which was based on general relativity — essentially Alexander Friedmann's model (which I describe in Chapter 18) — says that the matter, energy, and pressure in the universe generate attractive gravity that pulls in and slows down the expansion. How can the expansion speed up? What's worse, why did it change from a well-behaved expansion that slowed down to a runaway expansion?

Reviving the Cosmological Constant: Einstein Was Right After All

Something is pushing the galaxies apart now. Some source of energy is fueling the expansion of the universe. And it permeates the universe. What can it be?

It turns out that the best way to explain the runaway expansion of the universe is with Einstein's cosmological constant. The cosmological constant fills the universe with repulsive gravity — just what's needed to speed up the expansion.

The key to how the cosmological constant works is the contribution to gravity from negative pressure. The negative pressure, which creates repulsive gravity, is constant throughout the universe; it doesn't decrease with distance (like the part of gravity that comes from ordinary matter does). And it doesn't need the presence of matter or energy to operate. The cosmological constant operates in empty space; it's a property of empty space.

Tracking changes in gravity

The rate of expansion of the universe depends on a battle between two giants: the attractive and the repulsive parts of gravity (see Figure 19-1). As the universe expands and the galaxies move farther apart, the attractive part of gravity decreases. However, the repulsive part of gravity is the same throughout the universe and stays fairly constant even with the expansion. Which part wins out depends on how close the galaxies are to each other.

Figure 19-1:
The attractive part of gravity decreases with expansion, but repulsive gravity stays fairly constant.

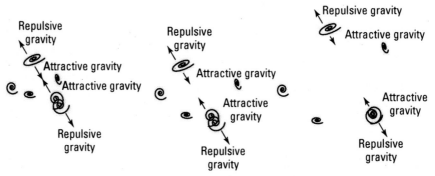

When our universe was starting out, its galaxies were closer together than they are now. As a result, regular attractive gravity was much stronger than repulsive gravity and held the galaxies more tightly together, slowing the universe's expansion (see the left side of Figure 19-1).

But after some time — about 5 billion years — the galaxies were far enough apart for the attractive part of gravity to decrease and match the strength of the repulsive gravity. At this point, the two canceled each other out; galaxies no longer felt gravitational force of any kind from other galaxies (see the middle diagram in Figure 19-1). But, even with no gravitational force, the galaxies kept moving away from each other, according to Newton's first law (see Chapter 4).

Gravity didn't disappear *within* galaxies, only *between* them. Attractive gravity from the mass and energy of objects depends on distance. And stars within a galaxy are close enough to each other that attractive gravity is stronger than repulsive gravity. The galaxies stay together with their stars bound to each other by gravity, as always.

As the galaxies continue to move apart, the attractive part of gravity decreases even more, and the constant repulsive gravity wins out, speeding the expansion of the universe (see the right part of Figure 19-1). This is the epoch that we are living in now.

In 1998, after their astonishing observations, Perlmutter and Schmidt suggested that Einstein may have been right: The universe does have a cosmological constant. It's what drives the current acceleration and what caused the earlier slowdown. Michael Turner, of the University of Chicago, proposed a new name for the cosmological constant: *dark energy.*

Taking a baby picture of the universe: Space is flat!

In 2001, another remarkable result came in from a NASA satellite, the Wilkinson Microwave Anisotropy Probe or WMAP. This NASA mission is taking a baby picture of the universe, measuring the leftover heat from the big bang, the origin of the universe. The WMAP satellite discovered that the universe is *flat.*

How is it possible to take a baby picture of the universe? The key is to realize how the universe began. A hundred thousand years after the universe began its expansion, protons and electrons came together for the first time to form atoms. Because atoms are neutral, photons (the bundles of energy I discuss in Chapter 16), which interact only with charged matter, started their independent existence, separate from matter. Two hundred thousand years later, the universe became transparent to light.

The lifetime of a photon is infinite. The photons from those early days of the universe have traveled through the universe undisturbed, giving us the baby picture that the WMAP is trying to snap. There are about 400 million of these original photons for every cubic meter of space today. (Here's a fun fact for your next party: If you tune a television set between channels, you see static; about 1 percent of that static is caused by the original photons.)

Today, 14 billion years later, these photons form the Cosmic Microwave Background, or CMB as scientists call it. When the photons first started their journeys, the temperature of the universe was about 3,000 kelvins. (As I explain in Chapter 5, a *kelvin* is the unit of the absolute scale of temperature.) This temperature was extremely uniform throughout the universe. Since then, the photons have been cooled as the universe expands. Today, the temperature of the CMB is only 2.7 kelvins, and it's still extremely uniform.

The results from WMAP show the small temperature changes of the CMB. The light captured in the baby picture image is from a region that's about 13 billion light-years from Earth. The image features patterns that represent tiny temperature differences, changing only by millionths of a degree. By measuring the distance between two regions and knowing the distance that the photons have traveled since their birth, scientists have been able to draw a big triangle in the sky with sides joining those two regions and the Earth. The angles of this triangle add up to 180 degrees, with a high precision. And that means that space is flat, not curved like everyone had been assuming for almost a century.

This finding is amazing. And there's more. If space is flat, the density of the universe is equal to the *critical density* (the middle value between an open and a closed universe, as I explain in Chapter 18). This density is a very small quantity. Write 28 zeros after the decimal point, and place a 1 in the 29th position. That's the fraction of a gram of matter (and energy) in every cubic meter of space.

From the discovery that space is flat, scientists have been able to use WMAP data to figure out the breakdown of matter in the universe. Their calculations show that ordinary matter — the atoms that make up the sun, the Earth, living things, stars, galaxies . . . everything we see in the universe — adds up to only 5 percent of the critical mass. (This result agrees very well with other calculations based on the nuclear processes that took place in the early universe.)

The data from WMAP also shows that dark matter accounts for 25 percent of the mass of the universe. That leaves 70 percent of the mass of the universe unaccounted for. The only candidate for the missing 70 percent today is dark energy, Einstein's cosmological constant. Figure 19-2 illustrates the breakdown of ordinary matter, dark matter, and dark energy.

Figure 19-2: Ordinary matter accounts for only 5 percent of the total mass of the universe. The rest is invisible dark matter and dark energy.

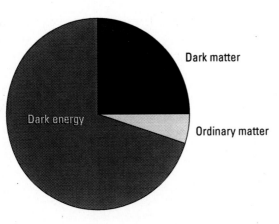

Dark matter

Dark energy

Ordinary matter

Think back to the Type Ia supernova studies I discuss in section "Speeding away: Accelerating expansion." These studies indicated that the universe's accelerated expansion could be explained by a push from repulsive gravity. More specifically, they indicated that dark energy (the cosmological constant) needed to contribute about 70 percent of the universe's critical density. That's a remarkable result. A completely independent experiment is telling us that dark energy accounts for the exact amount that's not accounted for already by dark and ordinary matter!

In science, nothing is ever proven. All scientists ever hope to see is that their predictions agree with observations. Right now, everything seems to be fitting together. The dark matter studies, the supernova studies of the accelerated expansion, and the WMAP data all point to the same conclusion: The universe has a flat geometry and is made up mostly of stuff we can't see.

What Is the Cosmological Constant?

What is dark energy, anyway? What is this exotic energy form that Einstein introduced in 1917?

Remarkably, the answer doesn't come from relativity but from the other branch of physics that Einstein originated, quantum physics. And the answer that quantum physics gives us is stranger than anything else I've discussed so far in this book. Dark energy, the cosmological constant, is the energy of the vacuum, the energy of nothing.

Creating particles out of the blue

This strange idea of the energy of the vacuum is at the very heart of today's physics. But today's physics has its roots in Einstein and the theories that were developed with his ideas, like quantum physics. When quantum physics was developed in the 1920s, physicists had a powerful tool that could answer questions like

- What is a force?
- How does the force between two electrons work?
- How does the electron know that there is another electron nearby so that it can repel it?

With general relativity, Einstein provided the answer to a question similar to this last one. The Earth knows that the sun is nearby because the sun curves the space around it. The Earth is moving in this curved space as best it can. It tries to move along a straight line, and the straight line in this curved space is the almost circular orbit around the sun. The force becomes geometry.

What about electrons? How do they know of each other's presence? In 1927, the English physicist Paul Dirac combined special relativity, James Clerk Maxwell's electromagnetism, and quantum physics, and he came up with *quantum field theory.* Two years later, U.S. physicists Richard Feynman and Julian Schwinger and, independently, Japanese physicist Sin-Itiro Tomonaga developed Dirac's theory into a beautiful new quantum theory of the electron that's called *quantum electrodymamics* or QED. This theory tells us what a force is and how an electron knows that there is another electron nearby.

According to Maxwell, when an electron accelerates, it radiates an electro-magnetic wave (see Chapter 6). That's how your cordless phone at home works: The base unit accelerates electrons back and forth along the antenna, and the accelerated electrons generate the electromagnetic wave that travels to your receiver at the speed of light. Quantum physics says that this electro-magnetic wave consists of photons. Accelerating electrons produce photons.

That's how electrons know of each other's presence: They send photons back and forth. If two traveling electrons meet each other, they exchange photons. The next questions you may ask are

- ✔ Where do these photons come from?

- ✔ Do the electrons carry photons around in case they meet other electrons?

- ✔ How do they know how many electrons they are going to encounter?

The push of the vacuum: The Casimir effect

In 1948, the Dutch physicist Hendrik Casimir came up with a clever idea to demonstrate that space is filled with virtual particles. He proposed placing two uncharged metal plates in an empty chamber. When the plates are moved very close to each other but not touching, the spacing between the plates excludes virtual particles larger than a par-ticular wavelength. Because particles with longer wavelengths can still appear outside the plates, there are more particles outside than inside. The imbalance should push the plates together.

When Casimir first proposed it, his idea was just an idea — a thought experiment — because the technology of the 1940s and early 1950s wasn't up to the task. But in a few years, several scientists attempted the experiment, getting encouraging results. In 1977, an experiment done at the University of Washington confirmed the *Casimir effect*, as it's now called.

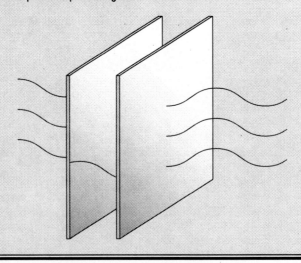

The answers to these questions may seem even more strange. Electrons don't carry photons with them. According to QED, the photons are created out of nothing. Their existences are allowed by Heisenberg's uncertainty principle (see Chapter 16). The uncertainty principle says that you can't determine with complete accuracy the position of an electron and at the same time measure where and how fast it's going. It also says that you can't measure simultaneously and with complete accuracy the energy of a particle and for how long the particle has that energy.

And this uncertainty is the clue to everything. It turns out that Heisenberg's uncertainty principle allows things to happen under the radar. You can borrow as much energy as you need and, as long as you pay it back within the short period of time allowed, you can use it for anything. If an unscrupulous kid "borrows" $100 from his parents, quickly invests the money in fast-rising stock, sells the stock at $110, and returns the $100 before his parents notice, he makes $10 from nothing, from money he didn't have. And his parents are none the wiser.

This illegal scheme is allowed in the quantum world. You "borrow" energy to create a particle, for example. The energy to create the particle comes out of nowhere, out of the blue. (Actually, it comes out of the black, the vacuum.) You borrow it, use it, and create your particle. The particle does its thing, lives out its life, and dies. You recoup your energy and give it back to the vacuum. If all of that happens within the time allotted, everything is fine.

Particles that are created out of the vacuum are called *virtual* particles:

> *A virtual particle is one that's created out of nothing and that exists only for the duration allowed by Heisenberg's uncertainty principle.*

Virtual particles exist for some fleeting moment and disappear. Real particles, on the other hand, exist for a long time or forever. Real photons are eternal.

Filling up the vacuum

As you can see, the conclusions that QED arrived at are very strange. Yet, the theory works — better than any other theory that humans have ever created. QED is the most accurate theory ever. Its predictions have been found valid to one part in a billion!

QED tells us that the vacuum isn't really empty. The vacuum is filled with these virtual particles that suddenly appear, only to disappear almost immediately. The vacuum, teeming with these virtual particles, has energy.

In 1967, the Russian physicist Yakov Zel'dovich showed that the energy of the vacuum is actually the energy that Einstein needed to create antigravity. The vacuum energy is the same as the cosmological constant, the dark energy that permeates the universe and is now driving its accelerating expansion.

Looking to Unify All of Physics

Einstein (and everybody else) thought that he'd made a big mistake by introducing his cosmological constant, and he reluctantly retracted it when he saw the evidence of the expansion of the universe. But his great blunder wasn't really a blunder. We now know that his cosmological constant, the dark energy (as scientists call it today), is the repulsive gravity that's causing the universe to accelerate its expansion. Dark energy is also the main component of the universe.

Even though he missed the opportunity to predict Hubble's discovery of the expansion of the universe, Einstein ended up being right, after all. But he wasn't alive to have the last laugh.

Einstein was at the University of Berlin when he published his cosmological constant paper. He'd moved there in 1914 from the Polytechnic in Zurich, lured by an offer of a professorship without teaching obligations. He also served as the director of the new Kaiser Wilhelm Institute for Physics. He remained in Berlin until 1933, when the danger of the Nazi regime forced him to leave Europe for the United States.

After the extraordinary success of the general theory of relativity and the confirmation of the bending of light by Arthur Eddington's eclipse expedition in 1919 (see Chapter 12), Einstein began to think about the next step. The general theory of relativity was the first extension. With it, he'd been able to develop a model of the universe. It was time to go beyond. Now he wanted to extend general relativity and merge it with the rest of physics into one, single unified field theory.

Recasting relativity into a five-dimensional spacetime

In 1919, there were only two fields in physics: the electromagnetic field and the gravitational field. Electromagnetism was itself the result of the unification of the electric field and the magnetic field. (As I explain in Chapter 6, that was Maxwell's great achievement and what, in part, got Einstein excited about physics when he was in college.)

Einstein wasn't the only scientist thinking about unifying electromagnetism and gravity. For example, Hermann Weyl, at the University of Zurich, developed equations attempting to unify general relativity and electromagnetism. And the German mathematician Theodor Kaluza rewrote Einstein's gravitational field equations into a spacetime of five dimensions (instead of four, as Einstein had done).

Kaluza's universe had four space dimensions, plus one of time. In space, you can go up and down (that's one dimension), left and right (two), and front and back (three). What could the fourth dimension be? Kaluza said that the additional dimension was the electromagnetic field.

Einstein liked Kaluza's approach but quickly saw its shortcomings. The main one was that no one had ever *seen* a fourth space dimension. There was no evidence of another direction in space.

Leaving his work unfinished

Even with its shortcomings, Einstein was encouraged by Kaluza's theory and soon began to work along similar lines. In 1922 and 1923, he published five papers with different variations of Kaluza's and Weyl's ideas.

In 1925, Einstein published a paper with his first complete version of a unified field theory, only to reject it quickly after publication. He'd seen that it wouldn't work. In a letter to a colleague, he said, "I have once again a theory of gravitation-electricity; very beautiful but dubious."

The following year, the Swedish physicist Oscar Klein extended and cleaned up Kaluza's theory and came up with a clever idea, one that scientists have revived recently. He said that the reason we don't see Kaluza's fourth space dimension is because it is curved, rolled up in a tiny circle that you can't see. It's a hidden dimension.

Einstein continued working on different attempts at a unified field theory, publishing his results and rejecting them later. Some attempts were extensions of the Kaluza–Klein theory, and others were different approaches.

Einstein died at 1:15 a.m. on Monday, April 18, 1955. He was 76. The day before, he had called his secretary on the phone, asking for a notebook in which he'd been working on his latest version of the unified field theory. He was too ill to make any progress on it. He died knowing that his work was unfinished.

Reviving Einstein's Dream

Einstein's lifelong dream of a unified field theory was unfinished but not forgotten. Today, similar ideas are once again being pursued by many physicists in the attempt to develop one single theory that can encompass all of physics.

In hindsight, we know that Einstein's approach couldn't work. When he started, there were only two known fields, electromagnetism and gravity. Since then, scientists have discovered two other fields:

- ✔ The strong nuclear field that generates the force that keeps nuclear particles together
- ✔ The weak nuclear field that regulates beta decay

Today, there are four fields in nature: the electromagnetic field, the gravitational field, the strong field, and the weak field. In their search for unification, physicists are looking for the single field that gave birth to these four fields.

Unifying the first two fields

The year before Einstein died, two physicists at Brookhaven National Laboratory, C.N. Yang and Robert Mills, started working on an idea that Heisenberg had come up with. Heisenberg realized that if you replaced every proton in the universe with a neutron, the nuclear field would remain unchanged. (Physicists call this type of process a *symmetric operation*.) From this apparently simple idea, Yang and Mills came up with a set of new fields. (Their symmetry operation was the motion of a particle in a circle in a fifth dimension.) After some analysis, they identified one field as the photon. QED theory had shown that the photon was the carrier of the electric and magnetic fields.

The other two fields described charged photons, and no one had seen such a beast. The Yang–Mills theory sat for decades until the 1960s, when three physicists, working independently, succeeded where Einstein had failed. Well, sort of.

Steven Weinberg and Sheldon Glashow of Harvard University and Abdus Salam of Imperial College London contributed key pieces to the first unification of fields achieved after Maxwell's unification of the electric and magnetic fields. Weinberg, Glashow, and Salam unified the electromagnetic field with the weak field, the field that regulates beta decay. One of the steps that made this unification possible was the identification of Yang and Mills's charged photons as the carriers of the weak force.

The three physicists called their new field the *electroweak field*.

> *The electroweak field unifies the electromagnetic field and the weak field, which is responsible for beta decay.*

The charged photons, the carriers of the electroweak force, were identified as the W and Z particles. The W and Z particles were discovered in a set of extremely delicate, ingenious, and complicated experiments in 1983 by a large team of physicists at CERN, the European laboratory for nuclear physics, led by the Italian physicist Carlo Rubbia. The experiments had to recreate conditions that existed during the early universe, when these fields existed. They don't exist today in nature. (The electroweak unification resulted in Nobel Prizes in physics in 1979 for Weinberg, Salam, and Glashow and in 1984 for Rubbia and Simon van der Meer, the engineer who designed the experiment at CERN.)

Attempting the next step

Encouraged by the success of the electroweak theory, several scientists started working on the next unification. The ones who have gotten the furthest are Sheldon Glashow and Howard Georgi of Harvard University. Their theory, which was refined later by Helen Quinn and by Weinberg, also uses symmetry arguments to introduce a set of new fields that have been identified with the W and Z particles of the electroweak field and with the carriers of the strong nuclear force (called *gluons*). Their *Grand Unified Theory*, as they call it, attempts to unify the electroweak force with the strong nuclear force.

Unlike the electroweak unification, Glashow and Georgi's grand unification hasn't been confirmed experimentally. And there are some problems with the theory. The theory originally predicted that protons should decay into other particles. After the prediction was made, several laboratories around the world started delicate experiments to look for the proton decay. None of the experiments found any evidence of that. Newer refinements to the theory don't include the requirement that protons must decay, but these versions of the theory haven't been confirmed yet either.

Today, most physicists think that the electroweak unification is correct and that the ideas behind the grand unification are probably correct. They believe that in time, these ideas will be refined into a successful theory. However, in recent years, another very different unification approach came up that's keeping many physicists busy.

Tying it all with strings

Gravity was Einstein's starting point in his attempts at a unified field theory. You may have noticed that none of the modern approaches at unification have started with gravity. In fact, none *include* gravity.

That's because scientists realized that starting with gravity wasn't going to work. The main reason is that general relativity, the theory of gravity, is a field theory but not a *quantum* field theory, like the electroweak theory. Before gravity can be integrated with the other forces, it must be quantized. Because the other forces operate in the realm of quantum physics, gravity must be modified so that it also operates in this realm. And so far, no one has been able to do that.

But there is another approach to unification: *superstring theory*. This theory proposes to marry general relativity with quantum gravity. With this theory, gravity doesn't have to be separately quantized and then unified. Rather, gravity becomes quantized automatically.

The theory started in 1968 with a young postdoctoral fellow at CERN trying to untangle the complicated mess of the many particles that were being generated in the particle accelerators around the world. Gabriele Veneziano discovered that a mathematical expression that the Swiss mathematician Leonhard Euler had discovered two centuries before would match very precisely the data on the strong nuclear force. But he didn't know why it worked.

Two years later, several other scientists showed that Veneziano's formula actually described the quantized motion of subatomic strings connecting particles that felt the nuclear force. At this point, however, almost no one was interested in this obscure approach. Physicists were busy working on the grand unification.

But a couple of physicists were interested. John Schwartz of Caltech and Michael Green of Queen Mary College in London kept up the work on these strange strings, cleaning the infant theory of certain mathematical inconsistencies. By 1984, they succeeded. The new version of the theory, now called *superstring theory,* proposes that electrons and all other elementary particles are tiny vibrating strings of energy. These strings are truly one-dimensional entities, with length but no thickness.

These strings vibrate like guitar strings, and each particle vibrates with a characteristic vibration. From $E = mc^2$, we know that the energy of the vibrating string gives the mass of the particle. Other properties of the particle, such as the electric charge, are also encoded in the strings. In fact, in superstring theory, all the properties of the particles that scientists observe in the laboratory can be calculated directly from the theory.

What makes superstring theory so appealing is that it automatically incorporates gravity with the three other forces of nature. Although it is currently a work very much in progress, it promises to one day be the true unified field theory. If it proves to be the right approach in the years to come, it would fulfill Einstein's lifelong dream, opening for us a window into the deepest mysteries of the universe.

Part V
The Quantum and the Universe

The 5th Wave   By Rich Tennant

After the circus, Bozo the Physicist went on to distinguish himself for his work on the Wave/Particle Joy Buzzer, squirting quarks, and Quantum Pratfall Theory.

In this part . . .

Quantum theory began with Einstein's paper on the photoelectric effect, during his miracle year of 1905. With that paper, Einstein created his second revolution in physics. In this part, I tell you why it was a revolution and how it changed our ideas of reality.

I also describe to you Einstein's famous letter to President Franklin Delano Roosevelt about the possibility of an atomic bomb and Einstein's limited involvement with its development. Finally, I show you the relevance of Einstein's work and the important role that it's still playing today in the current theories of the universe and in the unification of all of physics. This unification was Einstein's lifelong dream.

Chapter 20

Ten Insights into Einstein's Beliefs on Religion and Philosophy

*E*instein's religious beliefs constitute a very important part of who he was. These beliefs have often been misunderstood or quoted out of context. Some people, who want to think that Einstein would've supported their views, have used his statements to claim that Einstein believed in the God of their religion. Others have claimed that Einstein was an atheist.

Einstein's views on religion have influenced many people. The physicist Max Jammer said that after the publication of his book *Einstein and Religion,* he received some letters mostly from agnostic scientists admitting that they had been inspired after they read Einstein's concept of religion.

The philosophy of religion and the philosophy of science became the focus of many of Einstein's writings during the last years of his life. Einstein was not a philosopher in the academic sense. "I was always interested in philosophy but only in a secondary way," he wrote. His interest was in discovering how nature operates. His deep involvement with the meaning of quantum theory influenced scientists' views throughout the 20th century.

In this chapter, I give you examples of Einstein's thoughts on religion and philosophy. From just this short chapter, you can get a pretty good idea of who Einstein's God was. And you can see that he was not an atheist. You can also get a feeling for his philosophical ideas about how we think and how science works.

Wrestling with Judaism

As I explain in Chapter 2, Einstein was born into a Jewish family, but his parents weren't practicing Jews; they didn't follow the traditional customs and didn't attend the local synagogue. Einstein's father, Hermann, regarded religious rites and traditions as "an ancient superstition" and was proud not to follow them.

When Einstein was 5 years old, he entered public school. His parents chose the local Catholic school because it offered a better education. They didn't object to him learning about Catholicism, but they also wanted him to learn about Judaism. They asked one of their relatives to teach him at home. Einstein learned the teachings of the Catholic Church and those of the Jewish faith at the same time.

When Einstein entered secondary school at the age of 9, his religious education continued at school only, this time in Judaism. As a result of this instruction, Einstein suddenly began to follow religious rituals on his own, observing the Sabbath, eating kosher food, and composing songs in honor of God.

Einstein's religious fervor stopped as suddenly as it had begun. At the age of 12, he began to read popular science books. The stories of the Bible conflicted with the science he was learning. He thought that he'd been misled and began to distrust his teachers, as well as the school and church authorities. This distrust stuck with him and extended to every kind of authority.

Years later, when he was an adult, Einstein's religious feelings returned, but in a different form. He developed his own personal religious philosophy, what he called his religion. He never deviated from it.

Defining What It Means to Be Religious

During his mature years, Einstein often wrote and gave public lectures about his idea of religion. In a letter to a young girl who'd written to him asking whether scientists pray, Einstein said that a scientist does not accept that the course of events can be influenced by prayer — that is, by the wish of a supernatural being. However, he said, everyone seriously engaged in science discovers that "the laws of nature manifest the existence of a spirit vastly superior to Man, and one in the face of which we, with our modest powers, must feel humble."

The German novelist Gerhart Hauptmann once asked Einstein if he was deeply religious. Einstein replied that he was: "Try and penetrate with our limited means the secrets of nature and you will find that, behind all the discernible concatenations, there remains something subtle, intangible, and inexplicable." His religion was respect for this force that we can't comprehend.

In an essay that he wrote in 1930, Einstein said that his religion was "a knowledge of the existence of something we cannot penetrate, our perceptions of the profoundest reason and the most radiant beauty, which only in the most primitive forms are accessible to our minds — it is this knowledge and this emotion that constitute true religiosity; in this sense, and in this alone, I am a deeply religious man."

In spite of these statements, when it came time to decide about the religious education of his own children, Einstein said that he disliked very much that they should be taught "something that is contrary to all scientific thinking." How could he disprove of teaching his children something that he regarded as being "the most radiant beauty"?

To Einstein, religious education meant indoctrination in the rituals of a particular religion. That wasn't what he meant by being religious. To him, being religious was experiencing the emotion felt in the presence of the mystery of nature and in the veneration of its creator. That, according to Einstein, is something you can't teach in a class.

Reconciling Religion and Science

After 1930, Einstein wrote several essays on religion and science. In 1940, in an address at the Conference on Science, Philosophy, and Religion, in New York, Einstein said that he considered science and religion to be mutually dependent on each other. He wrote that "science without religion is lame, religion without science is blind."

Here again, he refers to his own meaning of the word *religion:* the feeling of awe brought about by contemplating the order in the universe and believing in a creator of this order.

In 1948, Einstein wrote an essay titled "Religion and Science: Irreconcilable?" in which he discussed two issues:

✔ "Does there truly exist an insuperable contradiction between religion and science?"

✔ "Can religion be superseded by science?"

Einstein said that the answer to both questions is no. Science and religion operate in different domains. Science, he said, is "the systematical thinking directed toward finding connections between our sensual experiences," while religion is "concerned with Man's attitude toward nature at large, with the establishing of ideals for the individual and communal life, and with mutual human relationship."

Meeting Einstein's God

Einstein's idea of God is based on two key beliefs:

- ✔ **Determinism:** The world obeys the precise laws discovered by science and, after the universe is set into motion, everything that happens is predetermined because the universe must obey these laws.

- ✔ **A denial of anthropomorphism:** God does not have human qualities.

In a 1930 essay, Einstein said that he couldn't conceive "of a God that rewards and punishes his creatures, or has a will of the kind that we experience in ourselves." And he added a beautiful description of what God was for him: "I am satisfied with the mystery and eternity of life and with the awareness and a glimpse of the marvelous structure on the existing world, together with the devoted striving to comprehend a portion, be it ever so tiny, of the Reason that manifests itself in nature."

In 1952, Einstein wrote that he didn't believe in a personal God. "The idea of a personal God is quite alien to me and seems quite naïve." And in 1954, in a written response to an interview, he said that he couldn't accept the idea of God based on the authority of the Church. "I do not believe in the God of theology who rewards good and punishes evil. My God created laws that take care of that. His universe is not ruled by wishful thinking, but by immutable laws."

Tracking the Development of Religion

In 1930, Einstein wrote an article for *The New York Times* titled "Religion and Science." In it, he laid out his (not entirely original) view of the origin of religion. He explained that the development of religion can be divided into three stages:

- ✔ The first stage, developed by primitive societies, is the need to appease fears: the fear of hunger, wild beasts, sickness, and death. Einstein called this stage "the religion of fear."

- ✔ The second stage is "the social or moral conception of God." This conception comes from the "desire for guidance, love, and support." This is the God that comforts, rewards, and punishes.

- ✔ The third and final stage is what Einstein called the *cosmic religion,* which is "very difficult to elucidate . . . to anyone who is entirely without it, especially if there is no anthropomorphic conception of God corresponding to it." This is Einstein's own religion. In his article, Einstein wrote that this religious feeling "knows no dogma, and no God conceived in man's image; so that there can be no church whose central teachings are based on it."

Holding On Tight to Determinism

Quantum physics was fully developed by 1925. This field started with Einstein's 1905 paper on the photoelectric effect, where he showed that light is lumpy (quantized). Quantum theory would become extremely successful over the years, "the most successful physical theory of our period," according to Einstein himself.

However, even with its success, Einstein never accepted that quantum physics was the final answer.

What was it about quantum theory that Einstein didn't like? That it abolished determinism. (See the previous section "Meeting Einstein's God.") Heisenberg's uncertainty principle (see Chapter 16), which is at the heart of quantum physics, says that you no longer can know at once everything you want to know about the behavior of objects. Although the principle applies to everything in the universe, from electrons to stars, the effects are noticeable only in the realm of the atom, when you work with subatomic particles.

If the universe behaves according to Heisenberg's principle, you can never know for certain the past or present of anything in the universe. And you can't face the future with any certainty about what you'll encounter. The outcome of everything became probabilistic.

"God doesn't play dice with the universe," Einstein once said. He wasn't ready to abandon classical determinism from physics. And he put up a big fight. He and Niels Bohr, who was the main champion of the new physics, argued back and forth about the meaning of reality. In many cases, Bohr convinced Einstein of the flaws of a particular argument against quantum physics. But Bohr couldn't answer Einstein's argument about the EPR problem, which I explain in Chapter 16. Einstein found a way to sidestep Heisenberg's uncertainty principle and determine, with complete accuracy, the outcome of the collision of two particles and their entire future history.

At the time, technology hadn't advanced enough for the extremely delicate EPR experiment to be performed. Now it has. Since 1982, several real EPR experiments have been performed, and the results show that Einstein was wrong. The basic premise of quantum physics is correct. The world is not deterministic.

Reading Philosophy

As I explain in Chapter 2, when Einstein was growing up, his family invited a poor medical student to dinner once a week. The student, Max Talmud, became one of Einstein's early influences, encouraging him to read books on science. When Einstein was 13, Talmud brought him Immanuel Kant's *Critique of Pure Reason,* not an easy read even for philosophy students. Einstein read the book and discussed it with Talmud.

A couple years after Einstein finished his undergraduate education, when he was working at the Bern patent office, he and two friends (who he'd been tutoring in physics) formed what they called the *Olympic Academy,* which I explain in Chapter 9. The three friends "had a wonderful time in those days in Bern," as Einstein wrote later. "Our cheerful 'Academy' . . . was less childish than those respectable ones which I later got to know only too well."

The purpose of the academy was to read and discuss books on physics, philosophy, and literature. The group read Plato, David Hume's treatise on human nature, John Stuart Mill's system of logic, Benedict de Spinoza's ethics, and Richard Avenarius's critique of pure existence, among other books.

These readings stimulated Einstein's thinking on the philosophy of religion and science. They also allowed him to write and speak with authority on the philosophy of science.

Defining Thinking

Einstein started his autobiographical notes with a discussion about what thinking is. Einstein explained that he did so because "the essential in the being of a man of my type lies precisely in *what* he thinks and *how* he thinks, not in what he does or suffers."

Einstein asked the question: "What, precisely, is 'thinking'?" When images pop up in our minds as a response to stimuli from our senses, he said, "this is not yet 'thinking.'" When such images form a series, and one of the images calls up another, "this too is not yet 'thinking.'"

Einstein said that the transition from free association or daydreaming to thinking "is characterized by the more or less dominating role which the 'concept' plays in it." A concept can stay in our minds in private thought.

If a concept is to be transmitted to others, it must be put into words, and sometimes that's not easy. But, Einstein said, the most important part of thinking occurs before reaching the communication stage: "I have no doubt that our thinking goes on for the most part without the use of words and beyond that to a considerable degree, unconsciously."

Einstein wrote that "the physical entities which seem to serve as elements in thought are signs and more or less clear images which can be voluntarily reproduced and combined." In his case, these elements were visual and muscular. Einstein's great success in working with complex abstract concepts seems to have been due to his ability to visualize them.

Interpreting the Scientific Method

In his inaugural address before the Prussian Academy of Sciences in 1914, Einstein described his ideas regarding the scientific method from the point of view of theoretical physics. In this respect, he described his own method of scientific research and his interpretation of how science works.

"The theorist's method," he said, "involves using as his foundation general postulates or principles from which he can deduce conclusions." The second part, drawing the conclusions, is the easy part; physicists are well-trained for that in graduate school. But the first part is difficult, Einstein said, because there aren't any methods or techniques already established that can be applied to do it. "The scientist has to worm these general principles out of nature by perceiving in comprehensive complexes of empirical facts certain general features which permit of precise formulation."

Einstein gave as an example his own development of the special theory of relativity. The first part, the difficult part, was to extract the principle of relativity from nature. After he did that, the second part came out easily.

To a certain extent, Einstein's method is the one that physicists still use today in the construction of their theories. It's what scientists call the scientific method. And it has been extremely successful.

Stating the Goals of Science

According to Einstein, physical theory has two main goals:

- ✔ "To encompass as much as possible all phenomena and their connections."
- ✔ "To achieve this on the basis of as few logically independent concepts and . . . relations between these as possible (basic laws, axioms)."

Einstein restated the second goal "crudely but honestly" as follows: "We do not only wish to know *how* Nature is (and *how* her processes develop) but also wish, if possible, to arrive at the perhaps utopian and seemingly pretentious goal to know why Nature is as *is and not otherwise.*"

Einstein's views on the goals of science and on the scientific method are part of his philosophical views on the nature of the universe and on our attempts to understand through science how nature works. His ideas influenced modern philosophers of science in their interpretations of how scientific theories are constructed.

Chapter 21

Ten Women Who Influenced Einstein

*A*s the rest of this book shows, Einstein obviously had a tremendous influence on the scientific community and the entire world. But unlike Isaac Newton, Einstein didn't live in isolation; he enjoyed people's company and learned a great deal from those around him.

In other chapters, I don't devote a great deal of space to Einstein's personal life. (Chapter 2 is the exception.) Here, I offer some insight by presenting short biographies of ten women who influenced his life.

Einstein's Mother, Pauline

Pauline Koch was 17 when she married Hermann Einstein in 1876. She was an educated woman interested in music and literature. She was an excellent pianist and enjoyed playing the piano as often as she could.

Three years after her marriage to Hermann, Pauline gave birth to her only son, Albert. In 1881, when Einstein was 2, she gave birth to a daughter, Maria, who they always called Maja.

Encouraging music

Pauline wanted her children to appreciate music and to play an instrument, so when Einstein was 6, she hired a tutor to teach him the violin. The lessons started out fine but, after a while, the boy grew tired of the rigid instruction. He threw a chair at his tutor and chased her out of the house. Patiently, Pauline simply hired another instructor.

Einstein endured the violin lessons, which his mother wouldn't let him drop. Pauline's strong hand in this regard paid off. When Einstein was about 13, he discovered Mozart, and his interest in music turned around. He started playing duets with his mother at the piano, a custom that he continued as long as his mother was alive. Music became an important part of Einstein's life.

Pauline was always very proud of her son and involved in his affairs. When he was in elementary school, she would write to her mother praising her son's performance at school. When Einstein wanted to apply to college two years earlier than the approved age of 18, Pauline contacted an old neighbor from Germany, who was then living in Zurich, to see if he could find out if the university might waive the requirement. Apparently, Pauline said that Einstein was a child prodigy (he wasn't), because that's what the neighbor told the university administrators. Whatever he said, it worked. The university dropped the age requirement, and Einstein was allowed to take the admission tests.

Discouraging Mileva

Not all was smooth sailing between Einstein and his strong-willed mother. The difficult times came when Pauline noticed that the relationship between Einstein and his college girlfriend, Mileva Maric, had become serious. Pauline never liked Mileva. She didn't think that she was good enough for her brilliant son. Besides, Mileva was older than him.

Pauline's strong opposition didn't go anywhere with Einstein, so she eventually eased up her criticism. However, when Maja told her to let Einstein and Mileva get married, Pauline flew into a rage. The confrontation caused a rift between mother and daughter that caused them to stop speaking to each other for some time.

Pauline never accepted Mileva. In later years, Einstein said that the relationship between Pauline and Mileva "bordered on hostility."

Despite that fact, Pauline loved her son and followed his success. Einstein, in turn, loved his mother and visited her when he could, sometimes joining her in duets at the piano.

After her husband's death in 1902, Pauline went to live with her only sister, Fanny, and her husband. When they moved to Berlin in 1911, she started working as a housekeeper in a nearby town.

In 1914, Pauline fell ill with cancer. In 1918, when her cancer was much advanced, Maja took her to a sanatorium. The next year, Einstein, by then married to his second wife, took Pauline out of the sanatorium and brought her to his home, where she died a year later, on February 20, 1920.

Einstein had said once that he wouldn't worry about his own or anyone else's death. But after his mother died, according to the wife of astronomer Erwin Freundlich, "Einstein wept, like other men, and I knew that he could really care for someone."

Einstein's Sister, Maja

When his sister was born, 2-year-old Albert, probably thinking that the new baby looked like a toy, asked where the wheels were. Maja (whose given name was Maria) was born in 1881.

In Chapter 2, I explain that before entering the Federal Polytechnic Institute in Zurich, Einstein attended school in Aarau, Switzerland, and stayed with the Winteler family. Maja later attended the same school, and she also stayed with the Wintelers. She then went on to the Aarau teacher training college for three years and later studied Romance languages and literature at the universities of Berlin and Bern.

While Maja was attending graduate school at the University of Bern, her brother was teaching his evening physics course as a *Privatdozent* or instructor at the university, the first step in his academic career. Maja sometimes would sit in his classes.

Maja obtained her PhD in Romance languages from the University of Bern. The following year, she married Einstein's good friend Paul Winteler. Maja and her husband first lived in Lucerne, Switzerland, but later moved near Florence. They lived there until 1939, when she was driven out of Europe by the Nazi threat. (Health problems prevented her husband from entering the United States.) After the war, Maja wanted to return to Europe and to her husband, but her own health prevented her from traveling. Instead, she went to live with her brother in Princeton.

Einstein's second wife, Elsa, had died in 1936, and when Maja came to Princeton, she joined Margot Einstein (Elsa's daughter) and Einstein's lifelong secretary, Helen Dukas. The three women ran the house and helped Einstein with his correspondence; shielded him from unwanted visitors; and offered companionship, advice, and affection. Einstein was very close to all of them, especially Margot and Maja.

Maja wrote a biographical essay about her brother, which was completed in Florence in 1924. This essay, which she titled "Albert Einstein: A Biographical Sketch," is the main source of family recollections about Einstein's early years. Maja's essay, which remained in manuscript form until recently, tracks Einstein's life only up to 1905 and is most likely an abandoned project. Her manuscript was published in 1987 as part of the *Collected Papers of Albert Einstein*.

Maja died in Princeton in 1951, four years before her famous brother. Einstein took it very hard. He had lovingly cared for her during her last months, reading to her every evening "from the best books of the old and new literature." Her intelligence was as keen as ever, but toward the end, she couldn't talk. "Now I miss her more than can be imagined," he wrote in a letter shortly after she died.

Einstein's First Wife, Mileva Maric

Mileva Maric was the only female physics major at the Polytechnic in Zurich, where Einstein went to college. During their second semester, Einstein and Mileva began to take interest in each other. Their relationship developed into a romance that eventually led to marriage, in spite of strong opposition from Einstein's family (especially his mother).

Einstein and Mileva's romance is well-documented in letters they wrote to each other between 1897 and 1903, which were discovered only in 1987. Not much was known about Mileva before the appearance of these letters.

In her early letters, Mileva wrote with enthusiasm about the physics she was learning in class. As time went on, the focus on physics disappeared, and her letters became love letters, showing her feelings for Einstein and her preoccupation with their relationship. Einstein wrote to her about his love for her, about his family's reaction to their affair, and about physics.

The letters are an invaluable and direct record of Einstein's early intellectual development. He proudly told Mileva about his ideas on relativity and about his discoveries of inconsistencies in some of the physics papers that he read. Mileva, with her understanding of physics, seemed to be his sounding board.

Starting a family

In Chapter 2, I explain how the relationship between Mileva and Einstein progressed during their college years. After graduating from the Polytechnic and before starting his job at the Bern patent office, Einstein took a temporary job away from Zurich, while Mileva stayed at the Polytechnic. (She had failed final exams and was preparing to try them again.) During those few months, Einstein came to see Mileva in Zurich every Sunday. During one of those visits, Mileva told Einstein that she was pregnant.

The pregnancy didn't help Mileva in her studies, which had been a struggle for years. She took her finals again and failed. She was devastated, and she quit school. Depressed, she went home to her parents in Hungary, who weren't happy with either piece of news. Initially, her father angrily prohibited Mileva from marrying Einstein.

During the winter of 1902, Mileva gave birth to a girl, Lieserl. The birth was difficult, and Einstein wasn't present. He learned about it in a letter from Mileva's father.

No one knows what happened to Einstein's only daughter. Soon after her birth, she disappeared, and no record of her has ever been found. Mileva may have given her up for adoption.

About a year later, on January 6, 1903, Einstein and Mileva got married in a civil ceremony at the courthouse in Bern. Einstein was working at the patent office, making an adequate salary as a civil servant. Life was relatively good for them.

A little more than a year after their marriage, Mileva gave birth to their first son, Hans Albert. Although he initially tried to help Mileva with the baby, overall Einstein wasn't a good husband. He was interested in his work and paid little attention to Mileva or to his son. It became worse during the burst of creativity of his miracle year (see Chapter 3). Their relationship began to suffer.

Struggling with depression

Einstein took refuge in his work. Mileva became depressed. According to one visitor, their house was a mess. Einstein tried to help, but his heart wasn't in it. He would carry the baby while trying to write his equations on a pad.

On July 28, 1910, Einstein and Mileva's second son, Eduard, was born. For a while, things improved between them, but that didn't last. Mileva continued to be depressed and was becoming jealous of the women Einstein flirted with.

In 1911, Einstein and his family moved to Prague, where he'd accepted a nice offer from the university. Mileva hated the city. A year later, Einstein accepted an offer from his alma mater and moved back to Zurich. Mileva was delighted. That lasted only a couple of years. In 1914, Einstein accepted an offer from the University of Berlin and moved his family there.

Mileva was extremely unhappy about moving to Berlin. Einstein's cousin, Elsa, lived there, and Mileva was jealous of her. Besides, Germans looked down on people of Serbian origin, like Mileva.

Heading toward divorce

Mileva was right about Elsa. Einstein started seeing her often, and that was the beginning of the end for Einstein's marriage. After a fight, Einstein moved out, and some time later, he wrote a contract for their separation that detailed the support he would provide. Mileva and the boys moved back to Zurich.

In 1916, during one of his visits to see the boys, Einstein asked Mileva for a divorce, which led her to have nervous breakdown. She recovered slowly, but their son Eduard then became a cause for concern. Eduard was extremely gifted. He read Goethe and Friedrich Schiller in first grade and had a photographic memory. He learned anything that he set out to learn with breathtaking speed. But he was troubled. (Eduard had to be placed in a psychiatric hospital in 1933 after he showed signs of mental instability. He died at the hospital in 1965.)

Mileva and Einstein divorced on February 14, 1919. After the divorce, Mileva spent a great deal of her life taking care of Eduard. In 1947, her health began to deteriorate. The next year, she suffered a stroke that left her paralyzed on one side of the body. On August 4, 1948, Mileva died.

Mileva had started out as Einstein's intellectual equal; they read, studied, and discussed physics together. By 1902, their partnership had changed, because Einstein's thinking had developed to a different level. But until then, her presence helped him shape his thoughts by providing him with the loving ears of another physicist.

Einstein's Daughter, Lieserl

Einstein's only daughter was born in 1902 in Novi Sad, then part of Hungary, where Mileva's parents lived. Einstein and Mileva weren't married at the time, and Mileva's pregnancy was kept secret from everyone but Mileva's family.

When the baby was born, Einstein was in Switzerland, waiting to hear from his patent office job application. When he heard the news about the birth, he wrote to Mileva wanting to know if the baby was healthy, what her eyes were like, and who she looked like. He had a thousand questions. "I love her so much and don't even know her yet!"

Mileva replied, but her letter didn't survive, so we don't know what she said. Einstein wrote again a week later, thanking her for her "dear little letter" but not mentioning Lieserl. Gone were the thousand questions he had only a week earlier. He wrote instead about his job application at the patent office.

In another letter, dated September 1903, when Mileva was pregnant with their first son, Einstein told Mileva that he was not angry that she was expecting a new baby. In fact, he said that he'd been thinking about a new Lieserl, because Mileva "shouldn't be denied that which is the right of all women." Then he said that he was "very sorry about what has befallen Lieserl." Apparently she had developed scarlet fever. "As what is the child registered?" he wrote. "We must take precautions that problems don't arise for her later."

Registered where? At a hospital while she was ill? What kind of problems? Health problems or name problems? No one knows. Lieserl simply disappeared. In surviving letters, neither Einstein nor Mileva ever mentioned their daughter again. Their son Hans never knew he had a sister.

There are no birth records in Novi Sad or any nearby areas that give any clues about Lieserl. It's likely that she was given up for adoption very early and that she was registered under her new family's name.

Einstein's Second Wife, Elsa

Elsa was Einstein's cousin, the daughter of his "rich uncle" Rudolf Einstein and his aunt Fanny (Pauline's sister). Elsa was first married to Max Loewenthal, a textile trader from Berlin with whom she had two daughters, Ilse and Margot, and a son who died shortly after birth.

Einstein and Elsa met often while they were growing up but lost contact as adults. During one of Einstein's visits to Berlin while he was still married to Mileva, he met his cousin again. She was divorced and living with her two daughters in an apartment right above her parents. Einstein felt comfortable with Elsa in this family environment. When he moved to the University of Berlin, he continued seeing her with some frequency.

After his separation from Mileva, Einstein saw Elsa often, and he moved in with her in September of 1917. Elsa was clearly interested in Einstein and kept the pressure on him to divorce Mileva.

After the divorce took place in 1919, Einstein felt free to marry Elsa. His main attraction to her was her cooking. He also felt grateful to her because she had taken care of him when he was ill with stomach problems. There was no passion between them. Nevertheless, they were married on June 2, 1919, three and a half months after his divorce from Mileva. Einstein was 40 and Elsa was 43. Their marriage seems to have been platonic.

Although some of Einstein's friends criticized Elsa's eagerness for fame, she was receptive of her husband's importance and was able to create a nice environment for Einstein to work in. Her efficiency in running the household made Einstein's life much easier.

As happened during his marriage to Mileva, problems developed because of Einstein's flirting with other women. He was very famous, and women all over the world were attracted to him.

In 1935, after Einstein and Elsa had moved to the United States, she fell ill with heart and kidney problems. She died on December 20, 1936.

Einstein had been very attentive and caring during Elsa's last months of her life. After she died, he adjusted quickly. "I have got used extremely well to life here," he wrote. "I live like a bear in my den . . . This bearishness has been further enhanced by the death of my woman comrade, who was better with other people than I am."

Einstein's Stepdaughter Ilse

Ilse was one of Elsa's daughters. When Einstein was considering marrying Elsa, Einstein felt attracted to Ilse, who was 22 and pretty. Ilse liked and respected Einstein. Einstein seriously and openly considered choosing between the two of them.

"Yesterday, the question was suddenly raised about whether Albert should marry Mama or me," Ilse wrote to a friend, asking him to destroy the letter immediately. (Obviously, he didn't listen.) "This question, initially posed half in jest, became within a few minutes a serious matter which must be considered and discussed." Einstein, she told her friend, was ready to marry either one of them. But she didn't have "physical feelings for him." She respected him and loved him very much, but more like a father.

Ilse went on to marry Rudolf Kayser, a journalist and scholar who later wrote a biography of Einstein, which was carefully edited by Einstein. Kayser published his book, *Albert Einstein, A Biographical Portrait,* in 1930 under the pseudonym of Anton Reiser. The English edition was published in New York the same year.

After the Nazis' rise to power in 1933, Kayser rescued Einstein's papers from Berlin and took them out of the country with the help of the French embassy. The papers were later brought to Einstein's home in Princeton and kept there until after he died.

When Ilse was 37 and living in Paris with her husband, she fell seriously ill with tuberculosis. She and her sister Margot had moved to Paris when they heard that the Nazis were going to kidnap them to get to Einstein. Elsa had to go alone to Paris to be with her daughter; Einstein couldn't set foot in Europe because of the Nazi threat. Ilse died shortly after Elsa got there.

Einstein's Stepdaughter Margot

Margot was also Elsa's daughter. She was married to Dimitri Marianoff who, like her sister's husband, was a journalist. He wanted to write a biography of Einstein and started dating Margot to gain access to Einstein.

Marianoff's plan succeeded, but unlike the biography written by his other son-in-law, this one wasn't edited by Einstein. As a result, personal details that Einstein wasn't interested in divulging appeared in the book, and Einstein was very unhappy with it.

The book, entitled *Einstein: An Intimate Study of a Great Man,* offered Marianoff's detailed view of Einstein's private life and his opinion of women. (The English version of this book appeared in 1944 and is out of print.)

The marriage between Marianoff and Margot didn't last. After the divorce, Margot lived in Paris until her sister, Ilse, died. She then accompanied her mother on her return trip to the United States and lived with her and Einstein. After Elsa died, Margot stayed with Einstein and took care of him.

Einstein's Secretary, Helen Dukas

Helen Dukas was Einstein's secretary from 1928 until his death in 1955. She emigrated to the United States in 1933 with Einstein and his wife, Elsa. In Princeton, Dukas lived in Einstein's house along with Elsa and her daughters. After Elsa died, she was one of the three women (Maja and Margot being the other two) who took care of all of Einstein's affairs.

After Einstein died, Dukas became a trustee of his literary estate and the archivist of his papers. She collaborated with Professor Banesh Hoffmann — who had worked with Einstein on his general theory of relativity — on two books, *Albert Einstein: Creator and Rebel* and *Albert Einstein, the Human Side.*

Einstein's First Love, Marie Winteler

Marie Winteler was Einstein's first love. She was the daughter of Jost and Pauline Winteler, Einstein's wonderful host family in Aarau (see Chapter 2). She was 18 when Einstein first met her, and he quickly fell in love with her. Their romance contributed to Einstein's successful year at the Aarau Cantonal School, perhaps the happiest year of his life.

But their teenage love didn't last. When Einstein left the Wintelers to attend the Polytechnic, he stopped writing to Marie.

Years later, in 1940, Marie wrote a letter to Einstein from Europe asking him for a loan of 100 francs because she was in a dire situation due to the hardship of the war. Einstein was known for helping many Europeans that were suffering because of the war. However, Helen Dukas, not knowing who Marie was, never passed the letter along to Einstein.

Marie Curie

The famous scientist Marie Curie was Einstein's contemporary. As two of the top scientists in the world, they crossed paths several times. One such occasion occurred in 1909, when both were given honorary doctorates at the celebration of the 350th anniversary of the foundation of the University of Geneva.

Marie Curie's discovery of radioactivity (with her husband, Pierre, and their colleague Henri Becquerel) played a role in Einstein's development of his $E = mc^2$ equation. In his paper presenting his famous formula, Einstein showed that applying his special relativity equations to an atom emitting light in a radioactive decay implied that energy carries mass with it. It would've been hard for him to think of the spontaneous emission of light from a body if the phenomenon hadn't been observed.

In 1913, when Einstein and Mileva traveled to Paris, they stayed with the Curies. The two families got along very well and became close friends. After that, the families visited each other several times to go hiking in the Alps.

Later, Einstein and Curie both served on the League of Nations commission, where they had the occasion to meet several times.

Part VI
The Part of Tens

The 5th Wave   By Rich Tennant

Einstein Working on One of His
Concepts of Time – the "Good Time"

In this part . . .

Einstein's life, like his science, was fascinating. Besides physics, he was interested in philosophy, particularly the philosophy of science. Einstein also said repeatedly that he was religious. In this part, I tell you what he really meant by being religious.

To complete our view of Einstein, the man, I've collected short biographies of ten women who influenced Einstein.

Appendix A

Glossary

● ●

alpha decay: The spontaneous emission of *alpha particles* by certain radioactive nuclei.

alpha particle: A bundle of two *protons* and two *neutrons*. Also, the nucleus of helium.

alpha ray: An *alpha particle.*

beta decay: The spontaneous emission of *electrons* and *neutrinos* from certain radioactive nuclei.

beta particle: An *electron.*

beta ray: A *beta particle.*

black body: An ideal object that absorbs all radiation. It's also a perfect emitter of radiation.

black dwarf: A burned-out *white dwarf* star. The sun will end its life as a black dwarf.

black hole: An object with such strong gravity that not even light can escape.

coherent: Light beams vibrating in step.

conservation law: The physics law that specifies that a certain quantity cannot be destroyed.

conservation of energy: The law that states that the total amount of energy you start a process with has to equal what you end up with.

dark matter: An unknown invisible substance that can be detected only by its gravitational effects.

diffraction: The bending or spreading of a light beam as it passes through a narrow slit or hole.

Doppler effect: The change in the wavelength perceived by a listener who is in motion relative to a source of sound. It also applies to light and other electromagnetic waves.

electric current: The rate at which electric charges move through a conductor or through empty space.

electron: A fundamental particle that can't be split and carries negative electric charge. As far as we know, electrons have no size.

energy: The capacity to perform work or the result of doing work.

entropy: A measure of the degree of disorder in a system.

epicycles: Circles that the planets were supposed to follow in their paths across the heavens, according to Ptolemy's model of the universe. The centers of those circles moved around the Earth. Copernicus showed that the model was wrong.

escape velocity: The minimum upward speed that you must give an object so that it leaves the Earth and never falls back. This value is 11 kilometers (7 miles) per second.

ether: An invisible substance filling all space that physicists of the 19th century invented to explain the motion of light in space. Einstein's theory of relativity did away with it.

event horizon: The surface of a sphere with a radius equal to the *Schwarzschild radius.*

field: The distortion of space due to the presence of a body that exerts a force on other bodies.

galaxy: A large island of billions of stars, held together by gravity.

gamma rays: Electromagnetic radiation emitted by certain radioactive nuclei.

geocentric: Earth-centered. Ptolemy's model of the universe, with the sun and the stars revolving around the Earth, was geocentric.

Heisenberg's uncertainty principle: You can't determine with complete accuracy the position of a particle and at the same time measure where and how fast it's moving.

inertia: The resistance of a body to an attempt to change its motion.

interference: The pattern that results from the overlap of two wave motions that run into each other. The overlap can be a reinforcement of the waves or a cancellation.

laser: **L**ight **a**mplification by **s**timulated **e**mission of **r**adiation produces a narrow beam of single-wavelength, coherent light.

mass: A measure of the resistance that you feel when you try to change the motion of an object; the measure of *inertia*.

neutrino: A subatomic particle that has no mass or a very tiny amount of mass — we don't yet know which. It plays a role in *radioactivity*.

neutron: One of the subatomic particles that make up the nucleus of an atom.

neutron star: An object only tens of kilometers across but with a mass larger than that of the sun. Neutron stars are composed mainly of *neutrons*.

photon: A *quantum* of light.

proton: One of the subatomic particles that make up the nucleus of an atom. The proton has positive electric charge.

pulsar: A fast-spinning, small, and very dense astronomical body that emits light and radio waves, like a lighthouse.

quanta: Bundles or packets of energy that can't be split. Light and all electro-magnetic radiation are made up of quanta.

quasar: An extremely bright astronomical body, usually found very far away, that shines with the brightness of trillions of suns.

radioactivity: The spontaneous emission of particles or radiation from cer-tain atoms.

red giant: A large, bright star with a low surface temperature. The sun will spend its late years as a red giant, eventually ending as a burned-out star called a *black dwarf*.

reference frame: A reference point for a moving object.

Schwarzschild radius: The largest radius of a star below which light will be trapped, as in a *black hole*.

singularity: Places where the laws of physics break down or don't apply.

spacetime: The combination of the three dimensions of space and one of time. It's needed in relativity because time and space are linked together.

spectrum: The array of the components of the emission of electromagnetic radiation arranged according to wavelength.

superstring theory: A new theory of the structure of matter that says that all elementary particles are represented by tiny vibrating strings. The theory promises to unify all the forces of nature.

thermodynamics: The study of heat and thermal effects.

uniform motion: Motion at a constant speed along a straight line.

virtual particle: A particle that exists only for the brief moment allowed by *Heisenberg's uncertainty principle.*

wave: A mechanism for the transmission of *energy.*

wavelength: The length of an oscillation; the distance between two crests or two valleys in a wave.

white dwarf: A small, dense star. One of the final stages in the life of the sun.

worm hole: A tunnel through space that connects two *black holes* at different places in the universe. We don't yet know if worm holes really exist.

Appendix B

Einstein Timeline

1879 March 14. Albert Einstein is born in Ulm, Germany, to Hermann Einstein and Pauline Koch.

1880 June 21. The Einstein family moves to Munich.

1881 November 18. Einstein's sister, Maria (Maja), is born.

1884 Einstein is fascinated by a compass. He remembers the event all his life.

1885 Einstein starts violin lessons.

1885 October 1. Einstein starts public school in Germany. He starts in the second grade. He has religion instruction at the Catholic school and Jewish religious instruction at home.

1888 October 1. Einstein passes the admission tests and enters secondary school at the Luitpold Gymnasium.

1889 Max Talmud, a poor Jewish medical student, starts his regular visits with the Einsteins.

1890 Einstein reads his "holy geometry book."

1894 June. The Einstein family moves to northern Italy.

1894 December 29. Einstein drops out of high school and joins his parents in Italy.

1895 Einstein is allowed to take the admission tests at the Federal Polytechnic Institute in Zurich, even though he is two years under age. He has an excellent performance in math and physics but fails the test because of his poor performance in other subjects.

1895 October 26. Einstein enters the Cantonal School in Aarau, Switzerland. He lives with the family of Jost Winteler.

1896 January 28. Einstein obtains a document releasing him from German citizenship. He remains stateless for five years.

1896 September. Einstein graduates from high school.

1896 October 29. Einstein starts college as a physics major at the Federal Polytechnic Institute in Zurich.

1900 July 28. Einstein graduates from college.

1900 December 13. Einstein submits his first scientific paper to the journal *Annalen der Physik*.

1901 February 21. Einstein becomes a Swiss citizen.

1901 May 19–July 15. Einstein accepts a temporary teaching position in mathematics at the technical high school in Winterhur, Switzerland.

1901 October 20–January 1902. Einstein teaches at a private school in Schaffhausen, Switzerland.

1902 January. Lieserl, Einstein's daughter with Mileva Maric, is born in Novi Sad, Hungary.

1902 June 23. Einstein starts working at the Swiss patent office in Bern as a technical expert third class with a salary of 3,500 Swiss francs.

1902 October 10. Einstein's father dies in Milan.

1903 January 6. Einstein marries Mileva Maric in Bern. Lieserl remains in Novi Sad.

1904 May 14. Einstein and Mileva's first son, Hans Albert, is born.

1905 March 17. Einstein completes his paper on the light quanta.

1905 April 30. Einstein completes his PhD thesis, "A new determination of molecular dimensions."

1905 May 11. The *Annalen der Physik* receives his paper on Brownian motion.

1905 June 10. The *Annalen der Physik* receives his paper "On the electrodynamics of moving bodies," the special theory of relativity. It was published on September 28.

1905 September 27. The *Annalen der Physik* receives his paper with the $E = mc^2$ equation.

1906 January 15. Einstein's PhD is officially granted by the University of Zurich.

1906 November 9. The *Annalen der Physik* receives his paper on the quantum theory of solids.

1907 Einstein discovers the principle of equivalence.

1908 Einstein starts work as a *Privatdozent,* an instructor at the University of Bern — the first step in his academic career. He publishes two papers with a collaborator.

1908 December 21. Einstein's sister, Maja, receives her PhD in Romance languages magna cum laude from the University of Bern.

1909 March and October. Einstein completes two papers on black body radiation.

1909 Einstein receives his first honorary degree from the University of Geneva.

1909 October 15. Einstein becomes a professor of theoretical physics at the University of Zurich.

1910 March. Maja marries Paul Winteler.

1910 July 28. Einstein and Mileva's second son, Eduard, is born in Zurich.

1910 October. Einstein completes his first paper on statistical physics.

1911 April 1. Einstein becomes a full professor of physics at the University of Prague.

1911 June. Einstein predicts the bending of light.

1912 August. Einstein takes a position as professor of theoretical physics at the Zurich Polytechnic.

1914 April 6. Einstein becomes a professor at the University of Berlin; he has no teaching duties and serves as director of the Kaiser Wilhelm Institute for Physics.

1915 November 25. Einstein completes his masterpiece, the general theory of relativity, and presents it before the Prussian Academy of Sciences.

1916 March 20. Einstein's first book, *The Foundation of the General Theory of Relativity,* is published by the *Annalen der Physik.*

1916 Einstein publishes a paper on gravitational waves and three papers on quantum theory.

1916 December. Einstein publishes his best-known book, *Relativity: The Special and General Theory,* which is eventually translated into every major language.

1917 Einstein publishes a paper on cosmology, introducing the cosmological constant.

1919 February 14. Einstein and Mileva divorce.

1919 June 2. Einstein marries his cousin Elsa in Berlin.

1919 Einstein receives a telegram with results of the British eclipse expeditions confirming his prediction of the bending of light.

1919 Einstein is awarded an honorary doctor of medicine degree from the University of Rostock, Germany.

1920 March. Einstein's mother, Pauline, dies in his home.

1921 April 2–May 30. Einstein first visits the United States. He is received by President Warren G. Harding at the White House. He also visits Chicago, Boston, and Princeton, New Jersey.

1922 Einstein completes his first paper on the unified field theory.

1922 November 9. Einstein is awarded the Nobel Prize for physics "for his services to theoretical physics and especially for his discovery of the law of the photoelectric effect."

1924 Einstein publishes a paper on the association of waves with matter, his last major discovery.

1932 October. Einstein is appointed a professor at the Institute for Advanced Studies in Princeton, New Jersey. Einstein is to divide his time between Princeton and Berlin.

1932 December 10. With his wife, Elsa, Einstein leaves Germany for the United States to start his first term in Princeton. They travel back to Europe but never return to Germany.

1933 The Nazis take power in Germany.

1933 October 17. Einstein, his wife Elsa, and Einstein's secretary Helen Dukas arrive in the United States with visitor visas and go straight to Princeton.

1935 Einstein leaves the United States temporarily and goes to Bermuda to make an application for permanent residency in the United States.

1936 December 20. Einstein's wife, Elsa, dies.

1936 December. Einstein's son, Hans Albert, receives a PhD in technical sciences from Einstein's alma mater, the Zurich Polytechnic. (The next year, he and his family move to the United States, where Hans later becomes a professor at the University of California at Berkeley.)

1939 Einstein's sister, Maja, joins him in Princeton, where she lives the rest of her life.

1939 Einstein signs a letter to President Franklin Delano Roosevelt mentioning the possibility of building an atomic bomb and alerting him of its military implications.

1940 October 1. Einstein becomes a U.S. citizen.

1943 May 31. Einstein becomes a consultant on high explosives to the U.S. Navy.

1944 February 3. A copy of his 1905 paper on special relativity, handwritten by Einstein for this occasion, is auctioned for $6 million as a contribution to the war effort.

1948 August 4. Mileva dies in Zurich.

1951 June. Einstein's sister, Maja, dies in Princeton.

1952 November. Einstein is offered the presidency of Israel. He declines.

1955 In Einstein's last signed letter, to Bertrand Russell, he agrees to sign a manifesto urging all nations to renounce nuclear weapons.

1955 April 18, 1:15 a.m. Einstein dies in Princeton. His body is cremated the same day, and his ashes are scattered at an undisclosed location.

Index

Printed in the United States of America
ED-08-17-11